GET THE

HELL OUT

AZURE GABRIEL

This Book is dedicated to my late Great-Grandfather
Nathaniel Corothers Sr.
My "Big Daddy."
I wish you were here to see how far I've come along,
and that your baby is okay!
Not a day goes by where I don't think about you!

I love you, "Tiger"
Your baby girl
-Azure

Foreword

By: Pastor, Jonathan D. Ellis

William and Tonja Gabriel have been a part of this church since before they were married, over 30 years ago.

They've grown together, have raised a beautiful family, and are a great example of a biblical godly couple. Azure and BJ have been raised in the admonition and fear of the Lord and I'm proud to be BJ's (Rocco) godfather.

As with all children, our parent's want the best for us and will do all they can to love and protect us. It doesn't always work that way as we have to carve our own paths when we THINK we know how to handle our lives as grown-ups.

This book shares the straightforward truth about being young and in love (my words). It will go to show that as any relationship goes, there must be a lot of praying, fasting, talking, and patience with somebody. This is an eye-opening book into the life of someone who's experienced a very critical issue in our society, domestic abuse.

Let it be a voice to those who feel nobody will hear them or who've been neglected to seek the help need so that you can "Get Out" and be healed and live!

This story you are about to read is true.

Some names and identifying details have been changed to protect the privacy of individuals.

Contents

**After Jesus had gone indoors, his disciples asked him privately, "Why couldn't we drive it out?" He replied, "This kind can come out only by prayer."
Mark 9:28-29 (NIV)**

When you try to do something without praying, what happens? Chaos right? But, have you ever noticed the difference in what happens when we pray first? You can try your very best and your very hardest; with the most effort, and the most perfection, that you think is possible, and still fall flat on your face every time without prayer!

BUT, when you PRAY FIRST it just seems like everything falls right into place doesn't it??. EVEN THE SIMPLEST THINGS WEDO!

With PRAYER and being BOLD in the things we ask God, we'll begin to see the Power of God manifested through:

- Souls saved

- The sick healed

- People delivered

- Burdens lifted

- Chaos at work gone

Perhaps you know somebody that may or may not be dealing with mental health issues, but they've got some "luna-tickish" ways. YOU may even have some "luna-tickish" ways. YOU may even have some "luna-tickish" ways. Ya' keep falling IN and OUT of the same SIN, (Self-Inflicted Nonsense)! Your FIRST man should have taught you a lesson; your first WOMAN should have taught you a lesson. But, NOPE, there you go again—falling back into the same old cycle. Moving from job to job, city to city, man to man, woman to woman but nothing has changed!

This causes you to fall back into the same ole' habits, and you find yourself going through the same stuff over and over again. You keep trying to figure out what is wrong with you, why you can't change, why you can't make better choices, discern the voice of God, hear the Lord

clearly, and wonder why things can't get better.

I've learned that prayer changes things. Even if you don't have a prayer life, or don't know God. If you just cry out "I NEED HELP, HE will hear you. You may say, "I'm going through HELL!" or "he/she is putting me through so much HELL, I don't know that I am going to do!" Well PRAYER, prayer can change all of that.

This is a guide and true testimony of all the HELL and abuse I was in. It tells of what I went through and put up with from someone I had hopes of being in a permanent relationship with. I thought he was going to be the ONE. The one I walked down the aisle to meet and take his last name. The one I thought that I would have a family and grow old with. That was just based on the outer appearance. If I had known what was on the inside of him, I would have RAN like Forest Gump a long time ago.

BUT through it all, I AM HERE TO TELL THE STORY!

Introduction

Now, this is a story all about how my life got twist all upside down. I'd like to take a minute just sit right there.... (go ahead and finish it; I'll wait.) Now that I have your attention. HEY! I want to first start off by saying THANK YOU! If you're reading this, you've purchased my book, or someone has blessed you with it. You are about to read a journey; my journey through one of the most trying, emotional and craziest year; yes, YEAR of my life. Are you in? Good! Now let's find out how I, GOT THE HELL OUT!

I remember growing up, there were some days I would raise the question, "Do I really have to go to church?" Don't get me wrong I loved going to church, especially Sunday School and Vacation Bible School, as a child. After my parents married, they relocated from San Antonio, Texas to Baltimore, Maryland where I was born. My parents attended First Apostolic Faith Church in Baltimore, under the leadership of Bishop Cornelius Showell. This is the city and state I was born in; (I only lived there for two years but I pronounce it like everyone else that's been born and raised -"Bald-da-more.") My Parents later moved back to San Antonio, to rejoin Greater Lincoln Park Temple, under the leadership of Bishop William A. Ellis then later; Pastor Jonathan D. Ellis (The Conquerors Assembly).

LISTEN! Growing up in GLPT/TCA was so dope! I love how church was back then. OMG Y'all VBS (Vacation Bible School) was the bomb! We would learn about the topic given for that year, have snacks and that Orange Hi-C from McDonald's; THE BEST (Where my GLPT/TCA kids at!?) I don't care what anybody says that good ole Greater Lincoln Park Temple had THE BEST Children's church, Vacation Bible School, Choir, Preacher…EVERYTHING! If you don't know anything about Bishop E because he's been set "FREE"; or if you don't know about the MORE THAN CONQUERING Suffragan Bishop Jonathan David Ellis! You have been missing out.

For as long as I can remember, my mother has always been in ministry. I remember her leading corporate prayer or reading the scripture on Sunday mornings; even to this day. While she was ushering in the presence of the Lord, I was either sitting with my Grandma and cousin Erika (cutting up and playing pity-pat on the floors between the pews.) or upstairs with my Dad in the sound room. It seemed like we were always at church, well, we were. My dad was not only in the Media Ministry, but he was a trustee as well; for those who are not familiar with having multiple roles in the church entails, let me break it down for you. Basically we (my household) was the first to come and last to leave church, OH and don't let it be a conference, convention, church or anniversary service; sometimes it felt like we never left. My older godbrothers Terrell & Marcus and when my little brother (BJ) was born; we all would be STARVING because we had to wait until after the last service to really eat, and our little corner store snacks wasn't cutting it. Now that's #realchurchhurt

I will never forget my first encounter with the Holy Ghost; I remember it like it was yesterday. Pastor Marvin Sapp preached one Sunday morning, while he was preaching, I had this unexplainable feeling that came over me, and all I remember was that when it was time for offering, he asked for a special seed. Now, I was like 10 or 11; I didn't have any money. I left my seat and went upstairs to the balcony; while I was going up the stairs, I felt my mouth starting to move rapidly; then my teeth started chattering, my lips were moving, and words were coming out that sounded weird. I approached my Dad; I think I scared him because he wasn't expecting me, and I probably had a look on my face that may have concerned him because I was trying to hold in my tongues. I asked him if he had five-dollars, he said his famous "huh?" with the confused look on his face. So with a little bounce in my stance and fidgeting hands, I said: "Do..y..yo... you have fi..fi..five dollars so, so I can give an offering?" He response, "Oh, hold…here." As he was pulling out the money, my bounce got a little heavier and my lips were rapidly moving and teeth we're chattering as if I was standing at the North Pole; All I knew was that I needed to obey what I felt and heard from God and sow my seed into the Word. It wasn't much, but I needed to do something. When he looked up, he saw me trying very hard to control what was stirring up in my belly. I didn't realize what happen or took place; I just knew something was different, and that was the day I received the gift of the Holy Ghost with the evidence of speaking in tongues! I didn't share what I experienced with my parents to see if that was what I experienced; I just knew!

Growing up in the church, I've witnessed miracles, signs and wonders; I've seen the blind being able to see, the lame walk, demons casted out of people, the deaf being able to hear and so much more; so, I know the power in His Name. I've also seen the good, the bad and the ugly in the church; it got to the point where I was getting tired of the "Church". Not God, but more so the business aspect of the church and how things were done and NOT done. With my parents being in ministry I saw A LOT of the behind the scenes things that could have really left a bitter taste in my mouth as far as the "church" is concerned. As I was getting older, I wanted to be more on the Kingdom level. I was done with the antics of the church, just give me Jesus.

Before I moved to Dallas, I felt the Lord leading me elsewhere, especially for that transition I was getting ready to take. So, I ended up leaving the church I'd never thought I'd leave; and that was the BEST decision I made. Being under the leadership of Apostle Kevin Duhart, I was challenged spiritually and mentally. Once I made that move, it seemed like everything that was inside of me just overflowed; my worship changed, my praise changed, the way I walked and talked all changed. I finally felt like I was living in the Kingdom.

Until I got to Dallas, it felt like I was losing my zeal for the Lord. When I moved to Dallas, church wasn't that mandatory to me like it was when I was a child; we didn't have a choice to decide if we wanted to go to church or not. Unless we were sick; even then it was "oh, you not feeling well? You're definitely going to church! That's where you need to be." I remember being young and on FIRE for the Lord; I was always excited about getting to church. So much that if my parents wanted a break on Sunday, I was calling my auntie or cousin to come pick me up. When my parents thought about moving membership, I was like NOPE! Not having it. I wanted to be all things TCA!

In Dallas, I was living on my own, and I didn't have anyone turning lights on a 6 o'clock, I didn't hear hands banging or tapping on our doors on Sunday morning. I was determined that I wouldn't find anything like The Rock. There were some Sundays I'd get up and wasn't feeling it, especially looking for a church. I went online and streamed services at The Rock; now All Nations Worship Assembly San Antonio. That was all good until I started to miss being at church being in the presence of the Lord just changes EVERYTHING. What made it harder for me, my boyfriend at that time didn't grow up in the same denomination as I did. He grew up Baptist; there is nothing wrong with the way he was raised; I just wasn't accustomed to how they operated. So I started going to his church where is his godfather was the

Pastor. It wasn't a bad church, I was able to get a Word, but it wasn't TCA and definitely not The Rock!

It was a point in time where I was working on Sundays, and I wasn't able to go to church like I normally would. He also started working on Sunday's. Yes, there were times where I would go without him, but it wasn't the same. I was scared of going to visit other churches, especially by myself, why? I honestly don't know. Growing up, I was taught, and I saw that the wife goes wherever the head of the house goes. Yes, everyone would have their own opinion; but my parents never made a decision without the other, and I took that with me to Dallas even in my relationships. A very wrong mindset to have because one; we were not married, two; we were very well unequally yoked, and three; it didn't help my walk or growth with God.

I remember having a conversation with my cousin, and she asked if I was going to church, because she could see a difference and honestly, I did too. I was just embarrassed to admit it. I told her, "I am just tired of church, don't get me wrong; I am not tired of God, just church. You know we didn't have a choice on whether we were going to church or not, we were told! Sunday service sometimes three services, bible study, choir rehearsal and such. I guess; when I moved out, I enjoyed that freedom a little too much." She understood what I was saying and feeling, and she gave me some advice, but there was still something missing in my spiritual life. It's not like I didn't know right from wrong; I was still in that stage of finding myself and my purpose. My older brother Marcus always said to me, "Sweets, you don't really find yourself until you hit your thirties or close to it." I know we hear that saying all the time, and it has become cliché, but it is the TRUTH!

Since the age of five, I knew that there was a calling on my life, as well did others. I was always on fire for God, and unashamed. At one point, thinking back, I know I took God for granted, I know I did; because of who I was and who I came from; my parents. The pressure became so real, and I was put on this pedestal and was TOLD from folk in the church, what my purpose in life was because of my Mom; everyone thought I would be walking in her shadow. I remember one Sunday, one of the elders in the church came up to me and told me, "YOU NEED TO STOP RUNNING FROM YOUR CALLING!" Like out the blue, he came to me. "You know you're called to preach like your mama; you have lives to save and bring to Christ and with you running and not walking in your calling, you're gonna have the ones who aren't saved's blood on your hands. Do you want other people blood on your hands when you could have saved them?"

Standing there looking at him like really dude? As well as trying not to say what I was thinking. I remember saying, "OOOOOOH kay!!! But Jesus and I haven't had that conversation yet. But okay." He said, "Okay, but remember, YOU DON'T WANT BLOOD ON YOUR HANDS!"

I don't know what dudes his motive was.

I do know I am called to reach young people; I have always had a heart for the younger generation, even the young people who were my age at the time. I loved seeing young people come to Christ and being on fire for the Lord.

In the next few chapters, you'll see how passionate I was to help those who were in need and to bring my peers to Christ. Often, we go through obstacles and life's challenges; even get broken down to the core to only realize our true value and worth.

You are about to embark on an emotional rollercoaster. Don't close the book; you'll be fine. You're probably saying How? Girl; you don't know my emotions... Let me tell you how I know. The experience you are about to read is about me, a bad relationship, and making bad decisions; all while still trying to be the best woman and Christian I know how to be. It broke me all the way down; but, I overcame it. Yes, there were times where I thought I was going to fall off and die, but it was nobody but God's Grace and Mercy that kept me alive.

While writing this testimony; I've learned one important lesson. ALWAYS HAVE A PEN! I learned that the hard way, you'll never know when God is going to start speaking. For me, when he started talking, it was like he wouldn't stop; and it would always be while I was working. I caught myself sometimes saying "Wait, Lord, hold on, let me get a pen or something." People at work would see me grab a piece of cardboard from one of their boxes so I could jot notes down. Some thought I was going to used it for a fan, others thought I was probably weird. I've caught myself talking to people or just having a conversation, and I'll stop mid-sentence to either write down or do a voice memo on what I just said so I wouldn't forget. It's easy to find something to write on rather than finding something to write with.

DISCLAIMER

Five things you may want to do or even say while you take this journey with me.

1. **Pray & Praise!** There will be some moments that will just be led to pray! You may know someone who is going through what your reading and made it through or it maybe YOU!

2. **Curse** Yes, I did just say "Pray and Praise". We are Christians, yes! But we are still human. There will be some cursing in the upcoming chapters, and some chapters will make you want to curse and that's okay; because I definitely did. After you get your words out, go back to Step one!

3. **"I need a drink!"** I don't even know how many times I've said this while living these chapters and even more so WRITING THEM!

4. **Laugh** This step comes from my Dad. He was reading some of the chapters in the beginning stages before he even got to the "forbidden chapters" as he would call it. Those are the chapters of the things I went through that my family nor him had ANY CLUE bout. I found him laughing, laughing to keep from crying and getting upset.

5. **Cry** You're going to need tissue; so, go ahead and have some handy.

6. **Call and Post** Some of you are going to want to pick of the phone to call and or text me, and that's fine, I'm ready. Others, I encourage you to post what your reading and share with men and women you know who may be going through this by using the hashtags #getthehellout #igotthellout #theycallherblue

Even though it may be a tough read for some, especially my family. I pray that by the end of this book, you have a better insight into knowing your WORTH! As well as understanding the signs of mental abuse, getting OUT and most importantly, gaining a closer relationship with GOD! I want you to know that you are not "too far gone" to where HE can't save you.

ARE YOU READY!? Let's go!

Mr. Right?

I was just getting out of a six-year relationship with my first love – my college love. In my opinion, things ended unexpectedly and kind of abruptly. Which caused me to have to move back to San Antonio from Dallas. I was NOT, and I mean NOT trying to go back to San Antonio, I was weighing every option. Using a spreadsheet for my bills, I would have to now take responsibility for everything all by myself since it wasn't being split. Ya girl would have been struggling every month just to get by, and to be honest, I was forcing myself to be okay with that because I did not want to come back home.

It ended up working out for the best as I was selected to be a contestant in the 2016 H-E-B Slim Down Showdown. It was a 90-day challenge with my job that would help me gain a better knowledge of nutrition, exercise and losing weight the right way and most importantly, the healthy way. It was based in San Antonio, so this helped me take advantage of the local events so I could get the most out of the program. I did not win the challenge, but I gained so much knowledge and was more aware of things that should and should not go into my body. I ended up losing 16lbs within that time span.

Although I was achieving my weight loss goal, I was borderline depressed. The breakup with my ex really tore me apart. I was okay during the program because it was a distraction from knowing that I was still single and nowhere closer to becoming someone's bride. I wouldn't say this made things worse, but during that time, I was also preparing for my cousin's wedding. We both dreamed of having a double wedding. more so her than me but hey, I was still down for the cause. I wouldn't say I was jealous about it, but, it was more like *"damn, what am I doing wrong?"* or *"what did I do wrong?"* I gave my all, and I mean my ALL into that relationship to think we're progressing to really find out that in the end, I was getting played! Don't get me wrong; I was uber excited for her to marry her high school sweetheart, I just imagined us doing it around the same time, if not together. But hey, life still went on.

I remember telling my parents one day after church; *"LOOK, I don't want nobody, I ain't looking for nobody I'm fine by myself!"* In all actuality, I was hyping myself up (this is me being a G (gansta) you'll find out more about that as you read) because deep down, I was dying. I just wanted to be loved by someone like I love others. My parents started laughing, and then made googly eyes at each other, smirked and my Dad pointed at my Mom; and I'm looking like… *"Umm, what I miss?"*

Mom: *"I said the same thing. Then I met your Dad! He was not what I was looking for in a man physically* (in awe my Dad looks at my mom while swinging his hands up and down like he's showcasing his body like he was the man!) *because I was attracted to other types of guy; guys that were no good for me. He may not have been what I wanted, but he was WHAT I NEEDED! God will send you what you need; it may not be what you want; but He knows what you need."*

Me: *"Yeah, yeah, that's cute, but I ain't looking for no one."*

Mom: *"I wasn't looking for your Dad, God sent him, your time is coming baby just be patient."*

July 12, 2016; Mom and I were sitting in the airport heading to Alabama to share and witness my boo (cousin) walk down the aisle. As we waited for our flight, I get a Facebook message from a friend, it says, *"Hey, how you been?"* I was a little shocked to get a message from this person. We were always cool, he used to play drums at my parents church a few years back, and we happen to friend each other one day.

We would always check in from time to time; then he would disappear. *RED FLAG #1* Right before I moved to Dallas, I ran into him at my Aunt's funeral, I got a message later that night saying *"Hey, sorry for your loss. I didn't know that was your Aunt; she was cool people."* Since then we would usually keep in touch from time to time; especially when I see one of his angry post about his "Baby Mama" and how he was going off and wanted to beat up and kill people *RED FLAG #2* over not being able to see his daughter. So, me being me, I'd hit him up asking if he was okay, try to calm him down, as well as sending words of encouragement.

He'd always joke and tell me *"Man, your dude tripping. Ya'll been together this long and he still hadn't put a ring on it?? Man, you'd be wifey right now if it was up to me."* I'd always ignore him and say, *"When the time is right for him, he'll propose."* Yeah right; but one thing I did not like was when he would try to talk down or ill about him. My ex may not have been perfect, but I wasn't going to let someone disrespect my man. PERIOD!

The week went on, and we started communicating on a different level, other than that "Friend Zone" I kept him in. He was saying all the right things, had his head on straight and everything. Brutha was coming correct; in church (noticed I said "in church", keep reading), educated, good job and was doing well for himself. I told my Auntie London who he was and everything — and like any good Aunt, she did her Facebook investigating; and for her, so far, he checked out; but she did say she was keeping her eyes on him because she knew the hurt I had just been through; and didn't want him to put me through the same thing.

The whole time I was in Alabama for the wedding, we were talking and getting to know each other on a completely different level. He was even there to calm me down through the hair crisis I was having on my cousin's big day. He told me that as soon as I came back, he was taking me on a date to a restaurant called Biga on the Banks, and he was determined to take me out that weekend. We went out a spur of the moment date; the morning after I arrived back in Texas. He was talking so much smack about how I can't bowl and stuff, so I felt like that was a challenge and most times I don't back down from a challenge.

So, I asked him when he wanted to meet up. He gives me a time but hits me with, *"Oh, you're gonna have to come get me because I ended up leaving my car downtown when I went out with my bruhs. Since we'll be downtown, I'll just pick it up after our day."* *RED FLAG #3* (the night before my flight I asked him if he could come pick me up from the airport rather than me taking an Uber, since we've been talking and he was very "interested" in me I figured why not right. that's when he told me that he was in a fraternity and they had a big BBQ that weekend and he was going to be drinking and didn't want to drink and drive.) **Months later, my speculation of whether he was a part of the Divine Nine was confirmed when I put him in front of my cousin and uncle who are both in the fraternity he spoke of and not once did he try to grip (the handshake) them up. When I told my cousin, *"Hey, he happens to be your frat."* Jahmel's response was nonchalant; and my cousin said, *"Oh yea, what's up bro."* Jahmel change the subject QUICK! I'm sorry; if I met a soror or a frat brother, I'd be like *"AAYO, FRAT!"* or *"HEEEY SOROR!"* As well I will have some type of paraphernalia or something, so that people would know I was apart of the greatest sorotity in the world. During our relationship, there was NO evidence of him being apart of ANYTHING…better yet a fraternity.** So I was like, okay cool, I believe you; because you work for USAA, so I know you legit and got wheels. (at least, so I thought) As I approach, he is standing at the corner, the first thought I had was, why am I picking up this nigga on the corner like I'm a side piece?

RED FLAG #4. We go bowling, he takes me on a boat tour on the Riverwalk, then out to eat. The time we spent together; it was a different feel and vibe; it felt adult-ish, it felt right so-to-speak. He treated me like a lady the whole time; it felt like something I could get used to. Leaving downtown, I said, *"Hey, where is your car? We can swing by there and get it so we won't have to come back after we eat. Where you park it at?"* He says, *"Naw, I'll get it later, I have my bruh picking it up for me. He took my keys last night"* Yeah Azure, that's like Red Flag #5; but I ignored it, trying to get all the pieces aligned and sorted before putting the puzzle together. We ended up going to Rudy's BBQ, as we ate, we got to know each other more over one of my favorite BBQ spots. After a long day of fun, I dropped him off at home. We hugged and said our good-byes and before I was able to get back in the car. He lifted my chin and went in for a kiss and said, *"I had a lot of fun. Let me know when you get home."* I low-key melted on the inside, blushing while I got in the car, looking at him with googly eyes. I said *"I had fun too. thank you."*

A few days went by, and it seemed like forever because I was excited about going out on a real date, and not to Olive Garden, or Cheesecake Factory, but actually go somewhere where I have no other choice but to get dressed up. This Biga on the Banks place looked really fancy from the pictures I seen on Google. Well, our formal date got changed to a spontaneous trip to the beach in Corpus, but the day before we got into a huge fight, and I mean huge; all because I was open and honest with him. At the start of our relationship, I told Jahmel that I wanted to have open communication with him regardless of what the situation may be. I felt strongly about this because this was one thing my previous relationship lacked. My ex always felt he knew how I would react if he was honest and just never spoke on the stuff that was going on or bothering him. So, I wanted this to be different with Jahmel and let there be no room for miscommunication. Well, he definitely took what I told him some type of way and went LEFT!

My ex; you know; let's give him a name...let's call him; Vince. So, Vince text me and asked, *"Do I still have my best friend?"* Vince still considered me as his best friend all though we didn't work out. During his break up speech he told me that he considered me one of his true best friends since we've been through SO MUCH together and I played a big role in his life and in his growth as a man and he would never forget me. (if I could insert and eyeroll emoji I would insert it here.) Before Jahmel came into the picture Vince and I would still text each other regularly, and it almost felt like something could be rekindled to only realized he was probably playing me again; so I just stop responding to him, which is the reason for the question; and at that time, I didn't consider him my "best friend" because he hurt me so much to even consider it especially after my last encounter with him well after our break up. I was officially done. I didn't want to keep throwing my heart out there to get played with.

This is what I told Jahmel, and he took it as if I was cheating on him and was trying to go back to Vince, so he went off on me. He said: *"You're pretty as hell but you're full of sh**."* The going back and forth went on and on— to the point I found myself begging him to believe me and not to be upset! LADIES LADIES LAAAADIEES! DON'T you EVER beg a MAN for anything! If you know you're not doing anything wrong or you try to plead your case so he can stay or no longer be mad at you. Baby, he ain't the one! (Keep reading) I was so afraid of being alone because all I wanted was to be loved the same way I loved. I called one of my good friends, Jade and when she answered the first thing I said was, *"I think I just lost a good one. Me and my damn mouth!"* She said, *"Zury* (one of MANY nicknames) *what you do now?"* I explained to her what happened, and while she was calming me down I had no clue she was messaging him on Facebook trying to be my advocate.

The hours went by and I hadn't heard from Jahmel, and at this point, the excitement I had for our big special date was dwindling down. Around 9 pm, I finally get a call; when the phone rang, I got excited but mad at the same time because it took forever for him to reach back out. We started talking, and he said that when he was pretty much ignoring my calls, he was thinking about what he wanted to do as far as moving forward; and that the ONLY reason he wanted to continue talking was because Jade reached out to him and advocated for me. I told Jahmel that we need to sit down and talk face to face. (this was for me so I can read his body language and see where he was.) He agreed and suggested we go to IHOP, but it came with some demands... *"Well since we're going to meet at IHOP, swing by and pick me up then."* Me, trying to avoid another confrontation or make matters worse, I gave in and said *"okay."*

We finally get to IHOP, and he gets straight to the point. He made it clear that he did not like the fact that I was in communication with *"the ex that did you dirty and played with your heart for six years."* Jahmel also made it clear that where he's from (California), that's considered being un-loyal. Not knowing the California ways and culture. I explained to him that that – that was not my intention and that my intention was to have open and consistent communication, so we can build and grow together and most importantly, gain trust especially if it's all out on the table, there would be nothing to hide or be secretive about. He was saying he would have to gain my trust again, because he thought I was different from the other girls he dated. So, ole naive me; took that as a challenged to prove to him I am indeed different from the other chicks and can be trusted. That whole time he was showing me who he was and how manipulative and controlling he can be.

We 'kissed and made up' afterwards and we were both excited to have a do-over and go on our date. Probably more so me than him though. Before I took him back home, we decided to go to Walmart at 1 o'clock in the morning and just walk around. As we were walking towards the toys and entertainment section, Jahmel ask: *"Have you ever gone fishing?"*

Azure: *"Nope!"*

Jahmel: *"Really, we should go. Would you go with me?"* Azure: *"Yeah, I'm open and down for new adventures; I'd go."* Jahmel: *"Well. LET'S GO!"*

Shocked and confused, I look up at him with a grin on my face *"RIGHT NOW!?"*

Jahmel: looks at me excited and says, *"Yeah, why not? We can go to the beach to fish. We just need to get some stuff…everything we need is here."* Grabbing my hand, he says, *"come on let's get a basket."*

Stunned at the spontaneity of what just took place…I get just as hyped as him. He asked if I had a swimsuit and if I didn't, he told me to go pick one out; cause we were going to the beach to fish and get in the water. He also told me that we were going to take my car because it would be easier to drive it on the beach. At that time, I had a rental car due to my car being in the shop to get fixed from a hailstorm we recently had. It was a Toyota Rav 4; cute little car too. I looked at him and with a sassy little attitude. I said "Well, you're driving because I ain't!" he looked at me and laughed saying *"Okay, okay. lil miss boss."* Excited. I placed one foot on the cart and used my other to sweep the ground so I can coast to the sporting good section.

I was, however, really looking forward to going on our fancy date he planned. I had all my girlfriends helping me pick out the perfect dress and everything. Who would have thought my little formfitting black dress would turn into a swimsuit, shorts, tank top and slides and we would end up on the beach. Nevertheless, we did have an amazing time and got to learn more about each other. Being out there on the water, I felt so free! I forgot all about the pain, hurt and betrayal I was feeling from the past relationship, I forgot about how I was blaming myself and trying to figure out what I did or what I was doing wrong because I wasn't getting married like my cousin. In that moment, I felt like he is the one and that I would soon be someone's wife and would be walking down the aisle. I posted a picture of the clear blue sky and beautiful water on Facebook and used the hashtag "baecation" and man oh man; the comments came in as well as the text and phone calls. One call, in particular, I could NOT ignore – My mommy! I didn't tell her WHO he was, but I did tell her I was with someone, and of course like any mother, she wanted ALL the details. If she could have snatched me from Corpus to Las Vegas through the phone she would have, because I wasn't giving up any information.

The day came for us to leave, and I did not want to go, I felt like that place was the only place I could be me. I've always loved water (even though I cannot swim) but being out there made me love it even more. Before we headed out to go back to San Antonio, Jahmel wanted to go to Walmart to get something for his daughter since it was her 7th birthday. He picked her out a pretty necklace, bear and a card. While we were driving back into the city, he called his baby mama to see where she was; because he wanted to go pick her up and take her out to eat. I made it clear that is should be something they do on their own and to not involve me. We have only been talking for a few weeks and I wasn't ready for all of that—I wanted to be team drama free.

The conversation between him and the baby mama went from 0-100! REAL QUICK! This was the first time I experienced any baby mama drama, so I didn't know what to do. They were both cursing each other out, she was telling his business. I overheard her say *"How you gon pick her up Jahmel? What car? You prob in some b**** car. You not about to have my child around no other b****."* I mean she was going in and he was going in just as hard. Telling her how dumb she was, that she's full of it and back and forth.

Shocked, as I sat in the passenger side, I wanted to jump out of the car because it felt so awkward. That should have been Red Flag #... something, (I lost count.) That phone call lasted about a good hour and a half, if not longer. I remember he got on the phone with her shortly after we got on the road and we were about 10 minutes back into the City when it ended. I felt like our ride coming back was robbed and we didn't really get to do a full recap of our trip. We arrived at the apartment where his daughter was living, and he asked me if I could write in the card for him because his handwriting was bad. He wrote happy birthday on a scratch piece of paper and it was horrible—so I gave in and wrote… "Happy Birthday Baby Girl; Daddy loves you very much." …in the card. He also wanted me to write something to her personally; I gave him the side eye and said *"Naah doc you're trying to set me up, I'm good. I don't want no problems."* He gets out to go give her the gifts; but what he didn't know is that I was thinking of an escape plan in case something popped off or shots were fired. If you would have witnessed that conversation, you would be thinking of an escape plan too. For me, my plan was solid. I had family who lived right around the corner and my Big Daddy was 10 minutes away so I would have been good; thank the Lord nothing happened, and I didn't have to execute my plan. Jahmel was able to spend the weekend with me on the beach and do what he loves—fishing and see his daughter for her birthday.

So that was definitely a win; I've heard the stories about the battle of him seeing his daughter on Facebook before we got together, so I knew how much she meant to him. If he was happy, then so was I.*WRONG MIDSET TO BE IN, with not even a month in; but that's just me as a person. I always want to see people happy.*

Jahmel was very adamant on meeting my parents; he really "wanted" to get to "know them" personally rather than the side he'd see at church; so much that he wanted to do a game night. So, I sent a message to the group chat and added him in the loop; (Communication is key right?) My Mom remembered him from his pictures and was all excited; he was handsome and "appeared" to have it all together and would be a good fit for me. During the chat throughout the day, Jahmel said he wanted to order wings and or pizza and just have a ball! He also suggested that we play Monopoly and he was talking trash already. *"Monopoly is my game. Ya'll going down."* he said. My Dad was hyped and Ready! He said, *"Ok, I see; he's talking mess! He's going down."* For me the scary part was being at work while the text messages were flying and not being able to regularly check my phone. I was praying hard that nothing crazy was being said and then my people would be like *"NOPE!"* God heard my prayers and none of that happened, so we were in the clear.

After work, I went over to pick up Jahmel (what flag is this?? Like 20? I know someone is keeping count) and then the food. I know, I know— he was the one that wanted to meet them. He should have drove his self or caught an Uber, because I still had yet to see this truck he had. In all honesty I wasn't ready for my parents to meet him this soon. Only because I wanted this one to be right and know that it wasn't a two-minute thing, but a relationship with potential and success. Although my brother BJ met him when he came back home from a tournament. We went bowling, and he was able to do his brotherly duty and scope him out before he got to the big honcho…DAD!

We finally arrived at the house, and I am more nervous then he is. I was trying to prep him on the ride over and before we walked in. He grabbed my hand, looked me in my eyes and gently said *"It's okay, this is going to be fun! Parents love me!"* Uneased in my stomach I gave a nervous grin with a sigh and said *"okay, we will see.* We walked in the house and it felt like I was meeting them for the first time too. My mom had the candles burning and cookies in the oven. It felt and smelt very homey and welcoming. Dad was chilling on the couch watching stats about the Knicks and BJ was sitting on the stairs chilling. Jahmel walked in and said, *"Hey hey, Hello hello!"* He sees my Dad first, he goes over to greet him and give him a handshake as I'm walking towards my mom in the kitchen, I hear him say to my Dad. *"Hello, my name is Jahmel nice to FINALLY meet you."* Dad responds with a similar pleasantry *"hey man, Mr. Gabriel, nice to me you too."* Then my mom, oh my mom. Excitingly turns around but not just any turn, she did a slight barney jump and said *"HEEEEEEEEEEY! Nice to meeeet yooou!"* With bucked eyes I looked over at BJ and then my mom like—whoa what just happened. After all the meet and greets were out the way we sat down to pray for the food and began to eat.

While eating dinner, the questions start flying; *"So, Jahmel, where are you from?"* *"What do you do for a living?"* *"Why, Azure?"*

He replies with *"I am originally from the bay...California. I was born and raised there. Until my last year in high school my mother wanted to follow her sister to Texas, and I been here since 2004. I work as a Mortgage Underwriter for USAA and I love it; and to answer your last question. Why not Azure, she's beautiful, about her business. Has a good head on her shoulders so why not?"*

I'm not going to lie; I was blushing while making eye contact with my mom thinking, *"Ohkaaay, Jahmel!"* While looking at my dad and BJ, they seemed intrigued and captivated so far. Then he goes on to ask...

"Mr. Gabriel, I have a question for you. What are your expectations of me?"

I see my Dad's eyes get a little big while he adjusts his position in his seat. BJ does the *"Say What?"* head motion while Mom and I hit the *"I been waiting for you at the doh"* neck snap. I think we all adjusted our position in our seat. That was a question that we never heard coming from a guy who is in pursuit of me, nor was expecting. I don't even think Vince asked that question at least to my knowledge, because the initial "Dad/Boyfriend" talk did not go well. AT ALL!

While we're still in amazement at his question, my Dad proceeds to answer.

"Well, for me, when any man comes to the table wanting to date my daughter, they need to have their things in order and or have a plan, working on getting things together. When I met her mother, I knew she was my wife because God told me. I saw her get filled with the Holy Ghost one evening service and that's when God told me. "That's your wife." We dated, and I didn't have much, but I knew what God told me, so I needed to get things in order, so I can be able to provide for her. During our engagement, I got a job offer in Baltimore, Maryland. I left her behind here in San Antonio. I didn't want to, but I knew what I had to do as man and provide the best life for her by going and getting established there. I started my new job stayed in MD for a few months got us an apartment. The next time I saw her was when I drove back a few day before our wedding."

Jahmel: *"Wow, that's commitment and dedication. So, what would you need to see from me that will show you I'm serious about your daughter? The last guy she was with was a bum and played with her, I mean six years and he couldn't make a move. He's stupid."*

We all kind of made a face in agreement to the comment and looked to my Dad to answer the question.

Dad: *"I need to see that you're able to provide for her. I expect you to be respectful of and to her. If your dating with a purpose to marry, I don't have a problem helping you get to that point; to where I feel like you are ready for her to come under your umbrella. Right now they're (pointing at my mom, BJ and I) are under my umbrella. There should be no lack or gaps while she's leaving under my covering and protection to yours."*

Jahmel: *"Okay, that's sounds fair. I'm not here to play games or toy with her heart. I plan on making her my wife in the next couple of years. Of course, with your blessing sir."*

Dad: *"Alright, that sounds fair. I'll have my good eye on you."*

That's pretty much how the "Meet the Gabriel's" went. We had a great night playing monopoly, and everyone getting to know Jahmel, it was right up his ally because it had to do with money and accounting; we were so into the game that Mommy burned the cookies; and I mean BURNT!! You could have played hockey with those things. After the initial meet with the parents, things started to progress. He would pop up at my job from time to time with roses, cards, candy and sometimes dinner. Then all of a sudden, the real Jahmel showed up and *"Mr. Right"* was starting to turn into *"Mr. Crazy!"*

"I'm Not As Think As You Dumb I Am"

(I'm Not As Dumb As You Think I am)

Things were going good and it was almost time for BJ's 18th birthday. He wanted to go bowling and hang out at the house with his close friends. Jahmel wanted to come and hang out with us to celebrate B's birthday. About an hour before it was time to head to the bowling alley Jahmel text me saying, today would be the day I meet his mother and daughter. Super nervous but excited I tell my mom what Jahmel said and she gives me that excited look. Jahmel didn't really talked too much about his mom as much as he talked about his daughter, so I knew this was going to be a fun experience but at the same time I never dated a man with a child so I didn't know what to say, all I knew was to be me.

Jahmel tells me that they were Ubering to the bowling alley and asked if I could take them home after the party was over because he still hadn't gotten his car from his house in Atlanta. Confused on how his car got to Atlanta when it was just downtown? Yea I was too; before we had the 'Meet the Parents' night. Jamhel asked if I could pick him up so we can go pick up the food and some games for the night—confused I asked him where his car was. He told me it was still in Atlanta, giving my phone the side eye I ask how his truck magically got to Atlanta when it was just in San Antonio when we went on our date and how has he been popping up at my job surprising me. He said *"Oh, no babe…I must have said it wrong. I had a rental car. Remember I was telling you my mom had a stroke last year and a few months ago she got worse, and I just hopped on the first flight I could get to come check on her? I didn't think I'd be in Texas this long. I just hadn't had time to go get my car and rest of my stuff."*

Not really buying his explanation, I brought it. Something still didn't seem right but I again, ignored the thousandth red flag that popped up. After the bowling part of the birthday party, we headed back to the house for movies, cake, ice cream and other things the birthday boy wanted to do. At the house I was able to mingle more with his daughter Ja'Nay, she's the cutest little thing too. When my mom saw her at the bowling alley, she said she reminded her of me when I was little. So much so that my mom snuck a picture of Ja'Nay and put it together with a picture of me when I was her age. LISTEN! If my mom was to post that picture you would hands down think she was my child, we look that much alike. Just spending a few hours with Ja'Nay, we became inseparable and she was stuck to me like glue. We went off and left Jahmel downstairs with the party to go do fun girlie things and watch movies in my room. Little Ja'Nay was slowly wrapping me around her finger, and I was pretty excited in knowing that if this thing worked with Jahmel, she would be my daughter too and I was totally okay with it all.

It's been about two months since Jahmel and I started dating, with him being an mortgage underwriter he told me his job requires him to do a lot of traveling and he would take Ja'Nay with him a lot of times and that he would love for me to come with him on one of his assignments. While we were going to the movies one evening, his boss called him to tell him that this couple was getting closer to signing on their new home in San Francisco and he needed to be there incase things needed to be taken away or added to the loan. She also wanted to know if I'd be joining him; if so, she needed my information so she can book my flight with his. All excited I said *"YEAH, I'LL GO! Just give me the dates so I can take off and I'll be there."* They both explained to me that all expenses will be paid all we had to do was get on the plane. After the conversation was over, I tell Jahmel that he's going to have to ask my dad for permission. He felt like he didn't have too, so I had to explain the whole respect thing to him and, it's only right that he ask my dad and let him know what his plans are especially if he's planning on taking me out of the state.

Now with my mommy and I being close, I couldn't keep this excitement to myself, as I was giving her the details and the run-down BJ walks in the room. So now I had to let him in on the big trip. A week goes by, Jahmel was just as excited as I was. He started sending me pictures of the suite we were scheduled to stay at and when I tell you it was nice, it was NICE! While the pictures of the view from our future room kept coming in, I asked Jahmel when he was going to talk to my dad, he responded saying he was going to come over that night. Dad not really knowing why Jahmel wanted to talk to him since there has been no improvement based on the last conversation they had. Jahmel explains the trip to my dad and BJ since he was in on the meeting. Mommy and I weren't invited but we had a front row seat to the conversation by eavesdropping from upstairs and Dad just goes straight into it…

"So, based on the last conversation we had about your current living situation and you bouncing back and forth to Atlanta; do you have an update for me? Why are we here?"

"Yes sir, I'm working on that. I was telling Azure the other day, that after I wrapped up with this client in San Fran my next trip would be to go back to Atlanta to get my car and grab the things I need from my house since I'm selling it. I have a friend living in it now, but I'm going to have to

sell it due to my mom being sick and I'm now closer to my daughter. Plus, with this trip to San Francisco, once the client signs I will go right into my new position and I'll get a $10,000 signing bonus." Jahmel pleads.

Dad responds, *"Well what if the client doesn't sign? You forfeit the new position and bonus?"*

Jahmel: *"Oh no sir, the promotion I'll get rather they sign or not, and I'll still get my signing bonus."*

Dad: *"Ok, I remember based on our last conversation you said you were already planning to go to Atlanta to get your truck that week. What happened to that? I already expressed to you once how I felt about Azure being out late at night especially having to take you home and having to come back by herself. That doesn't sit well with me, her mother and brother —and it shouldn't sit well with you either. Especially after you sat right there at that table and told us your plans for Azure and so on; and we have yet to see anything come from that conversation. Yes, we see you buying her shoes, make-up and stuff but that's not going to work. I need to see some action on that plan. Now as far as this San Francisco trip. Is her flight already booked?"*

Jahmel: *"Yes sir, we leave this Thursday and come back on Sunday morning."*

Dad: *"Okay, does she have all the information and the itinerary?"*

Jahmel: *"No sir, not yet. I'm waiting for the team at work to finalize the travel accommodations then they'll send it to me and I'll forward it to Azure."*

Dad: *"Okay, she can go. Just make sure you get that information to her."*

They talked a little bit more about his house and mysterious truck he had. I think I ended up taking him home that night, but Dad made it clear that it would be the last time I'll be out late taking *"this gentleman"* home. Jahmel was a little irritated after the conversation he and my dad had. Thinking on it now, this was around the time my parents started to see the true colors of Jahmel and knew that everything he was saying and has said was all a lie. They were starting to figure him out. So yeah, of course he should have been irritated because this plan of his was starting to fall apart. Being blind to all of this, I was super excited about our trip. I always dreamed about flying or going on trips with my boyfriend like you'd see on movies and like I'd see my friends and family do with their significant other.

I packed the night before, so that all I needed to do was shower, get cute and pack the little stuff. Jahmel was flying in from another 'business trip' so I was waiting on him to come and get me so we can catch our flight to San Francisco. Peeking out the window, I get caught by mommy. I turned around and she had this big grin on her face laughing at me. I ran up to her, saying *"Now I know how you feel, when you be waiting for Dad to come back from his trips."*

Mom laughs and says *"Yep, you have butterflies in your stomach huh?"*

Pacing back and forth checking my phone I finally get a text *"Hey babe!"* followed with a phone call. I excitingly answer the phone; *"HEY!*

You on your way!!??" Jahmel responds hesitantly.

"Yes and no, listen. That couple we were going to San Fran for. Something came up with them legally, so we have to push their singing back, so my job cancelled the trip. I know it sucks I just found out, BUT the good news is... thinking about the conversation your dad and I had the other night, I'm about to just hop on a flight to Atlanta; I was about to change my ticket, get my truck and drive back to Texas. Then we can go do something so your dad can get off my ass about the car and stuff."

My mom saw all of the excitement I had get sucked out of me while I was talking to Jahmel, and she knew that this trip was now a no go. I was sad and disappointed but at the same time I was happy that he wanted to use this opportunity to go get his car and take care of the things he needed to take care of back in Atlanta. My mom walks sad little me into her room so I can tell my dad the news about the cancelled trip and about him going to get his truck. Dad was like "well, sorry about your trip, but I'm glad he's taking action on this plan he's been having."

A few hours go by and my dad, comes and asked me if Jahmel got on the road yet, because it was raining pretty bad and some of the roads were flooded(it was hurricane season) and he wanted him to stay clear of IH-10 and he should take an alternate route to be safe since he was doing a turnaround trip; land, go pick up his truck and get back on the road. I texted Jahmel with the details I got, and he said it started pouring pretty bad so he just stayed at his house and would get on the road in the morning. The next morning rolled around and I figured I'd wake up to a 'Hey, babe I'm on the road, see you in a bit' text. Yeah, no. NOTHING! So, with my worrisome self, I panic and call him, phone went straight to voicemail. I'm thinking oh Lord, he got swept away by some water… HA! just being extra! Hours go by and still no word from him, then finally I got a call; he told me that he was back in San Antonio BUT! He didn't get his car; he flew back because the weather was too bad. Jahmel's plan was to rent a car and take me to the beach since our extravagant trip to Cali didn't happen.

I ended up meeting him at a food spot, so we can go over what the plan was. Jahmel was very admit about going to the beach, but I was more so going for the plan to go to Atlanta; if we're going anywhere Atlanta should be the spot, I can meet his people see the house and most importantly get this truck he's 'paying for and come back home. I tried my best to talk him into it, but it didn't work. The plans to go to Corpus was underway. Jahmel and I pull up to the rental car spot at the airport; Jahmel gave the lady his information for the reservation he put in while we were eating. Everything was good until it got to the payment part—Jahmel couldn't rent the car or put it in his name because he had an outstanding balance. All they needed was to have a card on file to pay for the amount that was due at the time of us taking the car. Now because I didn't have a credit card due to me maxing it out when I was with Vince, I had to put it on my debit card and it pre-authorized for a high amount, but the lady explained that it would lift in 1-3 business days since it was on a debit card and not a credit card. For all the trouble and super long wait, they upgraded our economy car to a SUV. It was a black Toyota 4Runner, the windows were even tinted. That truck was so nice I put it on my list for when it was time to look for a new car. All and all we had a good time at the beach like we did the first time, and we didn't have any baby mama drama on the way back. I kept telling Jahmel, I still didn't feel right about this whole rental car transaction but he promised and kept reassuring me that he would give me the cash for the total of the rental so I can put it into my account. I have YET to see that money!

I am a HUGE Dallas Cowboys fan; Jahmel called me and told me he was taking me to see the season opener against the Giants. With Jahmel not having a car, I wasn't trying to drive, and I know my parents especially Dad wasn't about to have me drive let alone take my car. I told him that he needed to talk to my Dad to let him know what his plans are so he can give the yay or nay on this trip; since he still hadn't come through on operation get the truck from Atlanta. Jahmel sent a group text inviting us to Chili's for dinner on him. In the main group chat between the four of us; Mommy sends *Hmm, well I guess he got his signing bonus.* Jahmel never said he did or didn't but the spontaneous trip to Dallas, rental truck, hotel and tickets to the game; sounded like he had received the signing bonus. Dinner was set for 7:30 of course we were on time, but we didn't see Jahmel til about almost 9 o'clock. My dad's patience was running thin…so thin we went ahead and ordered our food. Dad was like if he comes cool, he got the check, if not oh well we're still going to eat. (this is where I get my mentality of 'Imma always make sure I have me or I'm good.') I am blowing up Jahmel's phone like

"Bro! Where you at?"

"This is not a good look for you!" "Dad's getting irritated." "SERI-OUSLY JAHMEL!?"

"I'm sorry babe, I lost track of time wrapping up paperwork and waiting on the rental people to get here with the car for this weekend. But I am on my way." Jahmel replies.

What seemed like 1000 hours later, Jahmel finally arrives, upon him sitting down he greets everyone, shakes my dad's hand apologies for being very tardy. I ended up ordering food for him so by the time he got there he can eat, and we won't be "stuck" there waiting for his food to come out. Which was right on time, about 5 minutes after he sat down the food came out. An irritated dad, automatically jumps in… "So! Jahmel. What's the special occasion that you called this dinner?" BJ and I both gave each other the eye while sipping our drink with a smirk on our faces because we knew our dad was tired and annoyed, he had to wait on this dude.

Jahmel came right out and told my dad his plans to take me to the Cowboy game. Shocked and excited for me my dad asked Jahmel to repeat his self to make sure he heard him right. Jahmel chucked because of my dad's reaction and face—Jahmel thought it was a good thing for him because he thought my dad was shocked in a happy way. Nah, if I know my dad like I know my dad; shock he was indeed but it was more so…How you gonna take this extravagant trip to Dallas with my daughter and do all these activities and spend all this money on that and a rental car BUT YOU CAN'T PUT THAT MONEY TOWARDS GETTING YOUR CAR FROM ATLANTA! That's EXACTLY what my dad was thinking. (Dad if I'm wrong hit me up and let me know.)

"Sooo, how are you planning on getting to Dallas since you still haven't gotten your truck? (SHADE) *I'm going to tell you now; Azure driving and her car is not in the picture. So, if that was your plan for getting to Dallas, it's a no for me."* Dad quickly responds.

I felt like that hit a nerve with Jahmel because I noticed he clinched his hand under the table and kind of adjusted his self in the seat—but he was quick on his feet with his response.

Jahmel: *"Oh no sir, her car or her driving was not in my plan at all. I actually rented a truck."* He then turns to me and says *"Yo, they came and brought me the same truck we had a few weeks ago. How cool is that?"*

"Seriously? That's dope. I really like that truck." I say.

My parents look at each other; my mom shrugs her shoulders and says it's okay with me, I'll go with whatever you say. Dad turned back to Jahmel with a serious face and asks, *"So you have the tickets already?"* Jahmel responds, *"yes sir my best friend works for the FBI and he's on detail that weekend in Dallas, so he was able to get tickets for us."*

"Okay, if you're truly going to see game, I am all for her going. IF something changes to where you can't get the tickets or plans change. I'm calling the trip off." Dad says to Jahmel while looking at my mom for confirmation. Jahmel agrees to the terms and ladies and gentlemen the next day we we're on the road heading to Dallas, my home away from home, the city I lived in by myself for 3 years with Vince, the city I fell in love with and didn't want to leave.

We made it into Dallas late Friday night close to Saturday morning, I was able to meet up with some of my old co-workers and Jahmel was finally able to meet Jade, my friend that I mentioned in the chapter before that was in his inbox vouching for me. I took Jahmel to some of my old hang out spots in Dallas and around where I lived. While on my rendezvous down memory lane, Jahmel wanted to stop by the Sprint store to look into getting a new phone, because the one he had was absolute TRASH! I can't tell you how many times it kept freezing and I had to restart it. Oh, you didn't know? I'm a tech geek; my mom calls me 'Ms. Best Buy.' While Jahmel was talking to the Sprint guy I am minding my own business just roaming the store while Jahmel took care of *HIS* business.

He was looking into the iPhone and I was strictly team Android. Jahmel says *"you should get one, I know you we're saying you wanted to get another phone for your business and design company, you want it? I'll get you one."* Looking at him in shock I turned down the offer saying *"nah, I'll stick to my android, iPhone are whack, everyone I know has a cracked screen."* The sprint guy laughed and hesitantly agreed with me. He then showed me some of the features on the phone and he got me on the part where you can send a text message with fireworks (Fun Fact about me—I love water, lights and FIREWORKS) and invisible ink. I was then intrigued, next thing I know I'm giving my social to this dude while he's setting up a whole new account in my name. Then he says... *"Alright ya'll, ma'am you're all set to go."* hands me the bag, gave Jahmel and I our new iPhone's and says *"enjoy your new phones, thanks for stopping in."*

It was all happening so fast, I didn't realize I was being manipulated again, first it was the rental car then it was the phones. So what happen was—Jahmel was like you're going to have to put the phones in your name. My initial response was *"NOPE!"* I wasn't the one with the messed-up phone I had a phone that I was good with, under my parents' contract. He told me because of the type of work he does, his social has blocks on it and because of his baby mama too and he has to call and go through this whole process to get anything to go through. Some straight B.S right. He told me that he will pay the bills and whatever the down payment would be, and that he did. I can't remember what we had to pay out the door, but he indeed paid for it and also paid for the first few bills moving forward. I was excited because I finally had two phones. If Jahmel didn't do anything right in this relationship converting me from Android to Apple was the best thing he has ever done for me. Team apple all the way, I instantly fell in love with that phone. The iPhone became my personal phone and the Android was my business phone because that 210 number was already on my pages and business cards. Now because we got the phone in Dallas I had a 214 area code and I was hyped! I had a part of Dallas with me. I did text my family and told them this was a new phone and that Jahmel brought it for me. They didn't really say much, and I definitely didn't tell them it I was in my NAME! Mom wasn't too thrilled about it, she was just trying to understand the purpose, she felt like this was his way on keeping tabs on me and or controlling me. After she made that comment while we were talking on the phone I started to think, was that his plan? To control me. Nah! Can't be, God wouldn't have "The One" be controlling.

Before heading back to the hotel, I asked Jahmel what he was wearing to the game and if he wanted to hit up academy to get a jersey, shirt or something and that's when another let down came. He hesitantly says:

"Yeah, bae. About that game. It's not safe for us to go, I was unsure on how to break it to you but remember I was saying my best friend Twan was in town on detail? Well, he hit me up and told us to stay not go to the game, because it's 9-11 and they got a tip about a

possible terrorist attack at AT&T Stadium. I wanted to at least go to Arlington and watch the game at a club or bar there so we can be close, but he said it's safer for us to stay out of Arlington period. I'm sorry babe. I know you really wanted to go; but I'm sure your dad would appreciate me protecting you from potential danger."

Not buying his bullsh** story at all I respond *"If you just couldn't get or afford the tickets just say so. I would be more understanding of that rather than you trying to make up a story. It's okay to say you couldn't get the tickets, trust me."* After I gave him to opportunity to come clean, he still kept his story and it seemed like he was really going to stick to it.

Later that night my friend Jade and I decided to go out on the town, we went to this place that played live music and had a ball. I was excited to get back to the hotel for two reasons, I needed to get ready for this Cowboy game the next day and I was missing Jahmel. If knowing he was getting ready to humiliate me in front of my friend; I would have stayed out later until he was sleep or something. I got back to the hotel and he was just mad, just angry and I couldn't understand why or where it was coming from. He was taking it out on me, and I'm trying to figure out what I did wrong and IF I did anything wrong. He asked me if I knew where he could get a bag from, confused I wasn't sure what he was talking about. So I say *"HUH?"* he looked at me as if I was slow and said *"Really Azure? I know you're not that saved."* Still confused I look over at Jade and she says *"Weed girl, weed! He's asking if you know where he can get weed from."* After I tapped out of my blonde moment—*"OOOOH weed, yeah. I know someone here but that probably wouldn't be a good idea to reach out."*

"Then why even bring it up if you not going to call them?" Jahmel says in a tone that was very off putting. Then he storms out the room. Jade and I looking puzzled trying to figure out what just happened. Not

waiting to be caught in the middle of whatever was going on or what was getting ready to happen. Jade grabs her purse and says *"Well, I'm going to head out and let ya'll work that out, and oooh girl! He seems to have an anger issue; you need to check that boo."* Giving hugs and kisses closing her car door as we said good-bye. As Jade was driving off I went into instant angry black girl mode; walking back into the hotel like 'OH NO HE DIDN'T JUST TALK AND ACT CRAZY WITH ME IN FRONT OF MY FRIEND. OH HELL NO!'

Walking back into a still hotel room, there was no sign of Jahmel. Still trying to process what just happened, I gave him a call and of course, no answer. So, I went on about my night and started to prepare for bed, when I hear fumbling at the room door. Getting out of the bed to stand in the middle of the walkway so he can't avoid me, as the door opens, I see his face I exclaimed *"YO! What the hell was that all about."*

"Move! I don't have to talk" he says. I rebuttal *"I don't care if you don't want to talk, you owe me an explanation as to why you went off and embarrassed me like that in front of my friend. Over me not wanting to make a phone call?"*

"So why you don't feel like it would be a good idea calling? It's not like you the one smoking it." He inquires back.

"Jahmel, the reason I don't want to and why I am not going to call is because if I call X and ask him to meet me so I can get some weed it's going to raise A BUNCH of RED FLAGS. He's going to automatically call Vince and ask if he knew I was in town and he'll tell him I'm asking for weed. They BOTH know for a FACT I don't smoke, c a n 't s t a n d the smell, let alone be around it because of my allergies and ASTHMA! When Vince and I were around his friends they would purposely go outside or put me in a room where I wouldn't be affected by the smoke because they respected me that much; and the LAST THING I need is for Vince to try to be captain

save a hoe and call my people because he thinks I'm having a mid-life crisis or mental break down because he left me! NOW!!! If you want weed THAT BAD! You can go find it yourself. Forest Lane at the corner of Audlia or you can go over to 635 and Skillmen. But you'd probably get SHOT running up on unknown territory asking for weed."

"Maaaan you don't know what you talking bout." Jahmel say's jokingly. I chuckle *"Yeah, okay! You go ahead and try it. I lived on that street for a year and a half and in Dallas for almost 3 years. I've seen somethings and heard gun shots at LEAST once a week! A kid got murdered right in front of my building. So, If I don't see or hear from you in a few hours. I'm sure I'll see you on the first 48. IM NOT AS DUMB AS YOU THINK I AM JAHMEL!"*

I took my phones, slipped my shoes on, grab the hotel key and booked it towards the door. Jahmel call's out to me *"Azure? Where you going?"* Ignoring him, I let the sound on the door slamming answer for me. I wanted to cry, because deep down I was hurt, I felt like he wasn't taking me seriously, I almost felt dumb the way he talked to me. Sitting in the lawn chair by the pool trying to figure out who I can call and vent too, but at the same time I didn't want to invite people into my business. I just sat there scrolled through social media and sent all his calls to voicemail, on both phones!

The next day came, it was now also 9-11 and it was GAME DAY! Even though he gave me that B.S excuses as to why we were getting ready for brunch rather than the game, I was still hyped. You may be a Dallas Cowboys fan but you're not a fan, fan, until you experience game day in the city. Jahmel wanted a good brunch spot with mimosa's and good food, so of course I said let's go to Blue Mesa. It was my first time being there for brunch, but their happy hour and dinner is AH-MAZ-ING! We got the buffet deal and they had an assortment of everything. Even endless drinks that was included. While eating, Jahmel, asked.

"*So do you really think Vince would have or would call your people if you hit up his homeboy!?*" Looking up at him like really, you want to ruin a good time bringing this up again. Wiping my mouth with the napkin while chewing the bite I just put in my mouth, I start to nod my head "*Yes, Jahmel. He would!*"

"*He a weak lame a*** nigga then. You a grown a** woman, and you're not his chick anymore. So why he care?*" Not trying to get into it with him or open this conversation back up. I shrug my shoulders and asked him how he liked his chicken and waffles. The waiter comes over and brings us the check and tells us when we're ready we can pay at the front. He looks at me and says, "*Whenever you're ready babe.*" Finishing the last few sips of my mimosa I get up and we head towards the front. It was a few people ahead of us waiting to check out. Jahmel hands me the keys to the truck and tells me to go ahead and get in the car, because he didn't want me to have to stand in that long line because I had on heels. I push his hand away "*Nah, bae I'm good, I can wear heels for a long period of time.*" He kept insisting, he says "*nah go ahead cause it hot outside too, you can start getting the car cool and looking up where else you want to go.*" I finally gave in and went to the car, maybe about five minutes later, if that! Jahmel comes and say's come on babe let's go. Knowing the amount of people that we're in front of us. I immediately asked what happened. An out of breath Jahmel says "*nothing… they asked who could pay cash, so we can get out faster, so I just paid cash.*" Looking at him, praying he didn't just do what I think and felt in my heart he did.

JAHMEL! Did you just skip the check!? SERIOUSLY! WTH, WHY!!?" Ignoring me he said NOTHING! Just drove like a bat out of hell trying to get out that parking lot. "*Is that why you told me to go to the car!? Jahmel, I'm talking to you!*" Still no response. I thinking to myself this boy really thinks I am dumb. "*Jahmel! That's one of my favorite spots, now*

I probably can't ever go back cause they'll have our picture everywhere!" He finally has a rebuttal, *"You not coming back to Dallas anytime time soon, they food wasn't that good anyways. So I wasn't about to pay for that shit."* I'm thinking well at least let me pay for my food, this is my second home—I didn't want him ruining that for me.

The day went on, still in the back of my head I was uneased knowing that he didn't pay for our meal, we decided to head back to San Antonio, since we wasn't going to the game he promised my dad he was taking me to; but before we got on the road. I stopped and met up with my cousin Phil who also lived in Dallas. It was good catching up with him, we sat and drank coffee at Starbucks for a good hour or two. Jahmel came in for a little bit, but ended up going back to the car, because he said he had a headache and just wanted to rest a bit so he can drive us back home, but he didn't want me to cut my visit short with my cousin.

After my cousin and I caught up, it was time to get on the road, Jahmel said he was rested and was okay to drive back to San Antonio. We made multiple stops, I noticed Jahmel was a 'stopper' he stopped for everything. Me on the other hand I'd stop no more than two times going back and forth to Dallas. Not Jahmel, as we were getting closer to Austin, he was complaining more and more about not feeling good and his head hurting. Jahmel also started swerving and talking really crazy, saying he didn't know where he was and so on. I started pleading the Blood of Jesus, and directing him to pull over, while I got my parents on the phone.

Everything was happening so fast, the thing that I remember the most is that while on the phone with my parents—I was giving mom Jahmel's symptoms and what exit we were coming up on and mile markers; while Dad was on his phone looking at hospitals that were close to us. Jahmel was just rambling on and on and on talking really crazy. He said something in 'that tone', I felt like he was getting ready to act like he did at the hotel. I said, *"Hey ma, let me call you back and figure this out cause I don't want to hear his mouth."*

(Months to a year later…wheeeewwww chile! Mommy shares with me that the statement I made did something to her—and I believe it was in that moment she knew that I was in a situation/relationship that I should not be in. Talking about it now to her, she still gets this uneased feeling. She probably has that feeling as she's reading this.)

We were approaching a red light as I rushed my mom off the phone. I turned in my seat *"Jahmel, we not about to do this. I'm trying to get you some help. Don't START!"* He started to talk super crazy, passing a gas stations he says *"You SMELL THAT! It's gas it's gas! You trying to kill me, oh GOD YOU'RE TRYING TO KILL ME!"*

"Jahmel, ain't nobody trying to kill you, calm down." I say in a frustrating tone while rubbing his shoulder trying to console him. He looks at me and goes crazy. Asking who am I and where was his girlfriend; just complete crazy! I don't remember how but I was able to get him to pull over so I can drive. My mom still in consistent communication with me, by sending me addresses to plug in so I can see which one was close to us. Jahmel finally calmed down and knocked out which made it easier for me to safely and peacefully make it to the emergency room. While Jahmel was taking his cat nap, I was able to talk to my parents in peace and focus. Once I found the closest emergency room my dad called to let them know I was coming in hot with a passed-out patient. (Man, my parents are the truth!) While dad was talking to the nurse, I'm telling mom how far away I am so they can tell the nurses. As I was pulling up, they were coming out with a wheelchair, it felt like a scene from a movie or tv show.

They ran a bunch of tests and it came back that he had a bad case of the flu. Influenza B to be exact, they ended up admitting him, but through that whole admitting process he was super mean to me and was talking to me worse than he was when he was in the hotel room. I chopped it up to him not feeling well and having these hallucinations earlier on. I'm thinking dude! I'm trying to help you and be there for you, hell. I got you here, you should at least be a little nicer to me. It was getting late and I still had to go to work the following day, and I for sure wasn't going to stay with him; plus, the hospital didn't recommend it because he was highly contagious. I just wanted to get home and rest, so that's what I did. After he was admitted, and everything was settled I took the rental and drove the last hour and a half to get back home to concerned and loving parents.

Jahmel was hospitalized in Austin for about a week and I found myself making an hour drive almost every day he was in the hospital. I would get off about 6 or 7PM and I would hit IH-35N heading towards Austin to check on my babe. On my off day I received a phone call from loss prevention of the car rental place we rented the truck from. They were asking about the whereabouts of the Toyota 4Runner I rented almost month ago. Confused I told him that the truck was returned and that my boyfriend ended up renting the same truck this week. The lady on the other end sounded confused but more so perplexed, almost like she felt bad for me. She said, *"Ma'am I'm sorry but, that truck was never returned."* Trying to hear the lady tell me about this truck, it was nothing but RAGE coming from my body. My initial thought about this truck was right…while thinking about how I wanted strangle Jahmel…I hear the lady say at the end of her statement *"If the car is not returned by the next two days, we will report the car as stolen and if you or someone happens to be driving it they will be picking up a charge."* Still baffled, I just say yes ma'am I will try to find it and turn it back in. I wasn't about to tell her it was sitting in my parent's driveway. Heck no!

As soon as I hung up with her I called Jahmel going off; but I made it sound like I was scared and made it seem like they we're trying to pin everything on me with him "renting it again." Hope this would be the moment he would come clean… *"Jahmel, did you not return the tuck from the first time!!??? Like be for real this is my life that's on the line. Cause if you didn't the car is IN MY NAME and I would be caught up in some mess."* I stress to him. Just like he lied to my FACE about skipping out on the bill he did the same with the truck and gave me some BS excuse. I hung up in his face and got ready to go turn the car back in. My mom was actually off that day, I told her I was going to return the truck because Jahmel was starting to rack up late fee's since it's passed the day he was suppose to turn it in. She offered to follow me to the rental place, but I insisted she didn't and that I would UBER back, so she can still be able to get her work done.

When I got to the rental place, I walk up to the counter to return the keys, the young lady that was at the desk asked if I wanted a receipt, I said *"YES! Please!"* As she was checking the car in, she then tells me the account has a balance of $735 that needed to be paid, before I left. Eye's bucked, I looked at her *"Excuse me? Huh?"*

"Yes, $735 ma'am." She says.

Defeated I tell her, ma'am I don't have that at all, I was told that the truck was getting ready to be marked stolen and I needed to find it and turn it in. Probably feeling sorry for me as well, she says *"Okay, well hold on. Let me see what I can do to close the account."* She comes back a few moments later and told me she went ahead and closed it, but I need to pay it as soon as possible but the car is checked in and LP will not be marking it as stolen. Dodging a big bullet and possibly jail time for this boy you'd think I'd leave right. Yeah no, I still stayed like a dummy.

Jahmel was finally released from the hospital the weekend of my mom's birthday extravaganza. To only go back in a month later. I was starting to notice that when Jahmel, is getting ready to make a commitment, like signing a lease for an apartment and or getting a car. Something always comes up to where that date has to be pushed back, he'll keep the deal lingering to where it canceled itself, so he pulls a *"I'm sick something doesn't feel right I need to see a doctor stunt."* In this case it was the; I need to see the doctor because my headaches are coming back, and I could have the flu again. Mind you this was two days before he was set to sign a lease on a new apartment since he and his mother got evicted for non-paid rent. He claimed that while he was in Atlanta, he was sending his mother rent, but she wasn't paying the rent, she was pocketing the money or ordering stuff off QVC.

Jahmel and his mother were staying at a hotel, while they were waiting for their unit to get ready. All he had to do was sign the lese and pay the fees. The manager was willing to overlook the broken lease he had on his record. Again, all he had to do was SIGN! Yeah, no! Jahmel wanted to see me and hang out so after church I went over to scoop him up, our "hanging out" turned into another emergency room visit. I got to the hotel and he comes out with sweats, a hoodie and these red shoes. I could not STAND those shoes either. He gets in the car and automatically lays the seat back and went into straight grumpy mode, pulling a towel out of his pocket and wrapped it around his eyes. At this point, I was completely turned off and knew that it wasn't going to go well and just like I thought, we ended up across the street at the emergency room, he was admitted and was tested for meningitis because he had all the symptoms along with flu symptoms. It was the last week in October going into November, so the flu was definitely going around.

While I was at work, he text me and told me that one of the test came back the he had an aneurysm. After losing someone close to me due to the same diagnosis, I literally dropped everything and rushed to the hospital! To only walk into a chick, sitting in there with him, not wanting to make a scene I hesitantly say *"Heey, hey babe."*

Jahmel: *"What you are doing here, I didn't know you were coming."*

Me: *"WHAT YOU MEAN WHAT IM DOING HERE? I came running after the text you sent."*

Jahmel: *"I didn't mean to scare you, they're still doing test…Oh this is my friend, she came to make sure I was okay."*

"HM, oh okay. Nice to meet you." I say sarcastically.

"Babe, do you mind going to grab my mom? She walked down to the waiting area, when she came." Jahmel asks.

Putting my stuff down, I go down the hall to grab his mother, walking back in the room, homegirl conveniently disappears. *"hm, what happened to your friend Jahmel."* I say in a petty tone.

Jahmel: *"She had to get back to work, she was actually leaving before you walked in. But when you came she started tripping talking about that I was trying to play her and I was rubbing us in her face, and that I told you to come up here."*

"What do you mean, "RUBBBING US IN HER FACE!"'" I say.

Jahmel: *"We used to talk, and she doesn't like you and she's been trying to get me to talk to her since we've been talking."*

The doctors and nurses came in so we couldn't finish our almost heated argument. With the other few visitors he had the evening, it wasn't until later that night that we we're able to finish the conversation; and it ended up with him flipping the script on me. Because Jahmel liked selling stuff to get money, he didn't have a cell phone – so he ended up using one of mine. Jahmel went ballistic, I don't remember what triggered it but he brought up the fact that Vince sent me a message on Facebook asking me a question about a client we did work for back in the day and if I still had the contact on file. A simple business conversation right, Jahmel took that as if I was trying to still get back with Vince. He was cursing me out saying that he *"curves bi*****"* that be in his DM because he respects me and I don't.

Trying to reason and tell him he's tripping and it's not what he thinks…he grabs the IV pole and swings it across the room towards my direction. Jumping in fear but also concerned for him, I whisper *"JAHMEL! YOU'RE IN A HOSPITAL! You can't be doing that!"*

To say the least it was very stressful with all the going back and forth to and from the hospital, spending the night and still getting up early for work. There would be days I'd go home cook a meal for him and take it back to the hospital. Playing wife with this guy, going above and beyond. I felt like if I didn't show or do these things, he'd feel like I didn't care about him or love him. I was doing entirely too much without the commitment from him and then he has the audacity to yell and attack me in the hospital! If I was really "cheating" or "wanting to get back with Vince." I wouldn't be doing all that I was doing. When he swung the IV pole towards me, that was my breaking point. I threw my purse and keys against the wall in complete anger and rage. That night brought out another side of myself that was scary and for one I did not like. I couldn't wrap my mind around why he was treating me the way he was…after my blow up I grabbed my keys and noticed my car fob was broken because I threw it against the wall so hard, picked up everything that fell out, threw it in my purse and stormed out with my eyes full of tears. I didn't know where to go, I for sure didn't want to go home—I wear my emotions on my face no matter how hard I try, my family would have picked it up in their spirit that something wasn't right. I also didn't want to leave, because I knew if I did it would probably be another blow up. In that moment I did only what knew to do, pray and listen to my music. Although I wanted to run home and lay on my daddy because I know he we love me unconditionally so the closest thing I had at that moment was Fred Hammond; I played a song from his Worship Journal *"God Is My Refuge"*

"There is nothing I needed more than Your

Precious love upon me

Everything I've been searching for; I find in You Completely.

And we cry out, Oh, Lord, I need Your love

that's where I can find all my help…

God is my refuge and my strength a very present help in time of trouble."

You can listen to a song over and over but when you're going through something, those songs hit differently. Sure enough for me, it was everything I was needing in that moment. I wasn't ready to go back in a deal with Jahmel, but I had my overnight bag that I needed. Walking back into the hospital, I felt that rush of anger coming back, as I got closer, I realized that I was clinching my fist ready to start swinging in case I needed to—as I walked in.

"Where you been!? You didn't see me calling you?" Jahmel says.

"Yeah. I saw…don't feel like talking. Look you have food and snacks. I need to calm down before more things are said or done and someone gets hurt." I say with a calm attitude.

Jahmel's stay in the hospital went from a week to very close to a month. Test after test, scan after scan doctors still couldn't figure it out—and neither could we. The meningitis came back negative, but I didn't really hear anything about this aneurysm he claimed to have. To be honest, I really don't know what the actual diagnosis was! Obviously, there was something wrong because they kept him so long. It was definitely time wasted. While I was going back and forth to the hospital it became so overwhelming that it started to affect my sleep and some of my performance at work. To the point where I ended up being let go from my job of 10years. Then to be greeted with an unexpected loss.

February 26, 2017, Jahmel and I were hanging out with Erika and her husband enjoying good, laughter and movies. Around 10pm-ish. I get a call from my Aunt Lauren, and in that moment you're hoping it's not "The Call". Scared to answer the phone because I knew it was going to be about my granny and I wasn't ready to hear what I was going to hear on the other end of the phone.

"Hello?" I hesitantly say.

"He..he…heeey darling." My Aunt Lauren trying to catch her breath in a shaky tone… *"Are you by your mom? Aunt, Aunt Michelle just coded…"*

I don't remember if I said anything back or even responded; my cousin saw that something was wrong. I remember saying "I gotta go, JAHMEL, my auntie my auntie, I need to get to my mom." I don't even remember if I said bye to Erika, I grabbed my keys, purse and sprinted down the long hallway to my car. Jahmel insisted on driving, but I did not give in. Doing 80 MPH on 45-50 MPH street I was determined to get home and get to my mom. Not wanting to relive anymore of that night—when I reached the house and ran upstairs not knowing my Aunt Michelle was taking her last breath all I could hear coming from the speaker was my aunts Lauren and London in complete distress. I finally make it to the side of the bed where my mom was sitting, seeing my dad with a teary eyes, I look at my mom for answers, and she shakes her head and says *"No, no baby."*

Not wanting to accept what I just heard, I walk off heading towards my room. I figured if I just lay down and go to sleep it would be all over in the morning, as I was getting closer to my room door; I felt my legs go completely numb and in an instant I was falling to the ground with my brother there to catch me. My auntie Chelle was my twin, she didn't play about me and I sure didn't play about her. So, losing her was rough and I didn't know how to process it, you'd expect or think that Jahmel would be there to console me or be there emotionally while we planned for the services and I design and print to funeral program. No, not at all, I was down and depressed—I wasn't wanting to do anything and because of that I was *"weak, too emotional, needed to man up because people die all the time and I need to get over it."* I found myself yelling at Jahmel during that whole process; one night I wasn't giving Jahmel any attention and he did not like it.

While I was texting one of my aunt's to get things I needed for the program he decided to take my phone and throw it because my focus was not on him and the fact that I wasn't out Uber-ing making money so they can extend another night in the hotel. When he grabbed and threw my phone I got up and charged at him yelling *"HAVE YOU LOST YOUR MIND?"* Next thing I know he was threating to punch me in my mouth if I didn't back up because I was doing too much crying and I needed to get over my aunt's passing. Deep down I wanting to swing off on him—where this emotion of rage was coming from I had no clue, I was already not myself; that night auntie Michelle passed a part of me passed too and to have my boyfriend, they guy who sat and told my parents and brother he was the one for me and I was the one for him curse at me and tell me to get over my auntie. I was NOT going to accept that. If that meant me fighting over someone I cared about and my sanity I was going to do it, because I was losing it. He was supposed to comfort, encourage and uplift me. Instead my boyfriend gave me grief, discomfort and belittled me.

It was a about a week after we laid my aunt to rest that Jahmel came out and finally admitted he didn't have a job. I find it funny that his news came out shortly after I received my income tax. He gave me a bs excuse that because of the job he has; well had with USAA being an underwriter he was not allowed to file his own taxes and it was to be professionally done. With my savings, and income slowly vanishing…I was running out of options to provide for myself paying a car note for a brand-new car and provide for Jahmel and his elderly mother. Jahmel was able to get a payday loan that was able to keep him afloat for about a month; I was able to get a side hustle running a graphic design shop and I loved it. While I wasn't working there, I was Uber-ing making extra cash.

His money quickly ran out because he was spending money on hotel rooms, food and weed and he was stressing out big time. Sad to say I was using my God given talent to do things that weren't pleasing to Him, and honestly, I feel that's why I stopped getting work for d'Monje (my freelance custom graphic and events business). God was probably saying "OH, you want to go this route? re-create and fabricate stuff? Okay I didn't give you this gift for you to do things that are not pleasing in my eye! HMM okay watch this!" I know that may be a bit extreme for some. Let me tell you, God shut that thang down asap-ish OKAY; and it's only until now I realize that.

My mind was so consumed with making sure my "man" was straight and happy that I didn't even see that the things I was doing for him wasn't pleasing my *real man,* GOD. As I look back, I can say in the whole year of 2017, I had no business for d'Monje, none! Okay, maybe a few "Hey can you help me with this?" or "I need some water bottle labels real quick for the church." and of course, my brothers graduation announcements. I don't count these because it was basically family and there was no profit made. Proverbs 18:16 says *"A man's gift will make room for him and bringeth him before great men."* Sad to say at that time, my gift wasn't making room for me."

It is amazing how we go to church Sunday after Sunday; read scriptures after scriptures, hear sermon after sermon, but things don't really hit us (well, at least me) until we are going through it or have gone through it. The word proclaims in 2 Thessalonians 3:10 *"...if a man don't work he don't eat."* That didn't really hit home until I broke up with Jahmel.

In February of 2017, I lost my job of 10 years working at a popular grocery chain. Was it due to the relationship with Jahmel? Definitely! It played a major part, but some fell on me as well. I often found myself putting him first before myself, goals, dreams and etc. You may be saying "Girl you crazy, I would never do that for my man." When I got into this relationship, I went in looking not just to date. See. No, I went in with the mindset of growing together, hustle'n, making money moves, building our empire and most of all, MARRIAGE! Again, you may be asking why? After being blindsided after six years with being with the "love of my life" I wasn't looking for another long-term friendship. NO. I wanted love, marriage and a family. Jahmel came to the table CORRECT! If only I knew it was all part of his plan to use and break me all the way down, I would not have invested so much and put my all into this relationship. Hell, I probably would have left a lot sooner.

Did you all catch the one thing that was missing? GOD! God was nowhere in my values and principles that I wanted to build this relationship on. Not saying that I strayed away from God, in my heart I knew/know that without God I and everything I set out to do is NOTHING. I just didn't make that known, let alone a top priority.

BOOKED

I lost my job, it was a week after I purchased my new car; which left me with a $450 payment that I had no clue on HOW I was going to pay for. Due to the hits my credit was taking, using card after card to take care of the household bills from when Vince and I were together. (One day, I'ma learn to stop taking care of MEN, and let a MAN take care of me doggone it.) But tax season was upon us, so I knew I was good. Little did I know that some; well most of that money would be used to make sure *"my man"* and his were okay and had a place to sleep at night. That money ran out QUICK and I was still jobless, he was too. He never fully came out and said "Hey, I lost my job" or "I got fired" or whatever the situation was. To be honest, I don't think he even had a job from the get-go. He would always text me *"Hey babe, on my way into work"* or *"Headed to a meeting"* (yeah right). But he HAD MONEY and was always taking me to nice restaurants, buying me MAC, shopping and he even brought me a pair of my weakness…J's (Jordans). So, I figured okay, well he's definitely working cause he's bringing in money from somewhere; and to my knowledge he wasn't dealing either.

Every day I was stressing thinking about how I was going to pay my car note, take care of my other obligations and make sure he was okay. I often found myself in payday loan offices or at the pawn shop. It wasn't just for him; it was for me too! It was always *"so-n-so is sending me this or I have this coming"*, but it would always fall through; but because I was being manipulated (I wouldn't even call it *"In Love"*), I, Azure was left trying to figure out how HE was going to pay for a room for him and his mother and importantly eat. I had a home to go to, but at the same time, I didn't want my boyfriend and elderly mother on the street, in the shelter, sleeping at the airport or checking into the hospital just to be able to sleep and get some type of a meal.

The whole time I wanted to see him win and be great! Things started to look up; he was able to secure employment. I was feeling good and also excited for him. I was also excited for me, thinking yes! he can finally take on responsibility and help me with my car note like he said he would. This was in May, so it had been four months since I brought my car and I only was able to make two payments on it. I didn't say anything to my parents, because I've always felt like I was the problem child. It seemed like I could never do anything RIGHT! You're probably saying that you would have asked for help but let me tell you something; PRIDE is REAL! We'll dig deeper into that later. So, yes, with him landing this good paying job doing underwriting; would benefit me as well. You may think that it's kind of gold digger-ish, (yes, that is a made-up word.) but I didn't look at it like that. I saw it as, okay I carried you and held down the fort, so now you as the man. It's your turn. Yeaaaah, that was short-lived; in the same week of him starting his new job, his past caught up to him; which indeed set him, me and 'us' back.

Memorial Day weekend: we found ourselves going to go meet my Auntie, because some stuff went down, and I wasn't having it. I told Jahmel, *"Yo, I'm bout to go meet up with my Auntie so I can see what happened."* It was late and he didn't want me to go by myself, I get it, but if I had known what was getting ready to happen in the next 20 minutes, I would have made him stay; or better yet stayed sitting on the couch.

He decided he would drive so I can focus on the directions and my Auntie if she called, smart but not so smart move. We got on the toll road to connect to the highway before we took our last exit to our destination; we were like five-minutes away from my Auntie. Out of nowhere, in the rear-view mirror I see red, white and blue. No, it wasn't the colors of the flags waving in the air from the car dealerships we passed. It was the freaking PO-PO! I yelled

"Seriously, Jahmel!?"

he responds *"F***, I'm going to jail, I'm going to jail!"*

Me panicking; looking in my side mirror to see if he was indeed coming for us or if it was another car he was after…nope! He was definitely coming for us. I tell him—

"You're not going to jail for speeding"

he yells back *"I wasn't speeding though!"*

Me: *"So why are we getting stopped?"* I asked in a confused and scared tone.

He looks for a safe place to pull over we saw a sign for an exit and took it, but I told Jahmel to put on the blinker to signal that we're exiting so the cop won't think we're trying to run. While he's exiting, I start praying and tried to calm him down but at the same time I. AM. SCARED! Especially with the way "routine traffic stops" have been going; I didn't want him or myself to lose our lives that night. While we were waiting for the officer to come to the car, Jahmel is taking his wallet out his pockets, change, everything like he was getting ready. I'm looking at him baffled like *"Dude, you don't even know why he stopped you; I could have a light out or something CHILL!"*

The officer came over, and I must say, I was a little relieved when I saw that it was a black officer. We were pulled over because I had an outstanding toll balance that had not been paid from when I took the tolls back in March when I came down to lay my Aunt Michelle to rest, going for interviews, etc. The officer told us we could no longer use the toll roads until the balance is paid and if we need to get on the toll's we needed to pay instantly instead of doing pay by mail because if I was pulled over again, I would be taken in. The officer advised us to take care of it as soon as possible. He asked for Jahmel's license since he was driving because he still needed to run him.

When the officer went back to his car Jahmel *said*

"Call your Auntie, cause I'm about to go to jail!"

I look back at him with an annoyed look…

Me: *"You're not going to jail; you need stop thinking like that."*

This boy yells (not in a raised voice, but a tone that would make my skin crawl and stomach turn; shoot not just me, anyone. If I was to hear that tone today from anyone especially a male, it will definitely trigger something; and I won't turn the other cheek…I'd go STRAIGHT. OFF! When you've been verbally abused on a consistent basis, you don't want to put up with it moving forward. Ladies and Gents, it is NOT okay to be talked down to…believe it or not, it's VERBAL ABUSE.

"WOULD YOU JUST SHUT THE F*** UP FOR A MIN!? PLEASE!? GOD! Azure, I'AM GOING TO F***'ING JAIL! SO IMMA NEED YOU TO CALM DOWN AND LISTEN BEFORE YOU MAKE SH** WORSE! Just shut up, please!"

While he was yelling at me, my eyes were beginning to water and tears started to flow; one, because I was just trying to be positive and keep him relaxed. I have never been in this type of situation before, and then the fact that he yelled at me. I don't do well with people yelling; I don't process that well at all, especially if I was just trying to help and two, he was so concerned about him and didn't even think about me. Knowing good in well I've never been in this type of situation.

While we were still waiting (it was a long while already) I tuned myself in my seat and looked out of the window so he wouldn't see me crying, (I did this a lot during our relationship it always seemed like he had a problem with me expressing myself, it often felt like he expected me to bottle everything up and take his punches (NOT PHYSICAL-LY.)) While I was gathering myself, Auntie London calls to see where we were because the last time I talked to her we we're 7 minutes away and should have made it to her by now…while I'm telling her what's going on she hears him repeating *"I'm going to jail. I'm going to jail."* she starts to do the same thing I was trying to do, figure things out to get a better understanding. She says

"Wait! What? What he mean, he bout to go to jail!? Where are ya'll at?"

While I'm trying to explain everything that has happened so far to my Aunt while trying not to have him 'go off' on me again; especially with her on the phone. He tells me to go ask the officer what was taking so long. I look at him confused and said

"You just want me to get shot, don't you! I AM NOT ABOUT TO GET OUT THIS DAMN CAR. YOU CRAZY!"

Auntie London in my ear: *"Hell NO, you not getting out that damn car, you better sit your ass still, sh**!"*

So, he waves his hand out the window and the officer respond on his intercom *"I'll be with you all in just a second sir."*

Two minutes later, I see another squad car exiting. Then I knew, YUP his ass going to jail. Vince always said if you see two or more cars…somebody is going to jail. The original officer comes over to his window and says

"Mr. Edwards, can you step out of the vehicle please?"

At this point, I have so many thoughts and emotions racing through my body. It really felt like I was in a movie; you know when they get the person out of the car and everything becomes a blur and voices start to fade out…YUP! That's how it was for me. I hear the officer say

"Put your hands on the car… do you have anything in your pockets?

I realized Auntie London was still on the phone when I hear *"HEL-LO? HELLO? Azure? HELLO!?"* I look down to see my phone was on the floor. I reached down to get it to come back up to see the other officer standing at my door; scared the daylights out of me. I told my Auntie I would call her back, and she was going to call my Uncle to see where he was.

The officer (Hispanic) greets me and says *"Hello ma'am. I do understand this is your vehicle?"* Me: *"Yes sir."*

Officer 2: *"I will need to see your ID just to make sure you are clear to leave with this car or if not, we will have it towed."* I looked at him confused as well as trying to gather my words and tone so it won't come off as if I was being hostile or disrespectful.

Me: *"What do you mean if I can take MY car? I have my ID and insurance."*

He told me that since I was not driving they need to make sure I was clean. While all this was going on; I wanted to call my mommy sooo bad and just cry, because I was so scared! I didn't know what to do, how to act! I just wanted to go home and get there quick! At the same time, I was scared to call her because I knew it wouldn't go over well. Her baby being in this type of position with this *"BOY!"* I put on my big girl panties, wiped my tears and was still prayerful that everything would be a big misunderstanding.

Both officers come over to tell me everything checked out on me, and I would be free to go. They also told me that they need to take him in because he had a warrant for probation violation…again; I am confused because he was "supposed" to be done with that back in December. When we first started talking, he told me he was on probation due to an altercation he had with his baby mama and he busted the window on her car. Apparently, he violated, and they needed to take him in. The black officer was giving me different types of scenarios on what could happen. As he was talking, I was still trying to process all of this; I blacked out for a minute and when I came back to reality I hear him saying *"Ma'am? Ma'am…Ma'am? Did you want to go say bye to him?"* I looked at him with confused water-filled eyes and just nodded my head, wiped my tears while trying not to black out again.

He opens my door, I get out to a big gust of wind, bright lights and Jahmel cuffed in the back seat of the car. He say's *"I'm going to be okay, don't worry about me; just make sure my mom is okay. Are you okay?* (I'm looking at him like; Nigga do I look okay?) *Don't worry, I'ma get out, just get back to your Aunt's house* (he was staying at my other aunts empty house) *and I'll call you as soon as I can."* Leans over kisses my forehead and tells he loves me. I walk back to my car wobbling trying hard not to lose it! I get in the driver's seat, lock my car door and just screamed! Trying to hold it all together so I can at least find my phone. I call Auntie London back and on the first ring she says *"What's going on?* I don't remember if I had any words, I remember screaming, crying, and shaking trying to breathe because I really felt like I was going to pass out. I hear her saying in a calm voice, almost as calm as my mommy's (well, they are sisters)

"Ok Niecy, I know this is hard, but I'm going to need you to breathe for me okay…calm down baby, please calm down."

I hear her but I am a total mess. It felt like somebody just came and snatched life out of me, no I'm not saying he was my life, because he definitely wasn't. I just felt empty for lack of a better term.

I'm sitting in this big empty parking lot at damn near midnight BY MYSELF! My mama always told me nothing good happens after midnight. Now, because my mama instilled that into me, I was definitely looking, I may have been distraught, but I was aware of my surroundings. So aware; that I saw that a car pulled up behind me. I wasn't sure if it was parking security or what. So I immediately check to see if my doors were locked and grab my switch blade; then I realized it was a cop when I saw him approaching my car I said, *"Auntie* (in a shaky voice) *a cop is here!"* she says *"Ok; breathe and stay calm , don't go off or anything, just let him know your boyfriend just got arrested and your just getting yourself together. Okay?"* Thank the Lord I didn't have to repeat that because it was the same officer that pulled us over. He taps on the window and says

"Hey, I just came back to see if you were still here. I noticed you took it pretty hard, is there anyone I can call, or will someone come and drive for you? Jahmel was also concerned and worried about you, and ma'am I'm not going to lie I was too." Still shook, *"Yes sir, I'm actually talking to my aunt, do you mind talking to her and letting her know what happened and my location?"* The officer says *"Absolutely, I'll talk to her!"* I gave him my phone, and all I can think about is his elderly mother at the house and I knew that the responsibility that was his (when he would take it) now fell on me. Where was she going to go? She couldn't come back with me! Do I take her to shelter or a hospital? I didn't know so I started doing what I only knew to do while the officer was giving Auntie London the run down.

"Okay Lord, you are going to have to help me get through this one." and he was probably saying "GIRL, I JUST GAVE YOU AWAY

OUT!" I was deep into this manipulation and mindset that with him going to jail was another test God was throwing out there for us to get over and make us stronger. Tuuh, God was saying "Okay, I took him out of the equation…**RUUUUUUUNNNN!** You've been complaining about how you can't do it no more and this and that and you want me to help you…I'm helping you! GET OUT!"

You all don't *EVER* get to the point where your mind is so clouded to where you can't hear God clearly…don't let a relationship, friendship, man, woman, boy or girl…take you so far away from God the way I was. It's not worth it! TRUST ME!**

When the officer and my Aunt were done talking he said, *"Okay, you can stay here as long as you need to get yourself together. I called another officer; he's parked right over there* (he points towards the car) *he knows what's going on and he will keep a lookout for you. There's also standard security driving around so you'll be safe. Okay?"* I shook my head and he ended the conversation by saying: *"Alright get home safe."*

I finally made it back to my other Aunts apartment where we were staying, and when I walked through the door the first thing his mom says is *"Oh, ya'll back"* when she didn't see my shadow behind me her next question was *"Where is Jahmel?"* I took a deep breath and guided her towards the couch so she can sit down; I didn't know how she was going to respond to me telling her that her only child was in jail… AGAIN! Especially because we got into it earlier because I was trying to get her to take her medicine and she was telling me I wasn't the boss of her. When she didn't take her meds she was a whole different woman. I looked at her and took another deep breath and with my head hung low, I said: *"Well, we got pulled over and come to find out he has a warrant."* She says *"Whaaat? Oh GOD, for what!?"* I tell her what the officer told me *"It was for violation of probation on his criminal mischief charge."* She says confused *"VIOLATION? I thought he was off probation."* Our conversation went on; we both cried and were trying to figure out what we were going to do next.

The next morning, I get a phone call from "Scam Likely" I just knew it had to be him so I answered and heard a recording I'd thought I'd never hear *"You have a call from an inmate at the Harris County Jail* (he says his name) *if you accept this call press one"* It connects us and I exclaim *"BAAABY!??, are yo.."* he cuts me off *"...Azure, Azure, Azure... yes babe, I'm fine. We only have like five minutes so I need you to focus, get some paper and I need you to go do some work for me. Okay?"* He starts to tell me all he needs me to do...find a lawyer to see who can post his bail and represent him and so on. Contact his old lawyer who was on the case and got him probation, etc. Before we hung up, he goes on to say *"I really need you to get on this, not saying you wouldn't...I just got to get out of here, if the shoe was on the other foot I'd be doing all I can to get you out."* In my head, I said *"FIRST OF ALL...I wouldn't be in jail... but okay nigga."*

When my best friend Bianca heard what happened she immediate dropped all she was doing and was right there with and for me. She worked for a company that monitored people who were on house arrest, so she knew about the system as well as how Harris County worked. Since it was over the weekend, I couldn't do anything until that Monday. I thank God for Bianca because she walked me through everything, and I mean EVERYTHING! I was getting ready to go see him in jail; this was all new to me. I'm a morning person I wanted to get it done early so I can head back to San Antonio and get in MY BED and be at HOME with my FAMILY. Since visitation was not until 3:00 pm, I had to wait. My Bestie told me where to park, what to take and not to take in. When I walked in, I was automatically overwhelmed; I knew off jump this was not a place I should be in. PERIOD! I felt so out of place, confused, dirty everything. It was finally time for my group to go up to have visitation, I had to go through security and there were people getting turned away left and right due to trying to bring things in that was not permitted. While on the elevator heading to the floor, I saw mothers, fathers, wives, girlfriends, grandparents, and sad to say children even infants. It broke my heart. I don't know what each individual was in for but to see children in there like that broke my heart. I was a ball of emotions and when I saw him walk out and sit in front of me, I cried. I don't think it was because I was talking to him behind a window (like you'd see in the movies or on TV) the tears were more so for myself like how in the world did I end up in this type of situation.

What the officer told me the night of his arrest; my bestie told me as well. That if Bexar County (because that is where the crime was committed) doesn't request him he could be out by Monday Tuesday because Harris County can't hold him since the offense wasn't done in their county. Now if Bexar came and got him, then it's either we wait for the court date or bailout.

He gave me some names of people to reach out to, who can help me in any way on getting him out. We only had a few minutes to visit anyway because there was a lot of other people waiting to visit their loved ones. We said our goodbyes and I was unsure if he'd be getting out anytime soon.

On the way home, I found it funny that he was all sweeter and nicer, because he knew I could easily have chunked the duce like the Lord was telling me to do but I smoothly ignored it. He also knew that I was his only ticket out. He said what I wanted to hear pretty much; I call it 'Manipulative Reassurance' he was manipulating me by reassuring everything is going to be okay once I got him out. If I just would have taken that out that God was giving me for the UMPTENTH time, I would have bypassed all the stuff ahead.

Long story short – he got violated, which lead to their being a warrant out for his arrest; because his probation officer violated him the last day before his end date, due to a no show at his last check-in. He had a valid excuse he was in the hospital and was constantly sending correspondence to her. (SO HE SAYS.) I found a lawyer who was able to post his bail and all we had to pay was $500 to get him out. The lawyer would also represent him at his court date a few months down the line. (No, that money did not come out of my pocket; it came from his mom, I just did the leg work.)

"Houston, We
Have A Problem"

I often found myself going back and forth to Houston; and most of the time I was doing day trips sneaking down there and back; because if Billy and Tonja (my parents) knew, it would have gotten shut down with a quickness. During this time, his mom was still staying at my aunt's apartments and that within itself was DRAMA! Going back and forth to Houston just to bring her check so she can sign and cash it for me. So I can give my aunt money for the electricity and rent that her and Jahmel agreed on. Get whatever his mother needed, put some aside for this lawyer and lastly some for me so I can get back and forth from San Antonio and Houston. After Jahmel was released he still needed to go back to work. He had me send an email to one of his managers stating that he was in a bad accident, that's why he was not able to attend his second week of work. After he got out, I took him back to Houston and he was able to start back to work that following Monday.

While I, still J O B L E S S! Although I was actively looking for jobs and putting in application after application. I wasn't getting calls back from the positions I really wanted. It took my Dad to get me mad, so to speak, for me to really put myself out there and land a job. I felt like he came for me, and he felt I wasn't putting enough effort in. I had that "humph, okay, I'll show you buddy!" attitude, got dressed and drove to San Marcos for a job fair. I got there with 20 minutes to spare to find out I missed the last group for the day. They helped me get on the computer complete the application for the position and schedule my interview for the next day. Where I would come back, accept the job, take a drug test, complete I-9 and all that good stuff. The next day after completing everything even taking my picture; I walked out with a full-time job, benefits with a start date of July 5th as an associate at one of the world's largest online retail companies. I showed him huh!?

I was getting very excited because things were starting to look up! Jahmel was working and preparing to get an apartment in Houston. I was getting ready to start work, and I felt a load lifted off of my shoulders. I was thinking; no more stressing about not having enough money not only for gas but, not having to pay for a hotel room. God was finally answering my prayers; all for it to come to a screeching halt when he got fired from his job the weekend before I was supposed to start my new job. (how convenient) This is when things took a major turn, not for the better, but for WORSE!

Jahmel and I were planning to go down to Corpus and hang out on the beach. He liked to fish, and I love being in the water. He thought it would be a good idea to spend some time together before I started my new job. That Friday the plan was for him to come up after work, pick me up (in his rental car) and head down to the beach. I was excited, because not only was I getting back to work; but that things were really starting to look good for him, me and us. We could actually start that building process I've been longing for. Yeah, the construction on that got put on hold yet again; when I get a text from him a few hours before his expected arrival saying, *"So, I just got fired!"* Jahmel had a track record of giving up when things went wrong or not according to his plan. Don't get me wrong we all do but his was to the extreme, and it led to A LOT of bluffing and for me, emotional stress. I respond with the confused *"HUH?* Whaat?" then I proceeded to call him and he immediately answered and went in on the reason why he was fired. His story was, they let him go because he contacted the lender of one of his loans so he could get the file completed so he can move on to the next. Let him tell it he "felt" he was being proactive and going the extra mile. Well, that was apparently a no-no in the rules of Mortgage Underwriting.

Now, that could have been very well part of his sudden dismissal; but I believed he got let go because they found out either...

A: He wasn't in an accident; he got arrested, which caused him to miss his second week of work.

B: Him having to miss days/coming in late because he had to report every week to probation.

C: They saw that his criminal record was deeper than what the surface says.

D: ALL OF THE ABOVE.

I'll say **D. ALL OF THE ABOVE.**

Now, he never fully came out and told me the real reason that led to his termination. But I did notice later down the line when he would get mad or go into his moods; like you'll read in a minute. He would throw stuff out from the past to justify what was happening at that present time. In which would actually be true and the real reason he would be in that certain predicament. I don't know if he even realized he would do it since he lied so much. Jahmel wanted to get off the phone, so he could gather his "thoughts" and process what happened to see what his move will be. Here's where it took that turn for the WORSE.

We started texting, and he was saying things like his life will forever be messed up, God hates him, things will never change. Just really putting himself down and being negative. So, knowing that 'dark place' he tends to slip into, I respond with…

"Babe, breathe and focus, look at the bigger picture, okay? Get to me, and we can figure things out." (Why, because Azure always figures and works it out.)

Jahmel replies: *"Nah, F*** that! I'm done with life, I'm done with you* (hol' up! With me? Didn't I just get your ass out of jail?), *you can go and be happy and find someone your parents will like, cause I'm not good enough for you."*

He just went on; but what started the worry and concern was when he started a group message thread between my parents, BJ and I.

Before the text was sent, he ended up texting me *"Baby I can't do this anymore, I'm nothing"*. I was trying to be encouraging, pretty much telling him what I felt like he wanted to hear; just like he'd do me. See I was starting to figure out his bluff, so I was playing it back to him. Praying it will kind of cool him down a bit.

I say; *"But sweetheart, you've worked so hard to get to this place, don't throw it all away now, think about our future, our children."*

Jahmel: *"Please! I don't have no kids with you! I can't marry you; I'm not good enough. Like I said, I'm done! We're breaking up; we're over just know I loved you very much, I'm about to text your parents too. I'm cutting my phone off this is the last good-bye!"*

So, ladies; if your man just said all of that and talked about ending it all, or whatever "all" may be, how would you react? I know some people; one person, in particular would be like *"Oh, ok then, BYE; hope it works out for you!"* While others may go hysterical. Now, mind you this was all text. I couldn't react how I wanted to because I just picked BJ up from work and I had to play it cool so he wouldn't know what was going on. That ended quickly because that text he said he was going to send. He actually sent! My phone dinged, then BJ's. I saw that it was indeed a message in our group chat...the message read ...

"I love you guys! But I can't keep living like this, it's time to end it all. Tell my daughter her daddy loves her."

I kept a straight face and wasn't going to say anything unless he did.

Next thing I know BJ says

"Yo, what's going on?"

Then my phone starts ringing and it's my dad! OH LORD, here we go. I thought. I didn't want to answer but I did. Dad says, *"What's going on with J?"* I told him I would let him know when I got home. Meanwhile, I'm calling and texting, and it's going straight to voicemail and 'delivered' never turned to 'read.'

Once I filled everyone in on what happened earlier, Jahmel responded, I heard that chime and my heart dropped to my stomach. He was still in that so called 'Dark Place'. I needed to hear his voice to make sure he was okay and to get a feel for where his mind was. He did answer and said very short and angry *"I'm driving!"* then hung up. NOW! This is not the first time this has happened. Thanksgiving 16' was the first time I encountered this behavior.

It was around midnight if not later. All I kept thinking was how I was going to sneak out of the house. I felt like I needed to get to him and help (I feel like I can help everybody, I have a sponge mentality, we'll talk about that later) especially if he was serious about running into traffic like he said he was going to do or jump off one of our major highways. I was so confused at the turn of events; we just had a wonderful Thanksgiving meal, watched my Cowboys win, made up raps. It was a good day! When I dropped him back off, everything was fine; he was happy. Now he's talking about jumping off the highway??... Wait! What!? I didn't know what to do, so I did the only thing I knew best. PRAY! He was really adamant about not mentioning anything to ANYONE or calling for help. But I needed to get my prayer warrior; I had to go wake up my Mommy to have her pray and intercede on his behalf and bind every attack that the devil may be trying to do to take him out. We did just THAT, we called him out in prayer and came against the spirit of the enemy! Despite my mother's view and feelings towards him she never had a problem with praying for him or his situations.

With my Mom being in the field of Mental Health Care, she suggested that we call the hotline. She thought that would be the best thing for me to do than trying to go 'save' him. If he was indeed having suicidal ideations and was serious about it, me going to him he could have taken me with him as well. I was safer where I was, and we can do what we can to help him. We called the hotline and mom gave the operator all the information we had. What he was wearing, his location everything. I was so concerned because I didn't want it to end up in a Trevon Martin, or Mike Brown situation if the police approach him and he gets hostile or Jahmel-ish. They assured us the officer they were sending out has a special training for these types of situations.

My parents and I were having a conversation about what was going on, and I told them as crazy as it seems I felt like that he was okay. (Even though he sent live pictures of him definitely walking up the entrance ramp of the highway he was staying by.) I felt like he was in the room sleep or chilling just watching TV. The night went on, no response or text. I even called the hotel room and no answer. I asked God that wherever he may be, keep him safe, and I left it in His hands.

The next morning, I got myself ready to head over there. When I got in the car, I started to check the news sites to see if there was any breaking news or developing stories about a death and or hit and run over night. I already started pulling off to go outside of our subdivision. I went to KSAT news website and the first headline I see *"Man Hit and Killed by Car"* no lie! When I tell you I gasped so loud, hit the brakes and made a sharp turn into a vacant lot next to me. It felt like someone just punched me in my stomach and my heart felt like it was getting ready to explode. In an instant, all these thoughts came running through my head an all I can think clearly was go back to the house and get mommy. I can't even describe half of how I felt, like I entered a twilight zone or something. So I kept reading while I was sitting in a vacant parking lot. The first sentence in the story was the title followed by on Loop 410. When I saw 410, I felt a scream stirring in my belly rapidly rising up to escape my mouth. The hotel they were staying at was by the airport where Loop 410 and 281 crossed. I kept reading but hesitantly because I was afraid of what I was getting ready to read. I read a little longer and it said 410 and IH 10 EAST! When I tell you the relief I had; it was like the feeling of trying to see how long you could hold your breath under water, and you finally come up and take that first breath…OH.MY.GOODNESS. I really thought my baby was gone and I was going to be the one to blame.

Still unsure of him and his whereabouts (sometimes reporters get things wrong, and I wanted to make sure for myself.), I rushed over to where he was staying. As I was approaching the side the room was on (I entered the front and came around the back because it was a corner room) because I didn't know what I was getting ready to drive up on. As I slowly approached the corner, I see a black t-shirt and him; I saw him before he saw me. (I'm sneaky like that.) He was coming from the vending machine, just chilling looking pleasant. I sped up and parked all crazy, jumped out and ran up on him. When he realized it was me running up to him, his WHOLE MOOD CHANGED! Like he was angry, and he could spas at any second. What ya'll think, bluffing? When I finally reached him, you would think he would reach out to embrace me back and say something like "baby, I'm okay; it's okay." Or SOMETHING right? Yeah, no. I got a shove along with a *"MOVE; why you here?"* I went OFF! *"Are you freaking kidding me right now? I CAME TO CHECK ON YOU AND TO MAKE SURE YOU DIDN'T DO ANYTHING CRAZY!"* He felt like I didn't think he was important enough because I didn't come running the night before. We never really talked about that night moving forward. He did say someone came and talked to him. I never told him that I was behind it. He also said he reached out to one of his friends back in Cali and he talked him off the bridge. Because when we sent the text, he told me not to tell anyone, especially my parents. I was just glad he was alive and breathing! You're probably like yeah this is where she calls it off. Nope! Not with my dumb self.

So, now that you have a little back history of what the *'Dark Place'* is or could be. I kept calling, texting and still wasn't getting a answer. I was trying to see if he was on his way to SA so we can go on our getaway as planned and figure out what his next move would be. He finally answered my FaceTime call to show me he was indeed in the car and was on the highway driving; and then hung up the phone. I took that as…Yes, girl, I'm coming, I'm pissed right now let me get these few hours to myself to think. Leave me alone. NOPE! The text I got took things from zero to a hundred, real quick. It said.

"I'm about to die, the police are behind me, they're gonna have to shoot me, I'm not about to go back to jail."

WHOA, WHAT!? I'm pretty sure I rolled my eyes and said to myself here we go.

I called and kept calling, no answer. At this point, I don't know that to do, he's there, I'm here. I can't talk to him to calm him down because he is not answering; because if he is definitely in 5-0's presence, it's not going to be good. (He can't stand cops, or at least that was his story). He responds at least I think, and the text says.

"This dude is crazy! He's about to get killed by the police."

I reply with a confused *"HUH! what are you talking about?"*

A random person, we'll, call him "Witness": *"The dude, he threw me his phone and said record it and make sure some girl named Azure gets it."*

Me: *"WHAT!!?"*

Now I'm blowing his phone up, and now instead of it ringing, it will ring once then go to voicemail...I'm starting to get heated! All while trying to keep my cool because we are at the table having dinner. I text back...

*"By the way who the f*** are you!!???"*

Witness: *"I'm one of the people he threw his phone to, dude is going crazy!"*

I'm thinking this boy is on the highway surrounded by police like a shootout is getting ready to happen. Then my little wheels start turning. How are random people chilling and standing on the highway?? If someone gets pulled over, the whole highway isn't going to pull over with you and even if you are going "crazy" on the side of the highway, cars aren't just gonna STOP and gather around the scene. YOU'RE ON A HIGHWAY, I'm sure there will be barricades and police all around preventing bystanders to get close—but then again, he was in HOUSTON; but still, it makes no sense. At this point, I'm like Jahmel had officially gone crazy, something is seriously wrong with this guy...mentally! I'm calling and calling and still no answer. So I text this "witness" ...

"Can you answer my call please?"

(Stupid me, I'm somewhat falling for it. See he was the type of person in these types of situations if I ignored him or stop responding. He would go off on me and that was the last thing I wanted, even though 98% of the time he was bluffing. I didn't want me not responding or not showing him the attention, be that push for him to go off and hurt himself or someone Does that make sense?)

Witness: *"I can't, I'm recording."*

Me: *"Well dumb-dumb, I'm telling you that's my husband. Don't you think you should answer my calls??? Especially if you see that "Babe" is the one calling and texting, and how can you be recording and texting me?"*

Witness: *"OMG! They're about to kill him! I'm sorry ma'am."*

So, imagine me sitting at the dinner table with my family reading these text messages trying to keep my composure. They know something is wrong, because my thumbs were moving, I barely touched my food and my mood has all of a sudden change! As I'm sitting at the table, I begin to feel smothered, so I excuse myself so I can go outside catch my breath, get some fresh air and maybe walk a little. Yeah, no! They all followed me…all three of 'em. Mom asked, *"What's going on baby?"* While I was filling them in with all of us standing outside in the garage, I'm still texting. *"HELLO? Can you answer the damn phone!??"* My mom quickly reminds me that this isn't the first time this has happened. I told her, *"Yeah, I know. It's just the unknown that's killing me; and if this "person" indeed has his phone don't you think you should answer the phone and tell his "wife" what is going on"?*

I know that we weren't married, but I felt like that was the only way I can get this mystery witness to pick up and or respond.

A good 20-30 minutes goes by, and I finally hear the sound I been waiting for *'ding.'* This time it was definitely apparent that he was bluffing or "crying wolf" like my grandma would say, because 'Witness' tuned into HPD (Houston Police Department). Saying *"Ma'am he is okay and safe. We are taking him to the hospital where they will watch him for a few hours."*

Now, hol'up! Pause one quick minute. I've watched too many Law & Order SVU, NCIS, White Collar, Rizzoli & Isles, Burn Notice episodes and even binged watch Flashpoint on Netflix to know ain't NO way a POLICE OFFICER will TEXT the victim/ POI (person of interest) family member. ESPECIALLY on THEIR PHONE! Isn't that now evidence?? Police would make a call after the fact; send a detective over something...but TEXT!? FIRST OF ALL, they wouldn't use words like "watch" and "few hours" NO. They would say something like *"...where he would be placed under observation."* and *"if he needs or requires special attention, they will transfer him so he can get the help they need."* C'mon now, if you going to cry wolf...learn how to cry, my dude!

He had too many roles he was playing; he couldn't keep up. I don't know if he thought I was stupid, slow or dumb and thought I'd really fall for that. So, me being petty I played along....

Me: *Okay, sir. So, will he be in police custody or under watch??*

Ya'll, the "Officer" responded shaking my head.

HPD: *"Yes, and his phone will be turned off. He will contact you once he is able to and has calmed down."*

Here's where I got him though.

Me: *"Thank you sir! What is your name, badge number and best contact information for you or the precinct? That way I can follow up or if I need to contact someone. Can you also give me the police report number?"*

HPD: Oh, we're getting ready to take him in; I need to shut the phone off."

When I tell you my fear, worrying and concerned state turned into anger, frustration and irritation. It was like my own boyfriend was Cat-fish'n me with himself! I was like WTH just happened? My parents were so over it. My mama was like *"see that, that's manipulation, he's playing you, honey. He wants attention, and you're giving it to him."*

A few hours go by, and I get the *ding* again. *"Baby, it's me! I'm okay"* *They gave me some meds, so I'm kind of out of it."* I sat there baffled thinking he is really playing this game. Okay, then two can play this game. I just play it better. I respond, trying to sound so sad but I was really over it and was just going through the motions. *"OMG Baby you had me worried..!"* (In which he did) Laying in my bed perplexed like how are you okay with putting your girlfriend, the one you say you want to marry on these continuous emotional rollercoasters. While he was over there mad, I'm sure, but chilling and doing God knows what or who (sips tea). While I was the one stressed, tripping and worried.

This is the day I knew something was seriously wrong with him. I didn't brush it under the rug; I just thought okay Lord, I know the anointing that is over my life and the oil that runs deep in my bloodline. I knew how much power my family and I possessed and I figured that if I stayed a little longer, it will start to pour over on to him and his life will start to change. I was leading the horse to water, but I was trying too hard to make him drink.

"Light em Up!"

T he next day Jahmel comes into town as originally planned. I ended up meeting him at Wal-Mart because he was trying to avoid my house and my parents. I would be trying to avoid them too if I sent a message like he did. The purpose of meeting at Wal-Mart was so we can see if we were going on our getaway and to get the things that we needed. I told him I needed to go back to the house before we go so I can grab my things. He wanted to leave for Corpus right after we got done shopping; I don't know what he was thinking. I wasn't going to leave my car in the parking lot of Wal-Mart or he probably thought I'd leave it at the hotel where he was going to check his mom into.

My parents made it very clear to me while I was on my way out to meet him that they didn't have a problem with me still going but they indeed wanted to lay eyes on him. Especially after all the theatrics that happened less than 24 hours ago; this is what any sensible good parent(s) would do. I know my dad, well, mom too was thinking "you just basically sent me a suicide note, that you're about to kill yourself, now you want to come take my daughter without us seining you. Naw son." Now Jahmel also told me that he didn't want to come back to the house he just wanted me to meet him at the hotel. I felt like that was dumb no need to have two cars out. PLUS you're driving a car other than mine! I am going to take advantage of this and be "Miss Daisy" for the weekend. I told him no and to just follow me to the house so

I can get my things and we take one car. I also mentioned that my parents wanted to say hello and make sure that he was okay. Jahmel was okay with that plan until I mentioned the last part; he was VERY adamant about not seeing them.

We get to the house and if I would have known what was getting ready to pop off I would have just cancelled the whole weekend. I go inside to get my things and let them know that we were about to head out. My dad was on the phone, so I was trying to stall by taking a little bit out at a time. I go through the garage so I can put my stuff in his car, I walk out and I didn't see him in the driveway or on the side. I walk all the way out and noticed that he was parked two houses down from mine. Whoa, c'mon dude you're trying to start some ish like c'mon man. I walk down with one of my bags leaving my purse in the garage on the back of my mom's car. As I get to the car, he starts to go off on me… *"Why can't you just do what I asked you to do? I DON'T WANT TO SEE THEM, nor talk to them."* I tell him *"Well, Jahmel, they just want to make sure you are okay, WE ALL WE'RE WORRIED ABOUT YOU!"* We started going back and forth he is cursing me out and I'm just standing there. He started hitting the center console in the car saying *"I DON'T WANT TO SEE THEM! THEY GONNA WAN-NA TALK AND ALL THAT SH**. THE ONLY PERSON I WANT TO TALK TO AND CLEAR MY HEAD WITH IS YOU! YOU CAN'T DO SIMPLE SH** AND YOU DON'T F***ING LISTEN!*

By this time my parents and BJ are outside, and I see them looking like I was when they didn't see a car in the driveway. From two houses down all they can hear is a raised voiced in an unpleasant tone and the sound of his hands beating on the console. Dad being a protector and let alone MY DAD! He runs down to the car and goes straight into action:

Dad: *"YO, WHAT'S YOUR PROBLEM MAN?"*

I'm trying to explain that he wasn't yelling at me. (He was, I was lying, because I know my Dad; but he wasn't trying to hear that though.)

After Jahmel ignored him the first time my Dad repeats the question. *"Man, what is your problem?"*

Jahmel: *I don't have a problem; I just want to come and get Azure so we can go. I'm not here for all the extra bulls***. AZURE ARE YOU COMING OR NOT!?*

By this time, mom has gotten to the car. Now mind you, we live in a pretty nice and quiet neighborhood. My street is like a family and not too much drama or activity goes on. Yeeeeah this is probably the most action my street has seen since BJ's 17th birthday party.

Mom: *"No she isn't going anywhere, AZURE LET'S GO!"*

Jahmel: *"There they go, making decisions for you! Azure YES OR NO ARE YOU COMING OR NOT. IF NOT, GET YOU S*** AND DON'T CALL ME AGAIN".*

Dad: *"I'm so sick of this dude, all you do is talk."*

My Mom grabbed my bag and purse out the front seat and said, *"NO MA'AM you're going nowhere with him!"* BJ pulls the belt loop on my shorts to pull me back away from the car. Dad and Jahmel are going back and forth; Jahmel cursing my dad out (crazy part; all the while, his mom is in the back seat, just confused and helpless.) Now you're my boyfriend and all but at the end of the day I am a Daddy's Girl, and I will kill someone over my Fabio (Faaawb-e-o). It gets more heated and Fabio must have said something to trigger him and the next thing I know, Jahmel jumps out of the car charging towards my dad. Me being a daddy's girl, I run and jump in front of them ...BJ is trying to hold me back, and I'm trying my hardest to break away from him. I think I push the poor little guy, (my bad B!) I got away though and jumped in from of them yelling and pointing my finger in Jahmel's face…

"WHAT YOU NOT GONNA DO IS COME FOR MY DAD! YOU NOT TOUCHING HIM BRUH! WHEN ALL THEY WANTED TO DO IS SEE IF YOUR ASS WAS OKAY! ALL YOU HAD TO DO WAS SPEAK, SHOW YOUR FACE AND THAT'S IT!"

Jahmel: *"AZURE, MOVE, HE DON'T WANT THESE HANDS, YOU KNOW ME, IF I WANTED TO HIT HIM, HE WOULD HAVE BEEN ON THE F***ING GROUND ALREADY."*

Me: *"REALLY BRUH, YOU GON COME CHARGE UP ON MY FAMILY!!? AFTER ALL THE SH** I JUST DID FOR YOU!?* (you'd still be sitting in jail if it wasn't for me bruh! *I didn't voice that, because to my knowledge my parents didn't know he was in jail let alone I was with him when he was arrested.*) *NOW YOU JUST GOING TO THROW ALL THIS WAY!??"*

Fabio: *"I'm about to light this boy up. I don't have time for this clown; he's not worth my time anymore. I'M DONE…You're full of it."*

Jahmel: *"Mr. G., MR. G., I DON'T HAVE NO PROBLEM WITH*

YOU*!* (but you just jumped out of the car like you was about to fight him, but you have no problem? Oh kay!) *BE A F****ING MAN! I AIN'T SCARD OF NOBODY! YALL CAN ALL GET THIS WORK. BJ YOU TOO. YA'LL APPROACH ME HOSTILE I WAS STILL IN MY CAR. I GOT OUT SO I CAN SEE YOU BETTER. I FELT LIKE I WAS BEING ATTACKED SO I WANTED TO PROTECT MYSELF."*

Hol' up! My Fabio is one thing, but my little brother nope! This is when I got back in his face and tried…no, I didn't try; I squared with this dude! (I be forgetting I'm only like 4'9 and be trying to square up with niggas, I guess I ain't neva scared and I would really throw hands over my blood. I don't care who you are NO QUESTIONS ASK!) Jahmel felt that when I did this, I was ganging up on him and not "riding for him" so to speak. Sorry, not sorry! I'm going to protect my family FIRST!

BJ: Grabbing me aggressively, *"Sis! LOOK AT ME, LOOK AT ME* (I couldn't look at him because if I saw any type of tears or rage in his eyes, I would be going right back off on Jahmel, because this drama he caused is effecting my baby) *JUST LET IT GO MAN, LET HIM GO. HE AIN'T S***, THAT NIGGA AIN'T S***! HE AIN'T WORTH IT, LOOK AT ME! HE AINT WORTH IT! F*** HIM, F*** THAT NIGGA!"*

While BJ was checking me…Jahmel got back in the car. When I was done getting checked by my LITTLE brother; I went back to up to the car fuming…with water in my eyes looking at him in complete awe that he pulled this stunt that I'm so used to seeing behind doors in front of my parents.

Jahmel: Beating on the center console and punching the steering wheel again… *"Azure what are you doing? Are you coming or not!?"*

Mom: Reaches back in the car to see if she got all of my things saying *"BYE, JAHMEL, She isn't going anywhere with you! Especially with you hitting your hands with your fist…"*

Jahmel: *"…NO I WASN'T, I WAS HITTING THIS"* touching and hitting the center console.

Mom: *"…RIGHT and NEXT TIME IT WILL BE MY DAUGHTER. Azure, honey you're not going anywhere with him. HELL NO.*

Jahmel: *"WOOOOOOW REALLY!? Azure, really? Have I ever hit you? You know what F*** this, get all your s*** and leave and don't f***ing call me."* Then he speeds off!

We get back into the house and we are all livid! BJ cursed for the first time, Mom and Fabio are probably angry and shocked just as much as BJ and I are. My phone rings, and it's him! Talking about; *"Now you know I respect your parents."* Scuuuuuuuuuuurrrrrrrrrrrrt! *"HOW SWAY!? HOW? You just basically charged up and cursed out my dad and could have gotten into a fight with him. Yeah, that's very respectful! two, you come to their house to pick up their daughter and didn't even speak. If this was to happen to your daughter, you would have reacted the same way."* Growing up, they didn't care who it was when you go to someone's house to pick up someone or whatever the situation may be...YOU SPEAK.

He says, *"No I wouldn't, I would be understanding. If he didn't want to talk I would have respected that and would have been there when he was ready to talk. Azure, you know you hurt my heart when you jumped in from of me like you were about to fight me."*

Me: *"DAMN RIGHT, I was going to fight you. If you know me, you should already know how I am about my family!"*

Jahmel: *"...and your Dad was trying to fight me... I didn't do anything wrong. I told you I didn't want to talk to them and BJ bucking up like he had a problem and he wanted to fight me."*

Me: *"... Yes and BJ would have f***ed your ass up too!"*

Jahmel: *"Then your mom is going to say stuff like "next time it will be you" like really? F*** outta here man"*

There was more back in forth on over the phone. He was trying to justify his actions, and it came down to that the blow-up was my fault because I don't listen. All and all, I still wanted to go to the beach. My parents and I sat down, and I told them how I felt and vice versa. They did NOT want me to go but understood that I was an adult and need to make my own decisions and choices when it came to this relationship. I felt like if this was the end, I wanted us to be calm and level-headed and have a conversation like an adult! Growing up, we always talked about our problems, and that's the approach I wanted to take with this. I did feel guilty that in hindsight, I chose my crazy boyfriend who just caused so much chaos and hurt to my real protectors! But I knew what I had to do!

We went down to Corpus (I was prepared, I had my paper spray and pocket knife, in case he jumped stupid.) but it seemed like nothing was accomplished he was saying he was done, but for some reason I still wanted to fight for it and was determined to fix this, get him saved and everyone on one accord. All of this happened the Fourth of July; weekend right before I started my new job.

We talked and agreed to start over and take things slow. Like, go all the way back to the drawing board. The plan was that we take time away from each other. I start work, and he would look at places for new employment in Houston. Just give each other space and to see how things go or not go. Which I felt like was a good choice so I can focus on my new job. As well hoping this break would fix the stress that's been making me feel irritable, moody and having migraines like crazy.

While I was living in Dallas, I was diagnosed with Asthma as well as chronic migraines. We could never find the source of my headaches. About two weeks into working, I was very weak, having bad headaches and fatigue. I Googled to look up symptoms of bad headaches; and found things like; possible brain tumor, stroke and stuff. I pleaded Blood of Jesus! I put my hand on my body and prayed for the best. Little did I know the pain that I was experiencing at work and the struggles I was having in my body physically along with the emotional strain that was taking over, would be because of a diagnosis I wasn't expecting.

Oh, What A Night

August 6th, BJ turned 18 years old! We had a great day; we went to church, out to eat, and topped it off with a trip to Fiesta Texas. He was heading off to WSU (Wichita State University) the following week. So this was considered our last family outing before our road trip. What ended up being a great day with my family tuned in to a night I would never forget? I hear that famous "ding", and it read; *"I can't stay here, she (his mom) is trip'n again."* Mind you I brought him food that I had saved from Chili's on my way home from Fiesta Texas. I started getting into the habit of not finishing my food when we went out so I can give it to him later on in the day. I even left him a few bills I had so he can walk across the street to get his mom food and even swisher so he wouldn't bother me once I got home.

Jahmel and his mom had a love-hate relationship, more hate than love if you ask me. Some days they were okay, and most days; they were at each other's throat. A few hours go by then I get a call from Jahmel; he tells me he isn't feeling good again and wanted to go the emergency room. (He had a history of headaches; remember earlier in the chapter I mentioned that he was hospitalized for two weeks? Playing back all those ER trips and all the bluffing he was doing I questioned if that whole ordeal was even real.) I just got out the shower; put on some comfy PJ's and laid down because I was tired. I had a headache myself and was feeling worse than what I've been feeling. I just chopped it up to being in the heat and riding rollercoaster after rollercoaster.

I got up because I didn't want another "Houston We Have a Problem" episode or hear his mouth about how I don't care about him and if the roles were reversed, he'll drop everything. I don't know, growing up we went to the ER only if it was something serious. In my whole 28 years of living, I only remember going to the ER three times. When I closed my hand in the front door and severed the tip of my finger. The second time was when BJ thought he was a part of WWE and back-flipped off the couch and busted his head open. Lastly, when I had an allergic reaction to something just days before I went to accept my new job. My ID picture is the worse, face swollen and ALL. These types of incidents called for an ER run. Jahmel, if he coughed wrong. *"I need to go to the emergency room!"* Now if the cough or fever stayed longer than a few days we'd go to the Med Clinic or make an appointment with our PCP. My Mom is like Rochelle from *'Everybody Hates Chris'*. *"Just take some tussin!"*

My parents were sleeping, but BJ was awake. I told BJ, *"Hey, Jahmel isn't feeling well. I'm going to take him to the hospital. I'll keep you posted."* I think I went and told my Dad, I can't remember. When I was pulling up to the hotel, he was outside already standing on the corner. He gets in the car and immediately started his rant and mentioned that he was in a lot of pain. I guess I was going too slow for him because he wanted me to pull over so he can drive. In my head, I'm thinking; Uh. No. Your anger + you behind a wheel = ROAD RAGE to the MAX. He put up a fuss, and I was already irritated and tired because he took me out of my comfort to be out here, and the LAST thing I wanted to do was argue. We switched, he starts driving fast and recklessly. At one point, I really thought he was trying to kill us! He's driving towards downtown. I asked, *"Why are we going downtown. We're closer to Methodist on 35!??*

In all honesty I was scared to ask that question because I didn't want to get cursed out, let alone make him madder to where he really tries to wreck my car or just go completely crazy. I even felt that if he snaps on me, with the way I was feeling I would have gone off on him and we would really be arguing. With him still on his rant and he says *"I THINK I HAVE A MENTAL PROBLEM! No HOSPITAL can FIX THAT, F***ING THINK BEFORE YOU SPEAK, You SOUND-DUMB!"* There goes that tone I hate again…I take a deep breath and stay as calm, so I can and respond in a pleasant tone *"Well, let's go to the Crisis Center so they can evaluate you and see if they can help."* He looks at me with a look he would give me that would make me sick to my stomach. It was the look of pure disgust and belittlement; an 'Ike look'. You know how he look at Tina before he went upside her head? That! He gave me that look with an eye roll and kept driving. As we're getting closer to downtown, I still didn't know where he was going. He says in a frustrated, annoyed tone *"Azure, where's this place at?"* I start to give him verbal directions; he didn't want that. I guess he couldn't stand to hear the sound of my voice at that moment because he wanted me to put it in the GPS; even though he did not follow what it was saying. We eventually ended up at the Crisis Center; I was surprised he even took my suggestion into consideration.

With my mom working closely with them…well, it's technically under her company. I was hoping someone would recognize me and send an SOS to my mom. Farfetched, but hey, you never know. Jahmel goes to the counter and the guy asked how he could help, I don't quite remember what he told the gentlemen, but it was along the lines of he's really angry and he wants to hurt something or someone. He also mentioned a term I haven't heard of; IED. He hands Jahmel a clipboard of some documents that he needed to fill out. Not even a quarter of the way through he says, *"F*** this."* Puts the clipboard in the chair and walks out. Now mind you it's 11 pm or close to it, and I'm just trying to go back home. I give the clipboard back to the guy defeated and he gives me some suggestions on if his mood gets worse, I told him thank you and walked back out thinking…HERE WE GO!

When I get back to the car, he asked me for my phone to Google something. I couldn't tell what it was; it was symptoms for some type of disorder. I hesitantly asked, *"Jahmel, where do you want to go now?"* He says, *"I'm going to the hospital."* By this time he looked flushed, and it appeared like he was falling asleep or getting dizzy. I kept saying, *"LET ME DRIVE!"* For one, I ain't trying to die and TWO, we're downtown and around a lot of construction. A wrong turn can have my car in a hole! So of course, in Jahmel fashion; he runs a red light. I yelled *"DUDE! PULL OVER!"* Next thing I know, RED & BLUE flashing behind us and automatically had flash backs. I said *"NIGGA!"* I started to think of a way out of this ticket or whatever we were about to get. I could tell the cop I'm having stomach pain and trying to get to the hospital, or my blood sugar is low. I don't know something to get out of this ticket he was about to get. Thank the Lord the cop saw that something was wrong with Jahmel and asked if we were trying to get to the hospital. Jahmel tells the cop *"Yes, I'm sorry I ran the light, but I'm not feeling well."* He said, *"Okay, sir, ma'am" you're not far the hospital is right behind you. Just follow me."* As the officer was escorting us to the hospital, I notice the car started slowing down and he was becoming lethargic, I yell *"JAHMEL, JAHMEL!??"* Then all of a sudden, he passes out at the wheel.

(My initial reaction was—you all seen the gif of the little boy sitting at the table and he wanted McDonald's or something and his mom says no and he goes into a fit? That was my mood, cause I knew this was about to turn into an all-night thing. I know that's wrong, but I just wanted my bed!)

Then he just slumped over, Thank the Lord, the speed was low enough to where I can put the car in park without damaging my vehicle. I automatically freaked out; I tried shaking him to wake him up, I even punched him; he was OUT! With him being out…I was trying to figure out how to get him on the other side so that I can drive; he's a big guy so that plan was out. I went ahead and put the hazards on so oncoming cars can know that I am stalled. I also thought about sliding the seat back and sitting on him and driving the rest of way; even though the ER entrance was a few of yards away, he could come to, freak out and foot hits the brake or accelerator, so plan B is now out. I hooped out and ran around to the driver side so that I could try waking him up that way; it dawned on me to call 911. We were following the officer and the last thing I wanted him to think is that we lied and tried to get out of a ticket even though I was preparing to lie to get out of a ticket.

The operator comes on, and I tell her the situation and that we had a police escort and that's when my boyfriend passed out. She was calling for help; I look up, and the officer circled back around. **THANK YOU, JESUS,**! He gets out and says, *"Hey, what happened?"* He sees him hunched over and calls for back up. As the officer and I were trying to figure out how to get him to the passenger's side; a lady who was stopped behind us got out and ask what was wrong because she was a nurse. (God was looking out for ya girl that night. I could do a lot by myself, but THIS, nope; especially with me feeling weak. I couldn't do it alone) The nurse and I both thought it could be his sugar since he's a diabetic. She happened to have some candy, she directs me to rub it on his lips and teeth so he can get the sugar. While I'm doing that EMS and two other squad cars arrive (Listen, being with this dude, I had ENTIRELY too much interaction with the police than I was comfortable with.) Honestly, a part of me thought he was faking, I'm thinking he is such a character; but when I saw how flushed and clammy he was, I thought you couldn't fake that so this must be really real; but then again, people get paid for acting.

As we're still working the candy; EMS was trying to assess how they were going to get him out of this car. He comes to; and goes into a straight panic when we saw a crowd of people and bright flashing lights. I had to quickly reassure him that I was there and he wasn't in any trouble. Last thing I needed was him swinging and cursing out the people who were trying to help him. The original officer comes over and says, *"Hello sir, you're okay, you passed out. Do you think you can get up so we can get you on the stretcher?"* Jahmel shakes his head, yes. EMS comes over so they can take vitals on him to check is blood pressure and etc. While they were getting ready to take his blood pressure, this nigga passes out YET AGAIN! At this point, I began to plead the Blood of Jesus but was pissed at the same time. You're probably thinking that's hypocritical, mean and not Christian like; but something about this whole thing wasn't sitting right in my spirit. Fast forward, two Jolly Ranchers and five techs later; they were able to get him out of the car; on to the stretcher to take him to the emergency room which was literally walking distance.

I followed behind the original officer; he directed where he wanted me to park and escorted me inside. When I got back to the triage area; the first thing he says, *"They're f***ing rude! Me and this nurse are going to have a problem."* (Wait, sir weren't you just passed out like 5 minutes ago, now you can spot attitudes? Okay!) The nurse comes in and says something; I don't remember exactly what but I do remember her tone!

It was definitely off-putting and rude. I can see how he thought she may be an issue. She proceeds to ask him questions about what happened and he is telling her that he doesn't really remember. Jahmel told her that he was very angry earlier and that he may have IED (which is an anger disorder he looked up earlier.) She said *"IED? Like a bomb!? You have one on you"* he looks at me like this girl is stupid he replied *"NO! Do you even know what IED is?"* She responds with an attitude *"Um sir! Yes! I am retired military!"* I'm not sure if she then felt threatened because things escalated very quickly. Next thing I know he's cursing and getting loud with the nurse, to the point security came. Jahmel demanded that he sees the Dr. and get another nurse.

The Dr. comes in and asked what seems to be the problem. Jahmel is fussing at the Dr. telling him how rude the nurse is and that he thinks he has IED. At this point, I zoned out. I was getting tired of the same ole same ole with him. What got me a little more perturbed than what I was is what came out the Dr's mouth next. He says, *"Hmm, looks like you're fine to me. You're up, talking for someone who was just brought in by EMS."* I looked at the Dr. like REALLY!? Thinking that was the WRONG thing to say. I honestly thought Jahmel was going to jump on the poor man. Sure enough, I was right, the wrong thing to say; and it pissed Jahmel off even more. He now then turns on the Dr. he starts taking off the EKG pads, he even pulled out his IV literally trying to run up on people. I'm trying to restrain him and hold him back (yeah, me. My lil ole' self.) By this time, the security guard (black) comes and approaches Jahmel and said, *"Bruh Chil!"* I'm, still trying to calm him down while looking at the nurse and Dr. with the face of like ***HELP ME***! Obviously, something is wrong mentally with this guy! Yeah, no; It was total chaos! So much chaos that he was kicked out because he was erratic and also disturbing the other patients.

I honestly think if the nurse wasn't trying to be a jerk and actually took what he was saying seriously, she would have looked up IED if she didn't already know the medical term for it. Things would have gone differently; he may have actually gotten help that night. It wasn't until recently that I did full research on this disorder. I was sharing with my Mom and Auntie London; that I wonder how things would have gone if I knew what I know now. Maybe God didn't want me to know until now, because it could have ended a lot worse than what it did OR I would have stayed longer because I now know the causes and effects and would have felt like I could help him knowing what the issue was.

IED is also known as Intermittent Explosive Disorder. While I was reading up on it; it summed him up perfectly! *"Intermittent Explosive Disorder is an impulse-control disorder characterized by sudden episodes of unwarranted anger. This disorder is typified by hostility, impulsivity, and recurrent aggressive outburst. People with IED essentially explode into rage despite lack of apparent provocation or reason." –Valley Behavioral Health.*

You'd think he'd just walk out without a problem, NOPE! He was still talking mess to everyone. When we got outside, he was still very expressive, venting to me as we were going to the car. A white security officer that was walking behind us (accompanied by the black officer) says to Jahmel, *"You better leave before something bad happens to you."* Jahmel took that as a threat and high-key I did too! Especially with all the problems law enforcement and AfricanAmericans are having. Jahmel turns around and says, *"WHAT!"* while taking his shirt off running up on the cops. I'm standing there stunned like *"YOOOOO, What the hell man!?"* So, again my little 4'9 self-jumps in front of him (if they were reaching for a gun, I could have easily been shot; was I thinking? No, not really just trying to get him in the car before "something bad" indeed happened.) pushing him back, while yelling at him *"GET YOUR ASS IN THE CAR!"* While reassuring the officers that my 4'9 self-had him and will handle it. While walking towards the car; he picks up one of the construction sandwich boards as if he was going to throw it at them or something. I grabbed his arm in mid-rise; trying to make him put it down. NOPE! He throws it towards them. I grabbed the back of his pants and literally dragged him a block to the car! I tell you if I was on a reality show, this episode would have been one for the books!

I just thank the Lord for his GRACE and PROTECTION over my life; because that little blow-up he just had could have gone bad quickly, but it didn't!

I finally have him in the car; it's now like one o'clock in the morning. I turned and looked at him and in the calmest voice I could find, because I was out of breath from dragging this 300 pound man. I said, *"I need you to breathe and chill the f*** out."* He says, *"I want to go to another hospital."* I suggested the original one I was trying to take him to. He responds, *"I'd kill someone over at the hospital if they say something stupid."* He says, *"I want to go to SAMC."* I'm confused as to why he wanted to go to a United States Military HOSPITAL!! Like dude, they have NO PROBLEM shooting or detaining you if you jump stupid. But we went.

I approach the gate and I tell the guards that the hospital we came from could not treat him because he felt uncomfortable with the care that was being provided to him, and that I wouldn't be able to make it to the civilian hospital and that this was the closest one. He *says, "Okay ma'am, can I see your ID's please?"* We hand them our ID's, as they walk to check us out. At this point, I didn't care if my attitude came out in my voice; after all he just put me through, I had EVERY RIGHT to be mad. I looked at Jahmel and said, *"You sure you ain't got no warrants or anything?? Cause I don't wan..I CANT DO another Houston situation."* He exhales, *"Yeees; I'm positive I don't have any warrants, I just reported last week."* I just say, *"Alright, Jahmel."*

I can see the guards coming back to the car; this boy says, *"YUP, I'm going to Jail."* I snapped my neck to look at him so quick, yelling! "You just said that you were clear!" The guard handed me our ID's back and says *"Ma'am", you're all clear. Um, Mr. Edwards, you are cleared; but were you aware that you had a warrant* (says the city and state) *for Fraud?"* I look at him confused, but in the back of my head, I laughed and said to myself, *"why am I not surprised."* Jahmel says, *"NO, I wasn't aware of that."* The guard says *"Yes it shows up in our system since we run everything. I'm going to go ahead and let you all through to proceed to the ER, just make sure you take care of that sir. We can't really do anything since it's not in our jurisdiction."*

We get to the ER and got him checked in and everything; the staff there was very nice and genuinely concerned. Since he was a civilian if they needed to admit him for further treatment, he would need to be transferred to another nonmilitary hospital, but they would run all of his test and blood work there. It's now pushing four o'clock in the morning, and I was BEAT! Didn't plan on hospital hopping all night, but HEY!

While all of this was going on, I was texting my parents and BJ, keeping them in the loop and updating them on Jahmel and more so, my whereabouts. One of the tests they did came back, and it was something wrong with his heart, and he would need to be admitted. They let him pick which hospital he wanted to go to so they can order the EMS to come transport him. My first thought was THANK YOU JESUS! I can GO HOME! I told him I was going to go home and that once he got to the hospital and into a room to call me, so I can come up in the morning; well later. Not only was I tired and wanted to be home by the time my dad got ready to leave out for work. I still couldn't shake this feeling, and I myself even thought about getting checked out since I was in the hospital; but I prayed over myself and kept pushing. It worked out perfectly because as I was leaving his ride pulled up. I told him to behave, get some rest, and I was going to do the same. You'd think he'd say thank you for everything and that he appreciated me. I just got an *"Okay, please be careful and get some rest. I know you're tired."* I'm thinking, *"OH, now that you're getting some help, you can see clearly now that I am tired?"*

By now it's five-thirty in the morning, and I just KNEW my Dad would be heading out soon. I pulled up just as he was coming to get in his car. He asked how Jahmel was doing, I tell him that it was something with his heart, couldn't remember the exact diagnosis but he had a stint put in a while back, and they wanted to make sure that everything was still intact. He said a prayer for me and him, kissed me and told me to go to sleep; and I did just that.

A few hours later, I am wakened up by mommy. She, herself was heading to work and wanted an updated on Jahmel as well. She also informed me that it was raining pretty badly, and the highway that I needed to take to get to the hospital was flooded and I needed to take another route. I called Jahmel to check on him and to tell him how the weather was. I had to explain to him that I couldn't come right then and that I'd be there later due to the flooding and because I wasn't feeling well. *(I could have taken an alternate route, but I just wanted to be alone for a while.)* My headache had gotten worse; probably due to lack of sleep, food and stress as well I started cramping, which was right on time because it was that time of the month and it was a few days late. I began to feel a little better; thinking the reason I was feeling how I was feeling was because of my menstrual symptoms. I grabbed something to eat to have something in my stomach and laid right back down.

I get up to the hospital and I walked into his room he's sitting up laughing and joking with the nurses like nothing happened less than twenty-four hours ago. I said sarcastically, *"Well, you look better."* He says, *"I feel a little better. Still a little shaken up, because I don't really remember what happened."* Then he goes on to ask if I felt better and if my cycle finally came. Excitingly I said *"It's on its way! Now I can stop feeling so sick and weak! It should hit tonight."* Jahmel says, *"GOOD! Now you can stop being mean to me!"* I gave him that look, and then we both laughed.

I excuse myself to go to the restroom, and I felt and heard something fall into the toilet. It caught me off guard. I looked and it's a **HUGE! BLOOD! CLOT!** I panicked and remembered when I looked up how I was feeling, blood clots were one of the symptoms. I yelled *"BAAABE! GIVE ME MY PHONE! I need my phone!"* He responds in a concerning voice *"Are you okay?"* I yell back *"NO! YES! Just give me my phone!!"* I got the phone and immediately took a picture of what I saw! I got myself together. I was trying to hurry because I didn't want him to worry but I didn't want to leave a trace of anything.

While I was walking out of the restroom, I began to get dizzy and had unbearable pain. I tried to be a tough cookie, but it was hard to walk and stand up straight. I never really thought too much of the pain because I've had really bad cramps in the past that travel to my back at times. Jahmel saw that I was very week and kept pushing me to go downstairs to and check myself in. Crazy thing is I told him I didn't even have my updated insurance from my job yet so I couldn't go because I was uninsured. I called my jobs hotline; it's been a month, and I hadn't received my insurance card or anything. Come to find out it was submitted wrong, so I indeed did not have any insurance. They fixed the problem for me with no hassle; and I had immediate benefits. It's like God knew.

While he was still fussing at me to go to the emergency room; the pain was getting worse, and it started moving towards my back like it would sometimes do. I reach over to grab his hand, he looks at me and says *"Yeah, Azure; you need to go and get checked, you're looking flushed."* With deep and heavy breathing I say weakly *"I'm fine, imma just go home and lay down. I just need a hot shower and something to eat then I'll be fine."* He offered me his breakfast that he didn't eat, I looked at him and said, *"Well if you didn't eat it what makes you think I want that?"* With his head held down he says *"I'm sorry, I'm just trying to help."* In that moment I really wanted to be petty and let him know how he just felt when he was trying to help I how I feel EVERY DAY with him. But I was too week to pull my petty card."

I was sitting there trying to let the pain pass so I can get up and head to the car to go home. All the while, I was thinking, who I can call to get advice from. The first person that popped up in my mind was my Aunt Danielle (she's a nurse; but I was afraid of what she'd say. She never really came out and said it but she didn't care for Jahmel AT ALL! Plus I didn't want her to "accidentally" call my mom like she did when I secretly got my first tattoo) then my closest cousin pop's in my head. Erika, she's a nurse as well; I always call her when Google or WebMD tells me I'm dying or eternally ill. Then I thought about my Auntie London! So I sent the picture to Auntie London and Erika; yes I did a disclaimer message before I sent the picture. *IF THEY BOTH HAD iPhones, I could have hit them with that invisible text. SHADE!* I get an immediate response from both:

Erika: *"Uuuummmm, Babe, has your period come yet? If not, you could have had a miscarriage"* If it has come, you could have something irregular about period. I would just get check just to make sure!"

After what she said I felt like I was still good and I didn't need to go to the emergency room. *"Just give me some tussin and I'm fine."*

It was Auntie London that pretty much lit a fire under me, scared me and made me check-in. She called me, but I ignored it because I didn't want to talk to her in front of Jahmel. I left the room didn't say anything to him; just got up and left. Pain and all. Hunched over walking out the room clinging to the wall, one of the nurses saw I was in pain and asked if I was ok. I just shook my head yes and made it to the elevator to take me down to the lobby to have a conversation with my Auntie. She was asking me all types of questions; meanwhile, Jahmel is blowing up my phone, I guess because he was either sincerely worried or wanted to see if I actually left. Auntie London and I went through the process of elimination; all my cycles have been consistent; just the one for July came late; so we ruled out being pregnant. She thought it could be my gallbladder which would explain the pain but not the bleeding unless something ruptured. She was worried because if it was indeed my gallbladder or something else, she didn't want it to hurt my reproductive system; that sacred me because I do indeed want to have children one day. I finally got myself together, but I was so scared to hear what the doctor would tell me. I been feeling off lately and I didn't want to hear I had a spot or lump anywhere. My heart was racing going back upstairs to tell Jahmel that I was going to go check in and that I would call him once I got settled.

The wait was very short; they got me in very quickly after I told them what I experienced. They hit the ground running; blood pressure, temp and urine sample all less than ten minutes. They were determined to figure out what was causing me this pain to where I couldn't walk or stand up straight. The Dr comes in to meet me and ask general questions and tells me what his plan of care is going to be. Plan one was wait for the urine sample to come back to see and rule out pregnancy. If I wasn't pregnant, he was going to give me some medicine to help with the painful cycle that I was having. Plan two: if the urine sample came back positive next would be to get some blood work and ultrasound done, to make sure everything is in line. My last cycle was at the end of June, when "Houston, We Have a Problem" went down. So it was indeed late, but I would always have a late cycles because I'm stressed a lot, and the past few months ya'll cannot say I wasn't STRESSED! Plus, I had none of the early onset pregnancy symptoms, so the Dr wanted to quickly rule that out and get me on some medicine so I can start feeling better.

While I'm praying that there isn't anything eternally wrong with me; I'm texting Auntie London giving her updates. Auntie London is my mom's baby sister, and my go-to for everything. Things I'm scared to tell my mom, I go practice on Auntie London first, or if I need to vent in my ratchet mode, Auntie London is the person to go to. She will hype me up, get lit and be petty right with me; BUT if I am out of line, she will remind me QUICKLY that she is the Auntie and I am the Niece!

The pain started to become not as intense, which was making me happy because I just knew I wouldn't be here all day! I was just in the hospital all night, and into the morning with Jahmel, now I'm the patient. I just wanted to go home! The Dr. comes back in with a weird look on his face, and my initial thought was *"OH Lord, I'm dying!"* He asked how my pain was. I told him it's gotten better and that I was just cold. He said, *"GOOD! I got your urine sample back…* With a deep breath and sigh (in that moment I knew, YEP, I'm dying) he says… *and it is positive. You're pregnant sweetie!"* With a blank stare, I looked at him confused, yet shocked, shaking my head, *"HUH!?"* He goes on and says *"according to your sample you're about five weeks,* (I think at that time I passed out mentally) *we're going to get blood work done to check your HCG levels to make sure your count matches the five-weeks and to make sure the baby is growing in the right place, since you were having bad abdominal pain"* I guess I still had this confused look on my face and the Dr. asked *"Is this your first pregnancy?"* Mouth wide open, I just shake my head yes; he grabs my hands and says, *"You're going to be okay; we'll take care of you. I'll get the blood work ordered and get you some warm blankets. Okay?"* I just shook my head; I had no words. I'm trying to process what I just heard. Thanked the Lord I'm not dying, but I'M PREGNANT!??

So while the doctor was giving me the news, Auntie London is blowing up my phone *"????"*, *"What's going on?"* I replied… *"…Annie, they said. I'm pregnant."* She immediately calls me; I didn't answer. She texted, *"Don't you start that shit, answer the damn phone!"* (I had a tendency of not answering when I'd text her going off on how Jahmel made me mad, or after I'll send her something like *"I'm done I need to be alone, I can't take this no more"*) I was so shocked, because I honestly thought I couldn't have kids. Being in a six-year long relationship prior and not having not ONE pregnancy scare or false-positive test. I just knew something was wrong and I wouldn't be able to conceive. Well, I was wrong! I finally answered the phone for her; she said: *"You don't have to say anything, I just wanted to make sure you were okay."* She goes on to say *"The blood clot makes sense now, which is a symptom of a "threaten miscarriage"* IT MAKES SENSE! *You did go to Six Flags twice last week."* I instantly started to feel bad; I yelled: *"OH MY GOD!"*—and covered my mouth I was putting my child in danger just to have fun. I started thinking about all the roller coasters, water rides all the drops, twist and turns.

Like OMG! I was pregnant riding ROLLERCOSTERS! Auntie finally calmed me down and reassured me that I didn't do anything wrong, I simply didn't know. The random cravings of McDonalds French fries and Dr. Pepper every night at nine, ten o'clock on the way home now made sense. I'M PREGNANT! I suddenly remember a conversation I had with my Soror, she called me one night while I was in the drive thru.

She said jokingly, *"Sis you sure you ain't prego, cause every time I call you you're eating fries!"*

Me: I laughed and said *"Girl, I may be, you know I love me some fries, but I get them EVERY NIGHT! LOL"*

Soror: *"Your cycle must be coming!"*

Me: *"You know what, you sure right; plus, I hadn't really been eating."*

I was still a little scared, but low-key excited! Was I afraid of telling, Billy & Tonja? HECK YEAH! Especially after that blow up we had a month ago. I remember trying to comfort and encourage Jahmel, I said that he needed to live for his daughter and our children, and he said that we didn't have any kids together. Little did we know I was actually carrying his child. My mind was absolutely blown that I was pregnant. Then all of a sudden reality came rushing in. We're not stable; he didn't have a job, car and importantly a place to live; now we're getting ready to have a baby? At that moment, I made up in my mind that regardless of what happened or happens between Jahmel and I moving forward. I would take care of my baby! Now, I didn't see myself not married and prego; but hey! I made a vow that day to myself that I will take care of my baby and not be that dependent on no man to take care of my child. I finally called Jahmel; I was going back and forth on if I should tell him or wait until later. He answered immediately

"Baby, you okay!? I'm worried."

Me: *Yes, I'm fine, what about you?*

Jahmel: *"Waiting on the last EKG and test to come back and if everything is okay, they'll go ahead and discharge me."*

Me: *"Okay, that's good."*

Jahmel: *"What are they saying about you? Are you okay?"*

The tone of his voice you can tell that he was sincere and really concerned. He's never seen me like that before.

Me: *"Yeah. Um, babe?"*

Jahmel: *"Yeah, what's up?"*

Me: *"Jahmel...... I'm pregnant..."*

Jahmel: With some excitement in his voice *"REALLY?? What, how far along?"*

Me: *"Five weeks."*

Jahmel: *"IM ON MY WAY DOWN! I'm about to check myself out and tell them you're down in ER, and I need to get to you!"*

About an hour goes by he comes down to check on me as well to be with me. He wanted to ask me face to face rather than over the phone if the baby was okay. I told him we needed to see what the blood work and ultrasound said.

The Dr came back in and says *"Ms. Gabriel, you are indeed pregnant. Your HCG levels are high and based on that you're actually six weeks. We've ordered your ultrasound, once that is done we'll have you on your way. Just follow up with your OBGYN and be very careful because with the blood clot and bleeding, you were threatening a miscarriage. So just make sure you follow up with your OB and congratulations."* We had the ultrasound done, she had a hard time at first trying to find the baby, but we were able to see my...well our baby, and he/she was growing just fine. The Dr. gave me light duty, no; heavy lifting or bending.

After we left the hospital, Jahmel went into instant daddy mode! He took me to Wal-Mart to get some prenatal vitamins and food! He wouldn't let me lift or carry anything; I was thinking okay!! He's starting to step up emotionally. He could often be insensitive to situations where sensitivity is definitely needed. I was still unsure how things between us were going to go; so I asked him *"Jahmel? Are we going to be okay?"* He started giving me his goals and game plans and how he needed to for sure hustle to get things together and get a job so that he can provide for our child and me. I also told him that my stress level would need to be very low; *"so this staying out late, running all over San Antonio, especially after getting off work was going to have to stop. As well the yelling and anger. I'm not going to be able to handle that, you and your mom going at it, etc. If it happens baby and I are leaving and going home!"* I said firmly to Jamel. He responds back and says, *"Yeah, babe. I hear you."*

I had an appointment the next day with my OBGYN, but they couldn't verify my insurance! I had to wait until it was updated in my insurance company's system which would take 24hrs, so I couldn't do anything until the following day, but I had to work. So I had to cancel and reschedule until next week when I was off.

Later that night, I had family movie night plans to go see "Kidnapped". BJ and his friend were going to meet my parents and I at the movie. I was so tired and didn't feel like driving so I asked BJ if he could scoop me up from the house. Before we went to the movies we grabbed something to eat; I really didn't want Wing Stop because I was already nauseous and had a headache, but I gave in. I was only able to get two boneless wings down before I felt the urge to throw up. While we were eating, I get a notification on my phone! This boy, Jahmel signed me up for a baby progress app. While I was checking to see how big the baby was. I felt BJs friend looking towards my phone and out the corner of my eye I saw her looking over and I panicked. I was praying she didn't see it and if she did she wouldn't ask me out loud if I was pregnant in front of my brother or ask him later; because he didn't know yet. BJ saw that I barely ate my food, so he asked if my headache was getting worse and I told him, yeah, but I'll be okay. He packed my food up to go then we headed towards the movies.

Sitting there watching Kidnapped and seeing how Halle Berry was going above and beyond to get her son back in her arms. It had me thinking I would do the same. But I didn't want a boy! Even though I felt it was a boy! While watching her go to great lengths to get her son back, I remember holding my tummy looking down and telling my little baby *"I will always protect you!"* It was really setting in that I was going to be a mommy.

The next morning I woke up for work, Jahmel was NOT about to let me drive all the way to San Marcos by myself especially with me being under restrictions. So he made sure I picked him up on the way in. He stopped at Buc-ee's to get me breakfast. This boy comes out with kolaches, fruit, apple juice, yogurt, donuts, a breakfast sandwich and a Gatorade. Bless his heart, talking about I didn't know what to get so I got a mixture and whatever you don't eat I will! I make it to work, and after our team huddle, I stay behind so I can talk to my manager Tre'. He gives me that look like 'What chu want!?' I showed him my discharge papers and he quickly looked up at me with the same look I gave the Dr. He said, *"Okay! Go head to your station and I'll be over there in a minute to talk, but you good right!?"* I shake my head yes as I'm walking towards my station to get started working.

When he comes over, he says, *"BLUE!! What's going on?"* I told him I was fine and what happened with the insurance and that I needed to go see my OBGYN asap and that I rescheduled an appointment for next week. He says, *"HOLD ON!"* and then leaves. A few moments go by and he comes back and says *"GO...go to the Dr."* I look at him confused like huh he says, *"Get out my face and go!!"* (He didn't say it harsh;

more like go take care of your business) I don't know what he did, but I knew I had to go. He just became my manager like a week and a half before. So it was very refreshing to have a boss that barely knew me, but cared about me enough to let me go and take care of what I need to take care of.

We get to the office, my OBGYN is the BEST in the WORLD! He delivered BJ and 3 of my cousins, which included Erika! He walked into the room and gave me that you in trouble look. He greeted Jahmel, but just stared me down with a slight smirk on his face. My doc is like my dad but of OBGYN-ness. The first thing he says is *"HOW THIS HAPPEN!?"* in a stern voice. Then said, *"Don't answer that!"* and gave me a smile and fist bump. He examines me, and I asked him, *"AM I REALLY PREGNANT!!????"* He looks at me with that did you just ask me that question look and said: *"OH YEAH, You're definitely pregnant!"* He pretty much gave me the same restrictions as the ER doctor, until my next appointment. He also asked me. *"SOOO! Have you told mama bear yet!??"* with a raised eyebrow *"If you don't imma call her and tell her."* and he was serious.

I had so many questions, *"Can I fly?"* *"Will I be okay working in the fast-paced environment?"* *"What can I and cannot eat?"* *"Will the bleeding stop!?"* He assured me that I can fly and I would be okay and that bleeding is perfectly normal and would subside within a week; even though some patients bleed their whole pregnancy; but if I had pain with it to call him. As well, *"TELL YO MAMA!"* He said.

When I got home later that evening, I was feeling horrible after dinner. I went to my room to go to sleep and get ready for work the next morning. My mommy came in my room shortly after and laid in my bed next to me. I felt that 'it's time' tug in my heart. I said

"Mommy, me don't feel good, my tummy hurts." She starts to rub my stomach and surprisingly it started to feel better too. I said, *"I have to tell you something, I don't want too, but I have to."*

Mom: *"What? You're pregnant, aren't you!?"*

I put my head down in shame but confused as to how she knew. Me: *"Yes, ma'am, how you know?"*

I'm thinking; my doctor really called my mama and told her. Mom: She looks at me and says, *"GIRL, did you forget who I am?"* With a nervous and relived laugh, I say *"No, ma'am."*

Mom: *"Azure, your mood has been up & down...* (moving her arm like a wave) *you've been very snappy!"*

Me: *"Have I??? I'm sorry I wasn't trying to."*

She asked what happened and how I found out. I filled her in from the events in the ER and showed her the picture I took. She also asked about Jahmel and how he felt, she also gave me her motherly advice and then Elder Gabriel. She took the news a lot better than I thought. I got the concerned, but excited vibes from her. I was carrying her first grandbaby. I told her that I didn't want to tell her until I was further along, but we were getting ready to make that drive to Wichita to take BJ to school and I would be flying back by myself, and I would hate for something to happen and for her to not know. She said, *"YES! Good job and that's why you're going to tell your Dad and Brother, NOW!"* I got super scared and said, *"Mom don't make me."* She gave me a little attitude and petty-ness *"I'm sure London and Danielle (My God Mommy) already know so you need to tell your Dad! You know how he is about finding out stuff last!"*

I got a little snappish right back with her and said

"Only Auntie London and Erika know. Hmph"

Mom: in a calming voice, like my Auntie London gave me that one night, she says *"...and Jahmel and his mom right!? So that's five people who know and none of them are your DAD or Brother! We are a family baby; they need to know. I'll be right there with you, so you'll be okay! Let's go!"*

Mommy grabs my hand and pulls me out the bed; we walk out of my room and she looks into my brother's room and says *"BJ, C'mon, family meeting!"* Still holding my hand we walk to her room and I see that my Dad is sleep. I let her hand go and say *"Seee, Dad is sleep we gotta wait!"* She said *"AZURE! Nope, he'll wake up."* BJ looking at me confused like what's going on. Mom taps my Dad *"Bill, BILLY, wake up family meeting. Azure has something to tell you. Go head Azzie."* I look at BJ who is sitting at the top of their bed, with the body pillow over his legs, and then to my left where my mom is standing leaning over the bed and to my right where my dad is sitting up waiting to hear what's so important that we woke him up. I look back at my mommy and say

"Um, um" She says *"OKAY, I'll start it off and Azure you'll finish."* She begins to tell them everything I told her; she's saying this in a calming voice and everything. I'm looking at the boys' faces to get a read. BJ is sitting there holding the pillow, Dad still trying to wake up, but looks concerned because he knows it's something serious.

I'm freaking out on the inside, pretty much at this point I'm just trying to figure out what flowers I want on my casket because I knew I was dead. Especially Jahmel! I still hear my mom talking but it sounds like I'm under water. Then next thing I hear *"...so, she had an appointment with Dr. W. today and she six weeks pregnant!"* I was like wait, what? Not only did she start, but she also FINISHED!

In front of me, I slowly see the pillow move from BJ's legs to under his nose, and all I see was his bucked eyes. Dad is starting at

Mom then looks at me then back at her and says, *"HUH?"* with his hands between his legs shaking them back and forth. It was at that moment I'm like *"YUP, Hydrangeas are the ones I want on my casket. if I'm going out. I'm going out with my favorite flowers on me."* Dad was more shocked than anything and says *"WOW, ya'll scared me, I knew it was serious, but I wasn't expecting that. WOW!"* I looked over at BJ, and I can only see his eyes and eyebrows…but if I had x-ray vision, I'm pretty sure his mouth was wide open, which would explain the shock but excited look in his eyes. It was that look siblings give when they know the other is about to get in trouble or a whopping. YUP, that was BJ's face.

My dad asked if I was okay, then gave me his take on the situation, which was that I needed to step up. Not that I was immature or irresponsible of becoming someone's mother; but he was saying having a baby comes with a whole lot of responsibilities, which was pretty much what Mom said but is had that Daddy stamp on it. He then asked what my due date was, I told him April 19th. He nods his head and says, *"Hmm, imma have to have a real talk with that fella."* (They hadn't spoken or seen each other since the blow-up.) Then proceeds to say *"We got your back! We'll be here to back you up and pick up the slack where and if we can. We GOT YOU! Better than B.E.T!"* He reached his arms out to give me a hug. I wanted to burst into tears, but I held it in.

BJ was next to speak, and to be honest, I was a little worried about what was getting ready to come out of his mouth. Especially now because he is of age and he understands things better than he would if he was 8. His response to the news that he was getting ready to be an uncle to a little niece or nephew was P R I C E L E S S! Mom says; *"B, your turn."* He slowly uncovers his face with the pillow, sits up a bit and says, *"…well! Quincy, Durron, Charlie, Oscar, Tippy, and Jimmy* (which are some of our uncles) *ain't gon have nothing on UNCLE BJ!!!"* We all laughed! I expressed to them my concerns and worries, we hugged it out, and all went to sleep. I felt so relieved that my 3 Hearts knew the changes that were taken place inside my tummy. It definitely went a lot smoother than I thought. I didn't get kicked out the house or die. So, I'll say it was a good family meeting.

Shock the World

The next day was a Thursday, and we had plans to leave for WSU on that Saturday. Jahmel still had his rental car from back in July and of course they were looking for it (sigh, this guy!) Jahmel and his mother had been sleeping in the car because he had no money to get a room. When I got off work, we meet up at a McDonalds close to where he's been parking at night. He kept saying, *"You have nothing on you? I'm tired of sleeping in the car, ants keep crawling on me and stuff and my mom is getting on my nerves. I haven't showered."* and so on. Sob story pretty much. So he asked me, well not so much asked, he volunTOLD me that we're going to sell my iPhone 7 Plus.

When I got to this part while I was in the early stages of writing I was having a really hard time figuring out how I wanted to continue; Do I keep up with the bs lie I've been telling about my phone getting stolen out of my locker from, work; which is impossible because we have high and strict security or tell the truth!? I asked Erika on what I should do. The first thing she said was; *"The things you're writing that's going to be in this book, do Mom & Dad know?"* I said, *"NOPE! But they will."* She then says, *"Well, why not tell this? It's your story and YOUR TRUTH! You're letting it out, and it is okay to feel embarrassed, he manipulated you into giving up a phone you absolutely loved!* (I loved my iPhone too ya'll) *Which caused a lot of headache and issues especially for your parents, Aunt London and myself hell! This part of the story is vital for the next few paragraphs your about to write. It's okay, it happened, you've learned from it and you're getting your life back so just let it out!"*

She was right, it's my truth and story to not be all the way honesty and truthful about it. I been vulnerable and transparent with you all this far. Yeah, it sucks that I went through so much but at the end of the day. I'm still here! So, it's obvious that we sold my phone. I kept saying, *"I get paid tomorrow, it's less than 24 hours, you can't wait?"* He says, *"You're going to come back out at midnight and give me money so I can get out this car? NO! YOU'RE NOT!; because mommy and daddy won't let you."*

I really wanted to say *"HELL NAW, I AINT COMING BACK, You're gonna just have to wait! I have gone above and beyond, and more than some women would do! Now, you're wanting/telling me I'm giving up the only source of communication I have?"*

But I didn't say that, because I didn't want to argue nor cause stress on me and my baby. (The name that kept, coming to me for the baby was Harper, I just knew it was going to be a boy, but it could be for a little girl too.) The whole time I'm like *"Jahmel I get paid tomorrow, bruh, one more night isn't going to hurt, plus I'm going **OUT OF STATE** to take my brother to college!!! How will I be able to document this wonderful experience?"* I also had a guy calling me back from T-Mobile to help me with our account, because the person who committed to PAYING the monthly bill couldn't because he had no what....? MONEY! Let alone A JOB! So now you want me to sell this phone, so **YOU** won't sleep in the car!? BOY BYE! But I'm thinking, in the end, I'm going to have to pay $175 for the replacement and plus another $400 or whatever to keep it on, since the account had gotten behind! Like, I couldn't understand how he would do this knowing that the women carrying his child is getting ready to go out of state with no communication.

Nigga didn't give two sh**'s about me; it's only and was always about him.

So the phone that I absolutely love is now in a machine and no longer in my possession. Jahmel never looked at the bigger picture. It was only when he was high, it seemed like he was thinking straight; without that weed, it was only him that mattered. That day it was evident that he didn't care about me or Harper. He's now set! Got money to get the room, food and God knows what else. I just knew my Mom and Dad were blowing up my phone by now. Ever since they found out I was pregnant, having complications and the consistent bleeding; they would check in on me; especially when I got off work and had to make the forty-five-minute drive home.

I finally get home and tell them my phone was stolen out of my locker; they accidentally assigned my new locker to another associate because they didn't update my locker change. Just a bunch of BS; I know Mom didn't buy it! But that was my story and I was sticking to it. I didn't want to add stress and for them to know I was helping this lazy boy to the point to where it was costing me my things, my favorite things at that!

While he was more than likely chilling in the motel room, with food and a rented roof over his head; I was at home miserable without a phone. Not so much of the social media aspect of it. More so because I was getting ready to head out of town to embark on this amazing journey with my little brother and there were going to be memories made that I wanted to capture on my OWN device and not on my family's.

Saturday morning comes and we are WSU Bound! Despite the stupidity that took place the day before, I was HYPED and ready to hit the road with my family and baby Harper. Not even ten minutes into the ride BJ & I were cutting up— jokes upon jokes, shade on shade. I was sitting there thinking to myself; I am going to really miss my little guy.

The majority of the ride, Baby Harper and I were sleep and I mean sleep! It felt like I took a Benadryl or sleeping medicine; because when I would wake up my eyes wouldn't let me be great, they were so heavy. I was actually able to be at peace for a change and let my body, brain and everything else REST. With Jahmel, I couldn't do any of that. It was like a crime for me to be tired or want to go to sleep. He didn't do anything, I worked every day, drove everywhere— I'm the one that should be mad, right?

Dr. W. did advise me to make frequent stops on the way up so I can get out and walk so I won't develop blood clots, especially with me still bleeding the way I was. We finally made it to Wichita. SHOCK-ER NATION BABY: and I was so amazed! The campus was absolutely beautiful and the PEOPLE! OH MY GOSH, so nice! Wichita is small but the atmosphere was very family oriented. It made me want to apply and move to Kansas. One of the admission advisors was trying hard to get me enrolled too so why not! Ha, she thought I was a freshman along with BJ. Little did she know I was "27 & Pregnant."

Saturday BJ had a full day of things scheduled; move in, shocker lunch, meet and greet. Just A LOT! For those who know me, know I am a very hands-on person and I love helping people regardless of what it may be (I mean, hello! My helping people turned into a book!) Being on restrictions; lifting and carrying boxes was out of the question for me. The most my family let me carry was two pillows up to BJ's room. I was trying to compile the trash and move an EMPTY, EMPTY box out into the hallway and got BUSTED and fussed at by Harper's Grandpa! I said pouting, *"Daaad! IT'S EMPTY!"* he yelled, *"TONJA? Come get your daughter!"* while he looked at me like I knew better than to trying to pick up stuff. I hear my mom call out to me from the room; *"Azure? Come here sweetie."* While Harper's Grandpa and I are making funny evil faces at each other, I walked into the room in defeat, *"Ma'am?"* while holding a pack of sheets she says *"Here, you can make the bed, since you want to help."* I give her that side-eye and said, *"Really Ma!?"* she says *"Yeah, hmm. Make your brother's bed."* – and for the record I made the heck out of that bed too! While I was sitting down spinning around in the chair bored out of my mind patiently waiting for my next task. I looked down at my hands to see something out of the ordinary. My hands were peeling. I yelled *"MOMMY! LOOK! My hands are peeling!"* she shakes her head and laughs *"Azure, you're pregnant."* I remember looking up at her all giddy; I goggled it and sho nuff it was a part of expecting. No matter how many times I washed and lotion my hands, it would still look dry and kept peeling. It looked like I dipped my hands in Elmer's Glue and let it dry. I was so amazed, peeling the "glue" off my hands kept me entertained while they brought in the rest of the stuff.

By the time everything was in his room and somewhat in order, it was now time for BJ to attend one of his orientations. That gave my parents and I time to go shopping and get other things he needed for his room; electronics snacks as well as view the city a bit; since I missed the campus visit earlier in the year. We get to Wal-Mart and "Shocker Sister" and soon to be mommy went CRAZY in the little electric cart!!! I had WSU shirts, shorts, stickers, lanyards, license plates. I even saw onesies for Harper—but Grandma said she had to be the first one to by her grandbaby's first onesie. Thinking to myself, yep! She's about to lose it too.

Going crazy in Wal-Mart and all the running around we did definitely took a toll on me that night. After dinner we headed back to the hotel, my feet were swollen and I was just beat. I yelled out to my mom from the other room, in defeat. *"MOMMY I DON'T FEEL GOOD!"* When I came out and she said *"Come here, let me pray!"* because she realized she hadn't prayed over my pregnancy since we found out. After she prayed, she told me they were getting ready to leave to go back to BJ's room since he was out of the bowling mixer they had that night – but Mama told me that I couldn't go and I was put on bed rest! I pleaded and pleaded but Grandma put her foot down and bed rest it was.

Since I was room-arrest and wasn't feeling any better, I took a hot shower in hopes the swelling in my feet would go down and I wouldn't feel so queasy. When I settled down, I noticed my mom left me her phone so I can have some type of communication in case of an emergency since I was phone-less! I called T-Mobile to see if they can send me my replacement and they could have; but it wouldn't have made it to Wichita in time because they didn't ship on the weekends. I become irritated knowing that Harper and I will be flying from Wichita to St. Louis with a 2-hour layover before we got home; and in the event something happened. I would have no way to contact my parents. I didn't care about Jahmel, because he obviously didn't care when he fed my phone to the machine.

My last day in Wichita was very emotional. I was getting super sad knowing that my little brother was pretty much grown and would be on his own. I remember my college experience and my oh my; an experience it was. I remember the crazy roommates I had; one that wore my DIRTY clothes and the other who ate ALL MY FOOD. I also had struggles in the people I surrounded myself with, and I didn't want that for BJ. It was also settling in that one of my biggest supporters wasn't going to be around to see my growing belly. My little hommie would be thousands of miles away from me. My Fabio is my protector, but BJ is just as protective and always takes care of his big sister.

We all attended the program that BJ took advantage of kind of like an extended orientation for new incoming students. All of the students and their immediate family was invited to enjoy the last evening and dinner with their student (s) before classes started; basically the "Last Supper." This would be the last time eating as a family of four; well five, until Thanksgiving. Saying our last good-byes until the holiday break was so hard. I held my tears in as we stood there hugging and clinging to each other while Mom took pictures. Walking away with tears in my eyes, I didn't want to look back to see him walking into the building; but I did and ended up doing the ugly cry. He had a task in front of him that he needed to complete, so I had to let him go so he can become a greater man, get a great education and SHOCK THE WORLD.

The next day, it was time to head to the airport. My parents dropped me off, it was very early and nothing was open yet. The flight to St. Louis wasn't bad and went quicker than I thought. Once we landed, I was able to take advantage of the shops that were open so I can get breakfast, a GOOD BREAKFAST at that! I got paid that week and was able to enjoy MY MONEY since I didn't have to pay for things I wasn't responsible for. While walking through the terminal I walked upon a nice restaurant, ordered apple juice and an omelet and enjoyed every last bite! After I was done, I went to go sit next to my gate and saw a two young ladies sitting there talking. Seeing that they had cell phones I wanted to call my parents and Jahmel to make sure he didn't forget to get me from the airport. I timidly say to one of the young ladies *"Hi, um, excuse me. Do you mind if I use your phone to make two phone calls? I don't have my phone on me."* Without hesitation she said *"Oh, yeah sure."* and hands me her phone. I called Jahmel first to tell him where I was and to remind him of the time that I landed. Lastly, I called my parents so they know I landed and was safe and would give them a call when I got to the house.

I finally land in San Antonio and my "baby daddy" was there to meet us. He seemed so excited and happy to see me; with all of his excitement, he wanted to go to Babies R Us to look at some stuff for Harper. I was a little hesitant because I didn't need him cutting up if we didn't agree on something and quite frankly, I was not in the mood for it. Well we went; I actually had fun and surprisingly we did not argue. I was starting to think things were really going to start getting better. As we were leaving, he asked me want I wanted to eat. I was craving Mac n Cheese and Steak, and he sure did get it for me! After my big plate of mac and cheese and steak. I drop off Jahmel at his hotel, and I head home so I can unwind, relax the rest of the evening and get ready for my long day at work. I also checked in with my parents to let them know I made it home safely and to see how BJ's first day of classes went. He was officially a college student.

Heading out the next morning which was a Wednesday but my Monday for work, I go scoop up Jahmel; he asked me to use my car so he can put in applications and go to the TWFC (Texas Work Force Commission) office. While I was working, I already feel the effects of carrying. I was so sleepy; I noticed the frequent restroom breaks and I was extremely cold. My manager comes by to check on me, and he notices me with a jacket on in the middle of August. He says *"BLUE! YOU GOOD?"* I yell back, *"NAW man! I'm freezing!"* When he heard me say naw he started walking towards me saying, *"Hmmm, I think I know why;* (he leans in closer and whispers) *I think you may be pregnant Blue!"* I just look at him with that really face and say, *"SHUT UP TRE"!* 'He laughed and shuffled off.

After my shift, Jahmel was waiting outside to pick me up. When I got in the car, I noticed he was in one of his moods, guess the job hunt didn't go as well as he expected. So you know that ride into San Antonio was pretty quiet. We finally reach the hotel and I asked him what his plan was moving forward and gave him some options and places to look into and he just brushed it off with an attitude. With irritation I said to him, *"Jahmel, I don't need this right now! I'm already concerned and scared of being pregnant let alone someone's Mom and I don't need the stress. I just need you to be here for me, I'm sorry your day didn't go well. There is always tomorrow."* All he heard was *"...I was scared of being pregnant and someone's mom."*

He goes off and says

"REALLY! You don't think you should have said this when you found out!?" I'm looking at him confused thinking what is he talking about. I say, *"HUH?"*

Jahmel *"Don't play f***ing dumb! No one is ever ready to be a parent if you're this worried maybe you shouldn't be one!!!"*

I turned all the way in my seat to face him with and WHOLE attitude and said

"EXCUSE ME!? Let me make sure I got this right. Are you telling me to abort my CHILD!??"

Jahmel: Shrugs his shoulders *"If that's what you feel you need to do! Since you're scared of being pregnant and a mom. If that's the case, you should have done it that day!"*

Sitting there in complete shock, like this dude just basically told me to have an abortion.

Me: ***"FIRST OF ALL!*** *I'm not having an abortion, and you took what I said out of context! I never said I didn't want it! Like any first-time* *mother, there is anxiety! NOW if you don't want to be a part of his or her life, you need to let me know RIGHT NOW! Cause I'm not going to do this back and forth sh** with you! "*

Jahmel: *"Oh, so you're going to do the same thing my baby mama is doing, keeping me away from my child!?Azure your full of sh**!"*

I sarcastically say *"Oh, I'm sorry!"* By following up with—*I didn't know me, your girlfriend, the mother of your unborn child; expressing her emotions to you is considered being full of sh**! *claps* Well thanks so much Jahmel for that piece of information! I told you from the jump that this arguing sh** wasn't going to fly! But yet you can't even see when I need you the most because you're too worried about getting high and yourself! If you ask me, YOUR'RE the one full of sh**. I don't want you to be high in order for you to have a decent and sensitive conversation with me! Matter of fact, f*** this. You can go to my cousins' house by yourself. I'm done. "* Getting out the passenger's seat, Jahmel also follows suit getting out the car coming around to meet me.

Jahmel: *"You're not a parent, so you don't understand…and that fact that your pregnant doesn't make you a parent."*

Walking passed him to get into the driver seat. He tries to block the door so I couldn't get in, I push him out the way and got in the car. I wasn't about to continue to go back and forth especially after having a good day; putting my seatbelt on and putting the car in reverse I crack the window.

Jahmel: *"Where are you going? You're just going to leave?"*

Me: *"YEP!"*

He couldn't understand my logic; Ladies DON'T EVER get yourself in a position or situation to where you feel like your emotions don't matter. It was getting to the point to where I stopped sharing how I felt or expressing when he hurt me. I would just bottle it up inside. *"Cause when you bury emotions, you bury them alive. For them to only come back stronger somewhere later in your life."-Andy Mineo* . Sometimes to the point to where you can't take it anymore, and the end result could be suicide, blowing up or releasing it in an unhealthy way. Keep reading to find out how bottling and buying my emotions ended for me.

When he realized that I was serious. He yelled out *"WAIT!"* and started to change his tune. He apologized for letting his emotions from his day affect how he acted towards me. I verbally forgave him, but in my mind and heart, there was no forgiveness. I was literally backing out of the relationship mentally EVERY DAY!

My next workday, which was a Thursday; I was presented with the opportunity; to learn a different category to a path I was trained in two weeks before I knew I was expecting. This task wasn't as aggressive as my main job; its more self-paced. I still had a goal to meet but it was easier for me with the restrictions I was given. I was very excited to be learning something new; I was selected to be trained in this "higher level" of count because I was 100% in my quality two weeks straight, which means NO ERRORS. This was such a good day for me, I was even feeling better; I was still going to the restroom like every five minutes, but besides that it was a good day. I couldn't wait to get off and tell Jahmel about it; but in the back of my head I didn't want to get too excited. I wasn't sure which Jahmel I was going to get; nice, calm, funny and supportive Jahmel that I learned to love, or mean, nasty, short-tempered and full of rage Jahmel that I was starting to hate.

I get off to walk outside to notice my car not waiting in the line; IN-STANT RAGE, plus it was hot outside. As I look up, I see him pulling around the corner. God was on his side in that moment because he was about to GET IT! I just knew I was going to get the version of him I didn't like. I get into the car to be greeted cheesecake, chocolate mousse cake and my Yeti cup filled with ice cold lemonade (all sugar I know. Gesh let me have it. I'm pregnant!) I was in awe. He says *"I figured you'd be hungry and wanted something sweet so I decided to get you a snack to eat on the way home."* (Some snack, I'll take it though!) Ever since our little come to Jesus meeting the evening before, it seemed like it really resonated with him; and the little things that he was doing, was really making me less afraid that I would become a single mother and him being a deadbeat; but in the back of my mind I was still holding on the fact he insinuated that I should get an abortion and was this him really being sweet or was he buttering me up to have the abortion conversation again.

The week was slowly coming to an end and my parents would be coming back from Wichita on Saturday. Friday, I had planned on just chilling with Jahmel when I got off; maybe a movie and dinner since we really hadn't spent time together ALONE in a while. Jahmel dropped me off at work; he would usually catch a cat nap until traffic died down or hang around and bring me food for lunch. I got to my workstation and felt sick; I wasn't sure if it was considered morning sickness because I didn't know what that felt like. I just knew I felt off; kind of like I was feeling before I found out I was pregnant. I found my assistant manager and asked if was able to leave because I didn't think I would make it the whole day. He told me to hang tight while he checked. He comes back and tells me I am able to leave. As I was making my move to go clock out, I hear this loud voice yell *"BLUE!!?"* You guessed it right, it was my manager Tre'. Scared of turning around because I knew I was getting ready to get an ear full.

Tre': *"Blue, where you think you're going?"*

Me: with my snappy playful attitude, *"Uh…..............HOME!"*

Tre': *"Uh….WHY!?"*

Me: *"I don't feel good man! I mean unless you want me to throw up on these Pods I'll stay!"*

Tre': *"Yeah, no. BYE! Feel better."*

Praise the Lord, Jahmel was still in the parking lot, because if he wasn't…it would have been a hassle trying to get in touch with him since we BOTH didn't have a phone. I'd have to wait until he got back to the hotel to call him to have him come all the way back. When he saw me getting in the car; he panicked and first thing he asked, *"You OKAY; the baby okay!?"* Even though I was feeling like crap, I was hungry and craving an omelet so Ihop we went! After dropping Jahmel off I came home to lie down and was hopping I didn't throw up what I ate since I was feeling worse than earlier, I know I shouldn't have eaten it but I wanted it. Still feeling weird so I figured lying down and resting who help it pass.

About a few hours go by and I started to have extremely bad cramps, like bad! Worse than when I found out I was prego bad. I called Jahmel and told him he needed to find a way to get over here because I was having bad pain. I managed to unlock the door so that he would be able to get in if the cramps persist and I pass out; because I felt like passing out was next. He was able to get an UBER over to me; a since they have been staying over at the Motel 6 since he got fired, he became cool with the staff and they helped a brother out. He finally gets to me and the cramps have become so painful that I began to get weak and things get blurry. I think I was in the bed when he got there. He thought I may have gotten food poison from the omelet I had earlier.

I figured that if I got up to walk that the pain would subside; I was walking back and forth from my room to my parents' room. I sat down on the toilet thinking it could be gas. Jahmel asked if I had been able to make a bow movement since we ate and if I was bleeding. The answer to those were both no. He then says *"Baby, we should go to the hospital."* Ya'll know me…I was fine, give me some 'tussin', my bed and I'll be good in a few hours. I got off the toilet since I couldn't pass anything; and I remember walking hunched over back to my parent's room. Some type of way, I don't know who called who but I remember hearing is Auntie London's voice and a blurred image of her face on my iPad saying, *"What's the matter baby, what going on?"* All I remember saying was that *"it hurts; it hurts."*

I managed to get in my parent's bed and curl up in fetal position, and surprisingly it didn't hurt as much. Yeah, I talked too soon; it came back stronger. As I'm rolling back and forth in their bed, I yell out to Jahmel in a squally, faint voice *"Jahmel? JAAAAHHHMEEEEL, CALL MY MAMA, call… my… mama, callmymama"* I notice as I kept saying it, I was getting weaker and weaker that my words were running into each other. But! I was able to get out *"BUT DO NOT! Call my Dad!"* (Jahmel was smart and still kept the piece a paper I wrote all of our numbers down on.) I didn't want my dad to see the house number pop up; and hear Jahmel's voice especially after *"Light Em Up".* I figured Mom would be the best bet for a few reasons; her phone was probably glued to her hand, knowing I was home alone, pregnant and PHONE-LESS and she would be the calmer one for Jahmel to give information too.

By this time, I ended back in my bed (I was on a move; determined to get through this pain.) I hear Jahmel say *"Hello, Mrs. G? It's Jahmel, I'm here with Azure and she's in a lot of pain"* I'm not sure what my Mom is saying on the other end; but he responds saying *"No, she tried to use the restroom, and no ma'am she's not bleeding."* Then he gives me the phone, I wasn't crying at that point, but when I heard my mommy's voice, I felt the tears forming in my eyes. I was so scared, I wanted her here with me rather than Jahmel because it's MOMMY! I remember saying while crying, *"It hurts so bad, mommy! I'm scared I don't want to lose my baby."* (I thought Harper was my new breath of fresh air, that God was giving me for a new start, especially after losing my Aunt Michelle. Having a miscarriage was the furthest thing from my mind because mommy prayed for us in Wichita; and I knew we were going to be just fine.)

As she was talking to me, I hopped out of the bed and started running to my restroom. I was feeling that urge; dry mouth, tingling and a funny taste. I knew what was coming. I tried to make it to the toilet but the sink looked more promising. EVERYTHING I ate at Ihop was now in the SINK! It stunk too! It just kept coming, and I heard Jahmel, tell my mom, *"...aaaand, she's throwing up!"* He ran downstairs to get a glass of water, but I couldn't drink it. I had the urge to go the restroom and while I looked down and saw that the bleeding had started back again. I called Jahmel in a calm but scared voice; *"Jaaaahmeel! Yeah, let's go to the emergency room."* I was so weak and started to get drowsy; that I just laid down in my bed. Jahmel said, *"Mrs. G yeah she's bleeding again."* I'm guessing my Mom gave him some instructions because he handed me the phone and said I'm going to get the car ready.

I just remember hearing my mom in my ear praying, while I was going in and out. Jahmel comes back to get me. I had on my WSU shorts I just brought and a sports bra because the shirt I had on was wet because I had thrown up on it. He grabs a shirt (it happened to say *"To God Be the Glory"*) and puts it over my head. He then pulls up my arm to only feel something cold under my arms; this guy was touching up my deodorant! Haha! He put some lotion on my arms and peeling hands and slid my sandals on my feet. I still had the phone and I could hear my mom's voice, but I was so out of it I didn't know that she was saying. They told me I kept asking for BJ. Jahmel came back to get me to go down and get in the car. All I remember is trying to juggle holding the phone to my ear while putting my weight on Jahmel to get downstairs. I talked to my mom all the way outside until I had to hang the phone up. I told them I loved them and that once we get settled, I'll call from the iPad through Facebook.

Jahmel gets me to the car as he opens the door I see that he has the seat pushed all the way back and laid down. With a blanket draped over it with a pillow and extra blankets as well as my New York Knicks trash can "just in case". Bless his heart he was really trying to make sure I was comfortable. The last thing I remember was getting in the car, all of a sudden, I remember waking up to him yelling at all the slow cars to move and get out of the way then I went back out. Next, I remember waking up to two guys trying to pick me up. I started panicking until they told me who they were. With squinted eyes due the bright sun, *I ask "Where am I?"* one of the guys says *"Ma'am you're at the hospital, we're here to help you."* With the help of Jahmel, they lifted me into a wheelchair and rolled me into the entrance of the emergency room.

I get straight to the back and they started asking a thousand questions: the lights were so bright I just wanted to close my eyes and sleep! They took my vitals and for the life of me, I don't remember anything as far as results! The nurse asked basic questions that I was able to mumble through and answer, but the questions kept coming, and by this time, I was getting annoyed. So I told her to just ask Jahmel the rest I was drained, cold and just wanted to lay down somewhere and go to sleep. They needed to get blood work done, so they gave me a few warm blankets so I can warm up so they can effectively take my blood. Yeah right, effectively. They had me waiting so long that I finally got what I wanted…SLEEP! (Well, I don't know if it was really a long time, because I was out of it. It just felt like a long.)

I'm not sure how long I was out; I remember the touch of a cold hand on top of mine. It was the nurse; she wanted to see if I was still in pain. I said, *"Not really just very weak."* She then let's me know that it is time to get my blood drawn; so they can check my HCG levels and check on baby Harper through the ultra sound. OKAY! You would think the first thing that would have been done was the blood or an ultrasound, since I came in with bad pain, weak and SEVEN WEEKS PREGNANT! But hey, who am I. They wheeled me over to the station where the phlebotomist was waiting for me. I told him up front, *"LOOK! I have baby veins and they roll, so you'll need to use a butterfly."* He looked at me like did this girl just try to tell me how to do my job! He just said, *"Yes ma'am"* and proceeded to gather his supplies.

I hate getting poked especially multiple times, even more so when I tell them what works for me and then not heed my instruction. That's when 'Porsha' comes out… *Who's Porsha?* There was a time where I was somewhere and the people were taking forever and were giving me the run-around and my mom said *"Azure, did you have "patience" with you?"* I told her *"NO, I had her ratchet sister, PORSHA!"* and that just stuck with us. Patience is the patient calm sister, Porsha is the "you'll know she's there sister."

He was having a time finding my veins due to me shaking and being partially dehydrated. I didn't want to go off on the poor guy because he was really trying, and by this time, he already stuck me three times. I gave Jahmel that look, and he already knew; because he kept asking them to get the "Acu-vein" machine, because it highlights your arm and shows the vein. It's a pretty cool gadget. Now he did manage to get blood for two tubes from the three times I was poked but it wasn't enough for the other five I had to fill. Jahmel asked about the machine again, because it was kind of blown off the first time it was mentioned. So, the person waiting on me to get my blood drawn to take me to the ultrasound, responds. *"That machine is used upstairs in a different unit and it would take too long to get down to ER. The guy taking my blood tells me that he was going to get someone else to try because he didn't want to stick me for the fourth time.*

This big burly guy comes in; he didn't look pleasant at all. The previous guy told him everything I said to him before he started. He knew I was tired, weak and irritated and that I had been poked three times already. Do you think the new guy took what he said to heart... NOPE! He starts and was rough! He started hitting my arm to flush the vein out (I HATE THAT!) and out the corner of my eye I see Jahmel reposition his stance, Jahmel looked like he was getting ready to go off on the guy, and I wasn't going to stop him either! I noticed he was about to use a regular needle, so I pulled my arm back and said: *"No, you need to use a butterfly like he told you!"* He responds and says, *"I see a vein here, and I don't need to use a butterfly."* He pulled my arm back closer towards him and I gave him a little resistance. So he got the hint that he needed to chill and watch his tone with me; because I knew if I had opened my mouth it wasn't going to be pretty plus I had on a *"To God Be the Glory"* shirt, so I wanted my sure I responded and acted accordingly.

THIS DUDE HAD THEE NERVE TO SAY!

"Ma'am you're very dehydrated, so I don't know how they expect me to get blood. Why haven't you drunk any water today? You must have not had any in the last couple of days."

Ya'll know what happened next; I cut my eyes to Jahmel and the first guy who tried his best. They just took a step back because they knew I was about to let his Peter Griffin looking guy HAVE IT! I turned and looked at him with my Tamar Braxton 'You tried It' face, adjusted my seat in the wheelchair, got the neck roll going and with the biggest attitude I could muster up I said...

"FIRST OF ALL, SIR! NO! I HAD NOT HAD ANY WATER IN THE LAST FEW HOURS. I'M SORRY, NOT SORRY. I DIDN'T KNOW I WAS GOING TO BE IN PAIN TO THE POINT OF TEARS AND THROWING UP EVERYTHING I ATE AND DRUNK IN MY SINK! TO END UP IN THE EMERGENCY ROOM TRYING TO GIVE BLOOD STARING AT YOU; LET ALONE INCONVIENCE YOU!

Matter of fact, you can go ahead and just stop and I'll just wait for the machine to get down here. I been wai.."

He cuts me off *"Well I'm trying ma'am."* He should have just stayed quite; because I let him have it again. One for cutting me off and two for trying it! I say...

"WELL, you're not doing a good job; and I do not like your attitude. Come in here thinking you know it all. So, can you use the DAMN butter-fly like I said before; or get someone else to take this blood!"

Peter Griffin: *"Yes ma'am, I'll try again, and if I can't, I'll send you upstairs."*

I flop back in my seat and look over at the other guy and Jahmel, and they were looking stunned. God was on his side because he got the rest of tubes filled with the butterfly! I didn't mean to go off on the guy....well, yes I did! I had already been sitting there for forever and all I wanted was to make sure Harper was okay! There was NO sense of URGENCY. AT ALL! I finally made it back to their triage area to wait for the person that went in front of me to get done; as well as wait on the labs and talk to the Dr. He wanted a urine sample but I felt like I wouldn't be able to stand for a long period of time because of how drowsy I was feeling. I was scared of walking let alone standing by my-self. Plus, I didn't have the urge to go.

While waiting for the doctor, Jahmel goes to find a phone to call and check in with my parents to give them an update. I just knew they were worried. I had the iPad but it wasn't fully charge and the WiFi connection was poor. The Dr came in as soon as Jahmel left; he was ready to do his assessment and find out the events leading up to my ER visit. By this time, Jahmel had come back and the doctor begins to ask questions. He asked about food and activities for the day and how far along I was, when did the pain start; pretty much the same question they asked when I first came in. I'm thinking; dude, you don't read the notes in the chart? I was tired of repeating myself; the questions he was asking were annoying. I guess I felt that way because I didn't remember too much. I just had Jahmel answer the rest of them.

I remember the doctor getting testy with me, because he was ask-ing me the same question but wording them differently and my an-swers weren't changing let alone he wasn't making sense. According to Jahmel, I went off on the Dr as well because I kept calling him on his questions; and that I told the doctor that I needed to go to the re-stroom and asked if he still needed the urine sample I'd be able to give it. I remember him kind of snapping and was like *"If you were going to do a sample, it should have been done a long time ago."* So, of course, I couldn't let that slide, I looked at him and said *"Do you want it or nah! I'm so tired of ya'll and these attitudes....so either you want the sample now or never!"* I snatched the cup out of the nurses' hand, rolled my eyes at the doctor and walked towards the restroom. While I was walking away, I hear Jahmel say to the doctor while laughing *"I'm sorry doc, she's"* the doctor cuts Jahmel off and says *"Hey, it's okay, it's the hormones she's pregnant. I understand."*

As I start the urine sample, I feel something drop, which gives the cup a little weight. My heart dropped; I looked at the cup, to see what it was. The liquid in the cup was completely RED; and the same for inside the toilet. I panicked, I wanted to scream so bad and cry. I held it together because I didn't know what was going on. I tried to look at the cup to see what dropped. My mind was racing; I didn't know if I should pour the contents in the cup out. There was nothing in the restroom for me to use as a stick. I just needed to see if it was another blood clot, but I was scared because I knew there was a possibly it could be my baby!

I came out and told the nurse what I had experienced and that I was scared to flush the toilet so don't be alarmed when she goes in the get the sample. She helps me back to the wheelchair; and I hear the doctor say in a tone of frustration: *"Is that the sample!? We can't do anything with that, it's contaminated, it's nothing but BLOOD!"* I must have made a face, getting ready to say something because Jahmel said, "Chill honey." Finally! They're now ready to take me back to get the ultrasound done. The lady starts the imaging; and she's having trouble finding Harper, just like the other lady was. So she had to try to other route; the most uncomfortable feeling in the WORLD! The tech would not let me look at the screen at all; at that moment, I just knew it wasn't going to be good. She wrapped up the ultrasound and escorted me back to my room to await the results. I told Jahmel, to go ahead and call my parents so they won't be worried.

As Jahmel was coming back he tells me: *"Babe, I think you miscarried. I ran into the Dr.; I asked him if the results came back in. He said he rather tell you than me."* So I started pleading with God like; No, don't let this be true, my mom just prayed I'd have a healthy and safe pregnancy, so there can't be no way I lost my baby cause if any of you know my mother...SHE. CAN. PRAY! The doctor comes and he had this confused look on his face and said, *"Ms. Gabriel. It looks like you are miscarrying, your HCG levels are in the 500's and that too low with you being seven to eight weeks. I can't get your file from the other hospital to see what your original numbers were. So, based on the numbers we have right now. Your miscarrying if you hadn't already. Just follow up with your OBGYN to confirm. I'm sorry; we'll get you discharged soon so you can get home."*

I had no words, I started trying to take off my bands and yelled at Jahmel; *"LET'S GO, I'M READY TO GO HOME!"* I was even working to get the tape off where the IV port was so I can take that out too. He stands up to bend down next to me he kisses my forehead. I pushed him away; I didn't want to be touched or anything. The nurse comes with my discharge papers, and she was trying to be sympathetic, but I wasn't trying to hear it; I was just numb. As Jahmel was wheeling me out, the chick that does the registration comes. She says *"UM, Ma'am are you Az, a, ahz-u-raye? I need to get some information from you."* I'm like *"REALLY!? I've already been discharged; now you're trying to get my information???"* GIRL BYE! At this point, I was completely done and over it. I wanted to get home and talk to my mommy.

This lady had no sense of urgency nor was apologetic, which irritated me more. When she realized I was no longer in the mood, she says, *"Well, we'll have someone reach out to you and follow up with the rest of the information."* *"mmm-hmm,"* I replied and rolled out! LITERALLY!

The ride back home was like a twilight zone, and I don't really remember it. As we were getting closer to my house, Jahmel told me that he wanted me to stay with him. I agreed and told him I'd need to grab some clothes then we can head out. We got inside, and I remember there was still vomit in the sink and that I had to straighten things up in my parents' room because I had pillows everywhere trying to get comfortable. While I was cleaning up mine and my parent's bedroom; Jahmel got up and helped clean my bathroom and got the entire stink cleaned out. He even cleaned the downstairs restroom and kitchen to ensure everything was in tip-top shape for my parents' arrival. (This was the side of him I loved.)

After I was done doing my part, I called my mom while he finished up. I told her what the doctor said. She sounded sad, but I can still tell she was concerned. She asked what my plans were. I told her that Jahmel didn't want to leave me by myself. She jumps and says, *"You're going to have to talk to your Dad about that Azure. I know he doesn't, and neither do I feel comfortable with him in the house after that stuff he pulled outside."*

"Yeeeah, Mom, I know that's why I'm going to stay with him at the hotel. He just came in to help me clean up since I'm still out of it."

"Oh okay, tell him 'thank you' and call us when you make it to the room." (She sounded a little better, but I know she'd feel better if he was just out of the picture.) We finished up at the house and headed towards the hotel. I wasn't hungry, only confused and hurt, but yet still hopeful that my baby boy was okay in there and that my levels were low because of the bleeding I have been doing.

We pulled up to the room, and I remember Jahmel knocking on the door; in my head, I'm trying to figure out why he's knocking on the dang door, ain't nobody in there. As the door opens, it clicks his mom! I forgot that quick, and I think I could have mustered the strength to drive myself back home, because I didn't feel like hearing them go back and forth. I told him, *"Yo, I forgot about your mom, I'm not for the drama and yelling between y'all two tonight. You know, imma, imma just go home."* He shushes me and says, *"I got it; she'll be good; it's okay, just lay down."* I did hear him tell her I lost the baby and that I wasn't feeling good. (He's not a good whisperer) While he got the things out of the car, I remembered that the next day was Saturday and I needed to go to work; I went into a panic. Jahmel told me that I would be fine and I had to explain to him that isn't how my job worked. Stuff like that isn't an "excused" absence, I had to use a different time bucket if I went negative, I could be fired. I didn't have enough to cover my 10-hour shift. He then replies, *"You had a miscarriage, and you're bleeding, if they fire you for that you can sue them."* (That boy was always trying to sue somebody.) I did indeed call my jobs hotline, and they took care of it and sent a notification to my site HR. I just needed to bring proof in from the hospital.

Once I got all of that figured out, I called my parents to let them know that I made it to the hotel. Mom asked me if I was going into work; and that I needed to go at least and have them send me home. Jahmel overheard her and started fussing and yelling *"that's bulls***"* and he kept going on, I threw something at him to get his attention to direct him to go outside with all of his opinions. The last thing I needed was *'Light Em Up'* part II. I explained to my mom what HR said and that everything would be taken care of. She told me they planned on leaving early in the morning to get back to me and that she would call me in the morning. Jahmel came back in all pissy looking talking about *"f*** that, you're not going to work. With all that moving you do and stuff you could bleed out or pass out!"* I don't know if he was trying to scare me or what; I just know I got irritated and went to sleep. While he stayed up and watched CNN.

The next morning rolls around, and I'm just still in shock; I was blaming everyone in my head, even GOD! Jahmel pretty much left me alone but would periodically ask if I was okay or hug me. When he got hungry was when he bothered me because he needed money. My mom called me on messenger to let me know they have hit the road and also to check up on me and to see if I ate anything. I didn't have much of an appetite, but she suggested some broth. *"Tell Jahmel to get you some wonton soup, drink the broth to get something in your system, and we'll be home soon so I can take care of you."* She said

Jahmel agreed to get me the soup; I gave him my card. (I was starting becoming hesitant in doing so because my trust level with him was diminishing) Thank God for my bank; because they alert me every time my card is swiped and it did just that, so if he decided to do a withdrawal or go somewhere else, I would know. While he was gone, his mom and I had little to no conversation. She came over to hug me and told me that she was sorry. She even asked if we were going to try again. I looked at her like she was crazy and told her no. In the back of my head, I did think about it; not knowing God was setting me up for something, let alone someone else. Jahmel came back, and he walked in with more than what looked like wonton soup and Gatorade. Before I jumped to conclusions, I thought he might have gotten some extra money from his mom that she stashed somewhere. NOPE!

This boy used my card, but it was "all for me." (still doesn't make it right, even if I had it or not) He was very compassionate during this time and was doing everything he could to try to make me feel better, and his presentation of it was sweet until I realized he bought his favorites. Here's how he set it up though.

"Okay babe, here's your soup and some crackers; I got you some Gatorade so you can get your strength back. I also got you some cookies and ice cream. I know that's what y'all eat that when y'all on ya'll's period. So I'm not sure if it's the same thing in this situation, but I'm just trying to make you comfortable." Now he brought two flavors of ice cream: butter pecan (his favorite) and cookies and cream (also his favorite, but I liked it) I do feel he was sincere but also took advantage of me at this low

point. I couldn't be too mad; I mean it was his baby too. I barely ate the soup as it had a weird taste to it, so I just ate the crackers and drunk the Gatorade, and only ate a few scoops of the ice cream. Of course, what I didn't eat he and his mom ate.

Fast forward: I head home; I was very happy to see my parents and wanted to embrace them and just cry, but I also wanted just to be alone. I guess the fact of knowing that they were home made me better and SAFE! I was starting not to feel safe and comfortable with Jahmel. With this low level of trust I was having towards Jahmel and with my mind racing everywhere. I couldn't help but think and wonder if Jahmel put something in my food or drink to help me miscarry? He did bring up the abortion conversation earlier in the week and I all of a sudden, I miscarry! Far fetch I know, but to be totally honest I wouldn't put it past him if he did or thought about it. Again, I just chopped it up to my emotional state and thinking it was another "test" of our relationship from God. NO! That was the Holy Ghost telling me something, but I ignored it time after time. Until it was literally too late and things got out of control.

Blood Sweat and Tears!

After it was confirmed that I indeed miscarried Harper, I didn't say much to anybody, not even my parents. I can't even describe the pain I was feeling, but I do know that I was hurt, angry, and confused. I was mad at everyone and even questioned God, saying, *"WHY!? Why did you give me something so precious and that I've always dreamed of having and just snatch it away from me?* (He didn't answer me right away either, it was weeks until I got a partial answer and MONTHS until I got the real answer and got a better understanding of "WHY!?"

I was so angry with God; I just couldn't understand; so, I started to shut down mentally and emotionally. I built this wall to block my emotions and how I felt so people couldn't see my hurt and pain. Oh, but the ones close to me saw it and could tell. I even felt like I rebelled a lot during this time. I just didn't care about ANYTHING. It was like I was on autopilot; just going through the motions.

My Aunt Danielle sent me a message on Facebook; (still didn't have a phone) to call her. Deep down, I really didn't want to, but I also wanted to. I gave her a call, and she asked how I was and how I was feeling. I didn't even tell her I was pregnant. MOM DID! I was so mad at my mom. I was going to tell Aunt Danielle until I was further along, but since I lost the baby I wasn't going to say anything AT ALL to ANYONE!

After she heard that I was okay and heard my voice she automatically went into God-Mommy mode *"UHH…So when were you going to tell me."* That was how I knew Mom said something. I rolled my eyes and replied, *"…uh, I wasn't!"* She then says, *"…and, why not!?"* I explained to her that since I had complications, I wanted to wait, and my doctor as well said wait to announce it until I am in my second trimester. She wasn't having that! *"You know I would have torn that hospital upside down over you!"* she says; but she also understood that I wanted to keep it private, but felt that after my parents found out, she should have been the next phone call, which is true. I should have said something. We set up a time to meet up the next day to have lunch and to go into more details; also, so she can really see how I was doing.

I went to "confront" my mommy on telling my Aunt Danielle about my situation. She understood that I wanted to keep it under the table; but because she wasn't there physically, she felt that Aunt Danielle was the closest person to me and that made her feel better with knowing someone that loved me just as much as she does knew what was going on. Plus, she's a nurse and my godmother. Not only was the miscarriage hard on me, but it was also hard on my parents, especially my mom. She was so stressed, especially because she wasn't there physically and importantly couldn't pick up the phone to call me; she had to wait for a phone call. It took a toll on her emotionally, mentally, and physically. Seeing her in tears over this whole ordeal and seeing the pain in her eyes, hurt me. I know she didn't see it because I was hiding behind the wall I built for myself. Nobody wants to see their mother hurt. I still have the image in my head of that night with her sitting in her bed pouring out her heart and pretty much a cry for help for ME to ME. It was tough to see. Just thinking about it now is a tear-jerker. My mom was feeling sick at work that she had to see the nurse in her office because she wasn't feeling well. Come to find out her blood pressure was through the ROOF! Which played a big part in the headaches she was experiencing as well as the anxiety attacks. Her blood pressure was so high it literally could have, should have killed her or she could have had a stroke. When I heard that I was bawling on the inside, but that wall I built wouldn't allow me to express it. I COULD HAVE LOST MY MOMMA over a BOY!! A boy, that wasn't doing nothing for me except causing me stress, drama, and trouble. He wasn't pouring into me, uplifting, encouraging, or helping me build. He was literally a *'Bum ASS N****'* and I could have lost my mom behind it. NAH BRUH!

I was starting to notice that in my dealings with Jahmel; it was slowly separating me from and effecting the people I love and valued the MOST. Jahmel would always comment, especially after me sharing with him how Aunt Danielle felt *"…Man, I'm not in the mood, if anybody says anything crazy to me today, I'm not holding back, that goes for your god-mama too! I don't know what it is about her, I know she doesn't like me, and I don't give a f*. She thinks she's smart and be trying to challenge me and stuff like she knows it all."* This comment was also made before about my Church and my parents Church as well as my family and friends.**

I knew Aunt Danielle wasn't too much feeling him; although she wasn't privy to ALL the craziness I was going through, at least to my knowledge; BUT she's wasn't and is NOT stupid. I'm sure she had some speculations and had a conversation with Mom. Not knowing what was getting ready to happen on our lunch date indeed give her a frontrow seat to a sneak peek of how my life had been going.

I was so excited about our lunch date (I even put on clothes and makeup; I was still on bereavement leave and this was my second to last day before going back to work. My attire while I been out had been; t-shirts, workout pants and slides with socks; just bummy) I was finally doing something for me; ALONE TIME; without two shadows following behind me; and I could talk freely with my god-mommy, I had the intentions on telling her some of the things I was dealing with PLUS I needed a DRINK!

It was noon and time to meet Aunt Danielle for lunch at one of our regulars, Olive Garden. I wasn't even there for 30 minutes before the drama started. I was using my iPad for communication; once I sat down, I got a message from Jahmel asking why I wasn't responding to his messages (hello, I need to be hooked up to Wi-Fi! My car doesn't have built in Wi-Fi dude) and how long I'd be with Aunt Danielle. I told him I didn't know, and I just got there. I also told him that before we leave, I'll place a to-go order for him. I even asked him what he wanted. I felt like this was going to reassure him that I was going to stop by afterward and I was thinking about him, but it was for him just to let me be for a while. After we ordered our drinks and salad, the hostess comes up to the table, and says; *"Hi, is one of you ladies Azure?"* Aunt Danielle and I look at each other confused; I looked at her and said: *"Yes, I'm Azure, why?"* She says, *"Oh, okay, so your boyfriend is trying to reach you, he called and said you should be having lunch, and he wants you to call him back."* Embarrassed out of my mind I'm thinking 'you have got to be kidding me! I thanked her and used Aunt Danielle's phone to call him. In my head, I'm thinking, "What NOW!" I really started to feel like he didn't want to me have any type of fun. I didn't know then, but he was CLEARLY controlling me.

So of course, when I called the first time, he didn't pick up. So, my focus is now on my iPad and not my lunch date. I messaged him and said just this!

Me: *"Really!? You called me at OLIVE GARDEN!? What's is so important Jahmel!?"*

Jahmel: *"You need to get here quick; my mom is trying to stab me!"*

Me: *"HUH!? Jahmel what are you talking about?"*

Jahmel: *"She got mad at me because she thought I was mad that she ate my muffin. I brought her two plates of food this morning from the lobby. I ain't trippin about the muffin. I got extra food so we can have for later and just warm it up."*

Me: *"So how and why is she trying to stab you??"*

By this time, I was able to reach him on the phone, and he says

"She ran outside and got a stick and stabbed me saying she wanted me dead. Can you just come... (he's yelling *"STOP, MOM CHILL"* in the back) *Babe, can you come help me I can't fight her, she doesn't want to take her medicine or nothing. She'll listen to you and not me...just come as soon as you can."*

I hang up with him to only look at my god-mama in defeat holding back the tears, shaking my head saying after a sigh *"He just won't let me be great! I gotta go!"* She asked if everything was okay? I told her; *"his mama is trippin and not taking her meds; now she's trying to attack him."* She just says, *"Oh wow! Okay...You want some more to drink? You may need it. Lol"* She was right! I down my glass and refilled it two more times from the pitcher of Green Apple Moscato Sangria we ordered. That wasn't strong enough to face the pain, hurt and agony I was getting ready to walk endure.

As I was approaching the entrance of the hotel, I found his mother walking across the street to the bus stop with her purse and all her bags. I said out loud to myself, *"SERIOUSLY!* (while putting my hazards on to pull over and get out the car) *I don't have time for this sh** today!"*

I call out to her and ask what was going on? She says very upset *"I'm leaving him; I can't do this. I'm tired of his attitude and being in that room with him all the time!"*

Me: With an attitude; *"So being outside in the heat is better!?? C'mon man, get your stuff and get in the car! NOW!"*

Her: *"NO! NO! I'm Not Going!* (while I'm grabbing her bags and putting them in the car) *I'm going to stay here and wait for the bus to come get me."*

Me: *"TO GO WHERE? WITH WHAT MONEY!? You have NOTHING!"*

Her: *"I'll catch a bus back to Alabama."*

Me: *"... again, HOW, YOU HAVE. NO MONEY, and YOUR ID IS EXPIRED! TRY AGAIN."*

Her: (throws her wallet into the street) *FINE, I'll just see if someone will help a little old lady, or just I'll just sit, starve and eventually die!* (I don't know what it was with these two, but they were always talking about death.)

Me: *"NO! (while picking up her stuff) I'm not going to let you sit here in the heat.* (by this time, I have all the stuff but her and her purse in the car) Opening the passenger door for her; *"C' mon, get in this car! I don't have time for this with y'all today."*

She puts up a fuss, but I finally got her in the car. While I'm pulling into the hotel parking lot, I remember I was fussing at the situation and her like she was my child. As I angrily pull into the parking space, I exclaimed to her *"y'all got me out here, to fool with this sh**; I can't even enjoy a day to myself before I go back to work! Stay here!"*

I go into the hotel to figure out where Jahmel was. I banged on the door like I was the police! I was so annoyed, irritated, and hungry. I was trying to get this under control quickly. So, it won't be a "hospital hopping" type of night. As he opens the door, I rush in like I was on a mission. I just told him I found his mama walking across the street to the bus stop. He asked where she was, and I told him, "*I left her in the car, she was adamant about not being in the same room with you. So, to eliminate the extra drama, I left her, so I can figure out what was going on.*" Surprisingly he was very calm; he wasn't angry or nothing. I think because he probably was high before everything happened or got high afterward.

I don't remember so much that happened in between; but Jahmel said he was fine and wasn't tripping about the food. He was just trying to be peaceful and chill out. I went back to get his mother, and as soon as I opened the door she started saying:

"*I'm not going in there with him! I'll end up killing him, he's my son, but I cannot stand him!*"

Me: "*No one is killing anybody! Just come in, he won't be in there. We're going to go get a bite to eat, that will give you time to yourself to calm down and unwind, etc!*"

She was not having it! She started to grab her little suitcase and walk away. I immediately got in front of her to redirect her back to the car, and she was like "*Azure, I don't want to yell at you! Please let me go; I am done with Jahmel.*" I told her just to stay while I get Jahmel out of the room and into the lobby so she could come into the room. She still wasn't having it. I even told her, "*LOOK; I'll pay for you to have your own room for the night. I just need you inside!*" She says, "*No, you've already spent too much money and we still owe you for a lot!*" (well at least SOMEONE was paying attention to the money that was going into them) So she starts walking off again, and this time I wasn't going to chase after her. One, she ain't my mama, and two, this is where he needs to step in. I ran back into the hotel to tell Jahmel that his mom has basically gone rogue. He pleads with me to get her because I had a good 95% chance to get her to corporate rather than his 5%. He pleads and pleads for me to do it while he did some research on places to take her. He said he was getting to the point to where he could no longer care for her, and she needed her medicine that she kept refused to take.

When I came back outside, she was gone!! I said to myself again, *"I'm tired of doing this with these people!"* I get in the car and drive into the direction she was going. Praying that the Lord, would reveal her to me because that last thing I wanted was for someone to find her, rob, take advantage of her or worse case kill her; and worse, worse case she runs into law enforcement and says we abandon her. (she was good at that.) As I was approaching a street, I saw her on my left side, she walked fast; she was about two and half blocks away from the hotel. She was really on a mission to get away from him. I pull up to her, grabbed her bags, and put them in the car and told her she needed to stop acting like this and get in the car, and that is was not safe. She still wasn't having it. Sad to say I had to push and pull her to get her in the car. She sat in the back seat, literally having a temper tantrum like a 2-year-old kicking the seat and talking under her breath all the way back to the hotel. It didn't bother me; I just let her do it because I knew it was due to her not having some of her medicine. From what I was told, she had Dementia, so I just let her get it all out; at least I thought. She's still ranting about how Jahmel takes her money and doesn't care about her and always yelling at her. At this point, I kind of snapped, I was so tired of them both blaming each other for their problems and circumstances. I told her, *"YOU KNOW WHAT? Just stop! Y'all both yell, fuss at each other, and fight! Y'all the reason why I lost the baby in the first place with y'all stressing me the f*** out with all ya'll fighting and arguing."*

Her: *"Oh, so now you blaming it on us? I wish you just would have had an abortion like Jahmel said. I don't like you and didn't want you having my other grandchild."*

That really hurt me, like to the core. Who says something like that to someone? Especially to someone who has been taking care of you, and pretty much helps and most of the time buy all your necessities when no one else wants/wanted to???

We made it back to the hotel, and as I was getting out of the car to help her out; I hear her say, *"I am NOT going back in there!"* I open the door for her and reach my hand out, so she can hold on to me to get out, she slaps my hand away. I just looked at her and said: *"Really, I'm trying to help you gezz!"*

Her: *"I am a grown woman. I know how to get out of the car!"*

I took a few steps back, so she can get out comfortably and offered to take some of her handheld bags, you know being generous. While grabbing the bag, she grabs onto my wrist and demands I let the bag go saying, *"Don't touch my stuff! Let it GO!"*

Me: *Well, you'll have to let mine go first, but I don't mind; I'll carry your bags.*

Her: *"I will scream to the top of my lungs."*

Me: *"Stop, I'm just trying to help you so that you can get in the room."*

Her: while digging her nails deep into my left wrist, she says in a low aggressive tone, *"let my things go! Azure, I will slap you. Let it go and leave me alone."*

While I'm trying so hard not to mush this lady the face, I lean into her and give the same tone right back, *"you need to let ME go! Now you're starting to become physical, and you're hurting me. You may be my elder, but in the end, I WILL defend myself! SO, I strongly advise you to take your nails OUT of my skin and let my arm go! We are going to walk into this hotel, and you're not going to say or do anything to Jahmel, and he will not say anything to you as well. Do you understand me?"*

After that little talk, she got some act right. I let her walk in front of me because I didn't want to be chasing this woman down the street again. As we're walking into the room, I take a look at my wrist, and I have **BLOOD** forming in the area she dug her nails into my skin. She took some skin with her for sure (I still have that scar). As she went in, she walked past Jahmel like his 300lb self didn't exist.

I go into the restroom to clean my arm and gather my thoughts and emotions. Jahmel came in to ask how she was and how it went. I told him all that had happened and showed him my wrist. "SHE DID THAT!?" he exclaimed. *"Nah I did it myself,"* I said, rolling my eyes. He apologized and tried to help me clean it up. I felt so confused and hurt inside. What did I do to deserve this type of treatment? I kept saying, *"Azure, let the old lady make it. She is sick, and this could be all due to her not taking her medicine."* He confronts his mother while I go to the front desk to get the band-aid I called and requested. As I was coming back through the room door, I heard them at it. She was not taking her medicine. She kept running to the restroom to take them, taking her bag with medicine in the restroom with her; I told her no and that she needed to leave her medicine in the room. She listened to me, for once that day. While she was doing what she was doing, I took the medicine she needed at that moment and laid it out then put her purse in one of the drawers. Jahmel and I both felt like she was going to try to harm herself by taking more than the allotted dosage.

She came out of the restroom, and I was right there to hand her water, fruit, and medicine. She gave me that 'I don't want that' look and walked past me. *"Ma'am, you need to take your medicine!"* I say to her.

She flops down in the chair, holds her hand out, and says *"hmm"* like give it here. I looked at Jahmel like 'you better get your Mother before I end up going off on her.' I handed her everything, and she throws the fruit on the bed, throws pills on the ground and dumps the water on the floor. I looked at her and said, *"REALLY!? Was that necessary?* She then folded her arms and turned her nose up! I said *"Jahmel, talk to her, because I do NOT have time for this and if she keeps playing with me she'll get knocked out."* he turned his eyes off the TV (Yes! TV, he's watching TV while I was trying to get HIS mother to take her medicine. I could have been enjoying my Chicken Parmesan and Green Apple Moscato Sangria with my god-mommy right now.) He calls out to his mom, *"Mom, can you please do what Azure is asking? She's just trying to help."* She rebuttals, *"I don't have to listen to her! I don't like her no way!"* Jahmel looked at her the same way I did when I heard her say that outside in the car. *"What do you mean you don't like her!?"* Jahmel exclaims. Still sitting with her arms folded, and nose turned up, she says nothing.

While they're going back and forth about her not liking me and the reasons why like I am not in the room, I picked up the pill she threw on the floor as well as placed a towel down in the spot where she purposely poured the water out. I ignored their conversations because I knew it was all BS. I have done nothing but show love to him and his mother. So, I let it go.

Jahmel and his mom started fussing about something, and the next thing I know she goes starts grabbing some of his belongings; some clothes and a teddy bear I brought for him and runs to the restroom, locks the door and we hear her turn the shower on. A few moments later, she comes out to sit down but we noticed she left the shower running. Jahmel and I ran in to check because he felt that she might have stashed some of the medicine in her bra or threw them in the toilet or the shower. YUP! It wasn't the pills, but the clothes and bear she took in with her was drenched with water and was full of suds.

I stood in shock, confused, and thinking if this was really happening. But then, she has dementia, so I just chopped up the behavior of this being one of the symptoms of not taking the medicine regularly. An upset and frustrated Jahmel then finally spoke, *"I need to find a place for her. I can't deal with this anymore!"* *"Mom, why would you do that? Azure brought me that bear, that was special to me, and now It's ruined!"* At that moment, she didn't have no care for what she did! She yells back *"CAUSE I WANT TO, NOW! I don't like her! She's always here, always in our business!"* I just stood there and said nothing. But Jahmel pretty much said what I was thinking, *"Mom, if it weren't for Azure, we wouldn't be here; we wouldn't have a place to stay, food and you would have your medicine and everything else. Azure buys all of that!"*

Next thing I knew, she got up and charged in my direction, grabbed her medicine bottle, and ran to the restroom. Either the little old lady fast or my reaction was delayed. She gets to the restroom and pours the last of her medicine in the toilet and FLUSHES IT! Oh, I went straight OFF! I looked at Jahmel with hurt in my eyes and threw my hands up in the air *"I'M DONE! I CAN'T DO THIS ANYMORE! LIKE WTF YO! THAT WAS REALLY DISRESPECTFUL. You need to get her bruh!"* While Jahmel was trying to calm me down, I felt something hit me in my back and drop to the floor. This lady threw an orange at me. My initial reaction was to pick it up and chuck it right back at her face; but I didn't, I just picked it up turned and looked at her and said *"So we throwing oranges now? That's what we're doing?"*

Her with an attitude, *"I didn't throw anything at you."*

Jahmel: *"Mom, you need to chill; Azure didn't do anything to you!"*

Me: *"So, Casper threw this orange at me??"*

Jahmel: *"Azure, chill, yo!"*

Her: *"Yup, he's a ghost you can't see him"* while making a spooky ghost noise.

Jahmel: *"OMG, Y'all two chill. Mom don't say anything to her and stop throwing stuff at Azure and Azure, don't say anything back."*

Her: Throws another orange and a banana at me.

I looked at Jahmel angrily and told him to get her a she was getting out of hand. *"She's sick babe,"* he answered, with defeat in his eyes.

Me: *"…and that's the only thing that's saving her ass! Cause she's about to get knocked out."*

Jahmel: *"I don't know what to do; she's getting worse and worse; I need to get her some help. I'm going to go to the lobby to get on the computer and do some research."*

Me: *"UHHHM, you not leaving me in here with her. I will hurt this lady!"*

Jahmel: *"You'll be fine. She won't bother you, just stay on this side of the room."*

He leaves out of the room, and I asked her what was all that about, the medicine and the drama minute ago. Sitting with her nose turned up, and arms fold it, *"I did nothing, I don't have an issue with you; I'm mad at Jahmel!"*

Me: *"YOU THREW FRUIT AT ME! How is your problem not with me but with Jahmel? He hasn't said much of anything to you* (today) *you were the one that was trying to stab him and run away and sh**."*

Her: *"I'm so sick of him! He doesn't do nothing, he always says he's working or has a job, but he has nothing!!"*

I had to interrupt her because I had seen him work on applications. He even put one in for my job.

"He has a job lined up, just waiting for his start date."

Her: *"OH, WHAT? YO JOB!? Making $12/hr.? that's not going to help us."*

I snapped…sitting on the side of the bed across from her I leaned forward made one of my many faces, looked her in the eyes, and said, *"YEAH, THAT $12/HR JOB! Obviously it does something for you* (looking around the room) *that little $12/hr. you talk down on, makes sure you have a roof over your head; it may not be the best, but you're not on the STREET, you have food in your belly, clean and fresh underclothes that I WASH; it makes sure there is gas in the car to take y'all to and from to look at apartments, cash your checks, takes him in and out the hospital and buy the things you want, NOT NEED and lastly that $12/hr. buys the medicine that you DON'T TAKE and WHAT YOU JUST FLUSHED DOWN THE GOT D*** TOILET! So yeah, my $12/hr. is indeed worth something! I can't even pay my own bills and do stuff for myself because most of it goes to Y'ALL!"*

While bucking and rolling her eyes at me; she says, *"I'm tired of y'all, I want to get away from y'all."* Next thing I know, she started hitting herself on her arms and chest and punching herself in the head.

"What are you doing?" I asked, confused.

Her: In a determined tone, she said: *"I'm hitting myself so I can have a stroke and die!"*

Me: *"Well, you're not hitting yourself hard enough!"* I could have chosen different words to say, but that came out. I was so frustrated with the both of them and feeling disrespected and played. Now, I didn't wish anything bad would have happened to her but she did need to chill.

Her: She starts scratching herself and digging her nails into her skin. She replies, *"Well, I can say you did this! You made these bruises, and you'll go to jail for elder abuse."* She starts yelling out loud while still hitting herself, *"HELP ME, HELP ME, STOP, SHE'S HITTING ME!"*

I hopped up to grab her arms so she can stop "trying to give herself a stroke." I said to her, *"you really need to stop it."* While holding both her arms, she tried to kick me, but I moved in time. I told her that I was going to let her hands go on the account she stops hitting herself (if I had a stray jacket, I would have put her in it.)

She digs her nails into my skin AGAIN and says, *"you better let me go. I will slap you!"*

Me: *"You ain't gone, do SH**!"*

After she drops her arms, I let her arms go as promised. Then she swung at me; I grabbed her arms again while she was trying to swing at me again. I'm trying to protect myself; as well as check myself because my first instinct was to defend myself and fight her for real. I released her arms again and she manages to slap me in my face (my mama don't even slap me—well there was this one time but never mind). I tried to get her from slapping me again, but we ended up pretty much slap boxing. I felt myself getting ready to turn my open hands into a fist to beat the sh** out this lady. That's when I grabbed her arms again and said: *"IMMA NEED YOU TO CHILL THE F*** OUT MAN, IM NOT TRYING TO FIGHT YOU, BUT I WILL!"* While still holding her wrist, she kicked me in my stomach and I looked at her crazy and said, *"REALLY? MY STOMACH!?"*

"YEAH," she responded in a devious tone still kicking me in my stomach. *"Yeah, have another miscarriage and maybe you won't be able to have kids!"* she continued.

Grabbing my stomach, *"YOU BETTER BE GLAD I AM A CHRISTIAN WOMAN, and you're old because if you weren't, I'd be whoopin yo ass!"*

Jahmel's mom: *"Christian woman, yeah right nothing about you is Christian! You're a hypocrite."*

I was started to get bad cramps, so I held my stomach tighter and started praying to God that I wouldn't be bleeding. I was still trying to process what just happened when I told her, *"Yes, I am a Christian woman, I'm not perfect, but I try every day to live right. If I weren't a Christian, I wouldn't care about you all as I do, let alone do all that I do for y'all!"* That shut her up QUICKLY!

I was so over it. I ran to the restroom to make sure I wasn't bleeding or anything and praise the Lord I wasn't. When I looked in the mirror, I noticed a bruise and a big long scratch on my chest as well as a bigger cut on my wrist along with some other scratches. I just looked at myself in the mirror and began to shed uncontrollable **TEARS,** and asked God, *"What am I doing WRONG? I'm trying to live right and do the Christian thing. Why am I being attacked for having a good heart!? Please, God, help me understand why!"* He didn't answer right off the back. I wiped my face and just shot out the door running looking for Jahmel!

He was coming around the corner when I got outside! I told him, I was DONE and that his mother is crazy! I snatched my keys out of his hands and was walked fast by him because I was ready to GO! He started pulling on my shirt to get me to come back, so I told him, *"Jahmel, don't touch me, I am done with y'all, I lost all respect for your Mother. She's DEAD to me!"* I was getting ready to get into the car when he stood in front of me so that he could drive. He didn't want me to drive because I was really upset. (but it is okay for you to drive when you have rage in your heart? Yeah, okay!) I didn't want to argue, because I **SWEAT**ed all the energy I had mustered to get cute for lunch to end up slap boxing with his crazy mother! As we're driving off, he asks what happened, by this time I calmed down.

Jahmel: *"Okay, so what did my mom say?"*

Me: *"It's not what she said that has me pissed off, it was what she did! She slapped me and kicked me in my fu***** STOMACH JAHMEL, MY DAMN STOMACH! I wanted to beat her ass so bad man. I promise if she were like at least 20 years younger, I would have dragged and killed yo mama! MY FU***** STOMACH BRO!!! MY STOMACH!!"* I exclaimed with so much hurt and pain. You know what he did!? He quickly turned in to the next hotel, and parked abruptly and uttered…

"WHAT!!?? IS SHE OKAY!? Did you hit her AZURE!!???," he said while he was preparing to get out of the car. I sat there confused wondering if he heard what I just said because he was quick to run to his mother's "rescue!" Here's the thing, if he actually cared about his mother, I would have been somewhat okay with him responding the way he did in wanting to check on her. He didn't even ask if I was okay. Not even once. AT ALL! That, that right there…HURT! I just wanted to go find my mommy at work and cuddle in her arms; but I knew if I did she probably would have FINISHED HER (in my Mortal Kombat voice) for me, then prayed for healing and restoration. I'm just saying. I don't really remember what happened in the moments in between, but I did end up back in the room.

Jahmel had sat his mother down and was telling her what his plans for her were. He was telling her that he was looking for a place to get her some help or an assisted living place where she can go—but she wasn't having it. She felt like he was just putting her on someone else. Actually, he probably was. While he was giving her the run down, I started to clean up the mess she created with the water and food and other stuff. WHY? Because that room was under an employee rate and the last thing I needed was there to be something broken or messed up, and my friend loses her job over people she doesn't even know. I wouldn't feel right, and there would not have been any way I could help her financially.

While Jahmel and his mom were talking, I couldn't stand the sight of her. Just looking at her and hearing her voice made me sick to my stomach. I went and sat outside the room. A few moments later, the door opened and Jahmel he told me that he called APS (Adult Protective Services) and some places that could help get her somewhere to care for her. They advised him that if she tried to leave, he should not stop her or force her to stay, and that if and when it happens, he should call the police and explain to them what's going on and tell them that he already called APS and provide them with the case number, give a description and location and they will pick her up and take her someplace safe. He was trying hard to get me to come back into the room, but I know myself, and if she would have said anything slick or throw anything else at me I wasn't going to hold my tongue; **"I'm Saved, But You Can Still Catch These Hands!"**

While he was still trying to get me to come back in, the door opens again, it was her, with bags trying to leave again. She said she doesn't want to stay there, and that she was leaving. He calls out to her, but she ignored it and walked out the door. He looks at me with that "go get her" look. With a raised eyebrow, I look at him thinking "I ain't about to go chase after her." I tell him, *"Go call the police like they said and stop looking at me."* While he's on the line with the operator, I go to the window to see if I can see her walking, once I pulled the curtain back, I see her sitting outside on the bench. I laughed on the inside thinking; you put up all that fuss to go NOWHERE!

We got outside and met the police in front of the lobby, both officers came over to us, and we told him that she was sitting down at the end, one of the officer's went to question her and the other took our statement. I told them she became physically abusive to Jahmel and myself. I showed him my cuts and bruises; Jahmel did as well (although, I think his were self-inflicted wounds.) He asked if she had anything marks on her I told him no, he looked at me with an confused look. I guess he felt the same way I felt, if someone left marks on me like she did, they would have equal or worse marks. He says in a confused tone, *"Ma'am, and you did not fight back?"* I said, *"No, officer I did not, I mean look at her, she little and old and I probably would have killed her!"* He goes on to commend me for my response to the ordeal and apologize that I was attacked the way I was. Tuh, more than what Jahmel did.

We joined the other officer, and he told us that she did admit to attacking me and didn't have a reason for it only that I was the *"new girlfriend"* that she didn't like.

Officer 2: *"Did you and her son just get into a relationship, ma'am? She said you're the new girlfriend."*

Jahmel and I laugh.

Me: *"No, sir. We've been together a little over a year, and out of the blue today, she told me she don't like me so,* (as I shrug) *she cannot like me, that's fine. I just want to get her some help."*

Officer 2: laughs *"Okay, well there are a few options, the file you all did with APS says that she has dementia and she has had suicidal intentions. Is that correct?"*

Jahmel and I: *"Yes, Sir."*

Officer 1: *"Well, there are not a lot of options we can do. We can indeed take her, but the process is very intensive, it may be too intensive for her."*

Officer 2 chimes in *"Yeah, we'd have to handcuff her and take her downtown, and she'll get processed and all of that stuff, then APS will come get her. Now since she's talking about suicide or harming herself, the easier way would be for you all to take her to a hospital and let them know she has dementia and hadn't been on her medication, and then she became hostile, abusive, etc. They'll then admit her and do a psych evaluation and then go from there."*

Jahmel and I; both blown away. I say, *"WOW, Yeah, that's a lot!"*

Officer 1: *"Ma'am, do you feel comfortable with her being in your car?"*

Me: *"I rather her not be around me. Period, but if this is the step, I need to take to get her help* (shrugs) *then so be it, I guess."*

Officer 1 goes over to her and to explain the plan and to see if she was willing to go with us to the emergency room. While he's given her, the run-down Officer 2 continued to give us more information and answers to some questions Jahmel had.

So, she agreed to be taken to the hospital to get an evaluation. The officers assisted in getting her and her things into the car, so we can be on our way. While we're in route, she had something to say about everything we passed! We pass the Greyhound on the way you hear her in the back all snot-ish *"Oh, the Greyhound, you just gone drop me off and put me on a bus, huh? Hmph!"* I wanted to say, *"SHUT. UP!"* Passed a few restaurants; *"Hmm, I wonder how it feels to eat, since I hadn't eaten today, can't even take my medicine! Ya'll just going to let an old lady starve. Hmph."* I look at Jahmel; you know that look your mama give when she sees you acting up from across the church? Yeah, that's the look I gave him. Jahmel, didn't really want to "commit" his mom so he was trying to give her different options.

"Mom, okay. Do you want to go to the hospital to get evaluated? We can go get you something to eat, take you back to the room so you can eat, shower and relax. Me and Azure will leave you alone for a few hours so that you can have time to yourself, then in the morning, I'll take you to your Dr. that way you don't have to be in the hospital."

*He was also thinking that if she goes to the hospital, they're going to admit her, and if they did, he wouldn't be able to cash her check. So Jahmel was trying to convince her to just grab a bite and chill and honestly, I liked that idea a lot better—so we wouldn't have to make ANOTHER hospital trip. *

Her response: *"Whatever you and her* (me) *feel is best!"*

Jahmel: *"Okay, we'll just do that then, you just probably need food and rest. Okay mom?"*

We we're passing Travis Park and then she goes *"OOOOH TRAVIS PARK!? Just drop me off with the homeless people! I'm homeless anyway I'll just steal the food from the birds and wait to die!! JUST take me back to the ROOM! I'll kill myself while you all are gone!"* As she flops back in the seat." At this point, I had had ENOUGH of it.

I snapped my fingers and signaled Jahmel to make a U-turn *"UN UN, NOPE! Take her ass to the hospital, we not doing this sh** today. She's suicidal right now and leaving her alone is not the best and ain't no telling where her mind would be later tonight while y'all alone and you're sleeping. No, take her to the emergency room. NOW! I'm sorry, not sorry! TURN AROUND!"* He turns around, and we take her into the emergency room. They check her vitals and all of them we're OFF! They asked her questions, was she mad, what happened and so forth. She ended up incriminating herself by the way she acted and her responses. So much so, that they admitted her and put her in a confined room with others who were either having drug withdrawals or like herself who wanted to do self-harm. We talked to the doctor and they would be doing her evaluation in a while, but due to her age, would need to be transferred to another hospital. They assured us they would call with any changes and updates.

I dropped him back off at the room, and of course in Azure & Jahmel fashion, there's an argument; about the "fight" between his mother and I. He asked if I could stay with him that night because he worried about his mom and other BS I told him *"NO! I want to go home, shower, and lay down to get ready for work. I had a rough day! Your mother attacked me, and NOT ONCE DID YOU EVEN ASK IF I WAS OKAY or showed ANY TYPE of concern."*

Jahmel argued me down; *"you didn't ask if I was okay when your dad got in my face and was cursing me out."*

Me: *"DAMN RIGHT! YOU! Charged him up; and my dad never touched you, like he wishes he would have!"*

Jahmel: *"He wouldn't have done sh** but I didn't put my hands on him either, un-like you did my mom."*

Me: *"NI*** PLEASE! You mean to tell me if my dad would have thrown the first punch you would have stood there and took it? No, you would have fought back and protected yourself as I did! Don't act like you care about your mom now. Boy! Get out my face!"*

Jahmel: *"You gone get enough saying disrespectful sh** about my mom. We may argue, fuss and fight, but at the end of the day she's still my mom!"*

Me: *"EXACTLY! AT THE END OF THE F****ING DAY, HE IS STILL MY DAD, and I WILL ALWAYS PROTECT HIM, SO IF THAT MEANS BEATING YOUR ASS and DEFENDING HIM, IMMA DO IT NO QUESTIONS ASKED! I NEVER TOUCHED YOUR MOM, LIKE I WANTED TOO; BECAUSE I KNEW IF I DID SHE'D BE IN THE MORGUE RIGHT NOW AND NOT IN THE F***ING PSYCH WARD!"*

Jahmel: *"Alright Azure. Just go home and get some rest."*

I got home, at a decent hour if I remember correctly. While coming up the stairs, my mom greets me with her warm smile and loving hug. After she was done embracing me, the first thing she notices was the long, red, welted scratch on my chest. She says, *"hmm, what happened right there!?"*

I didn't do such a good job in covering up by zipping my shirt up all the way because the start of it showed. I looked down and at my chest and replied: *"Hmm, I don't know what happened there."* We both brushed it off and went on about the night.

End Result of what happened to his mom:

The next day, we went to the hospital to check on her because we got no phone call or updates, and whenever he or I would call, we would hit a dead end. We found out that she was indeed transferred to another hospital and admitted into the psych ward. She apparently told them that Jahmel abuses her and takes her money; so that check they were expecting never showed up to my house. It was obvious that the caseworker had it re-routed. It was a whole lot of back and forth with the hospital, Jahmel, and the caseworker. We were given a date for her to be discharged and we went to pick her up, but they had no clue on where she is. Turned out that since they "could not reach" him or myself; they marked her cased as abandoned and put her in APS custody, and APS placed her in a home which ended up causing more issues down the line.

"Who Are You?"

Growing up, I witnessed my mommy always praying and en-couraging her co-workers, colleagues, and staff. If someone was sick or going in for a procedure or may be awaiting test results. She first handled the business part of the call then ended with the spiritual business. She would pray over situations, sickness, and diagnosis. I remember one day I was in the car when one of her staff needed prayer and uplifting and just hearing her pray unashamedly ("HOLLA 1-1-6 IF YOU REP THE TRUTH") for the lady made me proud; like yeah that's my mommy, yeah! When the call ended, I said: *"I wish I had an understanding and praying boss like you."* She told me, *"Just, keep praying and asking God honey it will come!"*

Little did I know all those nights I cried, and prayed those prayers asking God to change and or get me out of the situation I was in with Jahmel, he was setting me up to be placed in the path of someone who would push me and coach me to greater and pull out my best me! When Tre' (my boss, my manager, he doesn't like to be referred by either of those; so, everyone just calls him Tre'!) came into my life; my prayers were answered! He started less than a month after I started; I knew it was nobody but GOD. He put the right person in place that would be equipped to handle the twist and life-altering events that were getting ready to take place in my life.

I had no clue how much he would impact my life when we first met. He seemed pretty chill and dope. He told me he was retired military and I was like 'Oh Lord. I hope he's not overly strict and all about rules…YEAH NO! Total opposite: BUT don't get it twisted, he will check you quickly if need be and as for me; I got checked A LOT, even still to this day.

Once I returned to work after I had my miscarriage, Tre' was happy to see me, but I could also tell he was concerned knowing the reason why I was on leave. He came over to my station to check in on me and asked how I was feeling. I told him that I was hurt and confused, and our conversations went a little something like this:

Tre': *"As you should be, that's an emotion. Have you thought about the good that came out of it?"*

Looking at him confused, *"What good could that be? I'm struggling right now. How could God give me something so precious then take it away from me like that!?? That, I don't understand."*

Tre': *"Look, think about your life! Think of how things are going on and the people in your life right now. Any time anything happens, you have to consider what you were being saved from. You have no idea what life would have been like for you and that child; and often times we misinterpret misfortune as a bad thing instead of seeing how it could have been a blessing. We rarely see misfortune as a blessing because we're blinded by the pain of it, which is human, but it is not spiritual.*

I stood there and thought about it for a moment then I flashed back to: *"Booked," "Oh What a Night," "Light Em Up"* and shook my head *"NO."* Also, while he's talking, I was baffled, like how he knew my life was not equipped right now for a child, especially with all the instability involving the 'baby daddy' without me even saying a word about my situation. Now I'm looking at him thinking, *"Who Are You!?"*

Tre': *"Be happy, that baby don't have to be in this world with all the craziness going on. Think about your life right now, would you want her or him to see that or live that? No Right?"*

Me: *"Yeah, you're right."*

Tre': *"Oh, I know I'm right!"*

I chuckled and continued: *"My life right now is so…OKAY so his mother ended up attacking me the other day. I have done nothing wrong but try to help and make sure she's okay. SHE KICKED ME IN MY STOMACH, like really! I wanted to beat her ass, but at the same time, I let her have it because I was always taught to respect elders; but at the same time… DEFEND YOURSELF!"*

Tre': *"One, you take on too much! I think a lot of time; we try too hard to show strength, when the strongest human that ever walked showed every emotion. Why do we put the pressure on ourselves to be stronger than him? When he doesn't ask you to be strong, he asks you to trust. There's strength in trust; it's just simply letting go and having the courage to trust even when you can't see it. And based on the altercation; I think a lot of time we react to things based on our character and who we are. Not everybody in that situation would have done it the same way. You had motive and reason to react differently, but you somehow managed not to react at all. You hadn't done anything wrong; she had no reason to take it out on you; so, what was she really fighting you for? Believe it or not, you have the gift to absorb, but the problem is, like any sponge it has a max capacity. You've always been able to absorb. The problem is you've reached the maximum capacity of absorption, and the only way to release that to be able to soak up again is to what…?"*

Tre' and I at the same time: *"Squeeze it!"* Again, mind BLOWN!

"…that's right, that's how we start new. You release everything you've absorbed thus far to start new. But now that you're new, you have the

absolute right and control over what you decided to absorb; because now you know what it's like to absorb everything that comes your way. The discipline and discernment that you have now will let you absorb what you can and squeeze out what you can't. You'll never reach full capacity again.; because you know what it's like when you reach that. You can't do the same thing twice."

I'm looking at him as a deer in headlights, speechless and in awe at the words that are coming out of this man's mouth. Still thinking *"Who Are You!?"* I been admiring my mom and how she handles her staff's issues and her praying for them with no hesitation wishing and hoping I could have a manger like her. To not even realize the answer to my prayers was literally staring me in the face.

He continued; *"CRY! It's okay to cry. I use to tell all my soldiers they get a day to cry, let it all out, snot-nosed and all. Whatever you feel you need to do in that 24hrs DO IT! JESUS DID IT! All the hell he went through. He took one day. The scripture says Jesus…"*

Me: *"…WEPT!!! OMG! WOW!"* I interrupted him and just stood there with my mind BLOWN. I hear that verse all the time; we sometimes say it as we bless the food. But it was at the moment; I understood the context so much clearer.

As he walks away, he says, well yells holding his finger up *"ONE DAY BLUE! 24 HOURS! GET IT DONE!"*

When Tre' walked off after telling me he was only giving me 24hrs to get all of my emotions out about losing Harper. I stood there a minute thinking WOW! OKAY LORD, I hear you…and honestly, I heard him, but I didn't listen. I seemed like I only listened once I reached my full capacity! From experience, that is not a place you want to be before you to really say OKAY GOD! Not only did I hear him; but I needed to heed his direction and instruction. That is one crazy place to be but what makes God so DOPE is that He never left my side! WHOOOO! MY GOD! All the stuff I had absorbed to this point, even to where I asked God; *"WHAT HAVE I DONE WRONG? WHY ARE YOU TAKING ME THROUGH THIS!?"* When I was losing sight of who *He* really is, and who *I* am in *HIM* and wanted to give up and end my life, HE WAS STILL IN THE MIDST OF IT ALL!

If you don't get anything else from this book get this—Don't ever get so far away from God like I was that you're not able to hear his voice clearly. Take it from me; it's not worth it. I'll end this chapter with these two scriptures; 1 Peter 5:7 *"Give all your worries and cares to God, for he cares about you."* **NLT** and 1 Corinthians 10:13 *"No test or temptation that comes your way is beyond the course of what others have had to face. All you need to remember is that God will never let you down; he'll never let you be pushed past your limit; he'll always be there to help you come through it."* **MSG**

Enough

THE BLOW UP's

It felt like dude was getting crazier as the day went on, he was coming up to my job and requesting me to come down, either he was Uber'n and was running out of gas and needed money, or wanted me to leave. They'll be days he'll come get me from work, and he'll be pissed at only God knows and will try to take it out on me. One day, in particular, I got in MY vehicle, and I say *"hey babe"* only to get a nasty response. He said: *"I'm pissed, and I don't want to hear your fucking voice right now!"*

EXCUSE ME WHAT!!!?

So, a lot of times, I would sit like a prisoner in my own car. Then other times he's having an episode, thinking on it now, probably a psychotic episode; he would want me to pull over or stop the car in the middle of the highway to let him out because he couldn't take being in the same space with me and or his mom. This particular day he was having an episode and was just not having it. I'm driving and he was not able to sit still for nothing it looked like he was having withdrawals from something. Now back when Jahmel was staying with one of my aunts, she mentioned to Aunt London that she felt like Jahmel was doing more than just weed. She came over to the house one day and said what she smelled didn't smell like ordinary weed. She never told me that but comparing how he was a week before his mom's little episode.

Jahmel was acting and looked like he was definitely having withdrawals of more than just weed. One day after work, Jahmel wanted out of the car and he wanted out that instant! I couldn't just stop the car on IH-35; one of the busiest highways in Texas, yet alone in the "fast lane". I would suggest getting off at the next exit; that wasn't good enough for him to the point where he took his seat belt off, opened the door and tried to get out; while I am doing at least 75 on a TEXAS HIGHWAY! *Ya'll I can't make this stuff up!*

"JAHMEL, WHAT THE HELL IS WRONG WITH YOU!?" his mom in the back screaming *"AAAAAAHHH JESUS, JAHMEL, JAHMEL... OOOOOOOOOH JAHMEL JESUS JESUS JESUS!"* At the point I still didn't care too much for her and felt she was in on this bluffing game with her son...Hearing her scream the way she was, definitely showed there was love in her heart for her only son.

Finally finding a way place to pull over that was safe and off the HIGHWAY. Jahmel immediately jumps out the car with clinched fists screaming *"AAAAAHHHHHHHHH HMMMMM HMMMM HMMMM"* Going completely crazy, we we're parked in the back of one of the shopping centers off IH-35. Waiting for him together his thoughts and come back to the car, was taking longer than normal I drove around to the store fronts to see if he was walking there. NOPE no sign of Jahmel. By this point I knew it was getting ready to be a long Friday night. Finally saw him, I pulled over and got out to talk to him and he was not responsive at all. He was pulling away from me, cursing me out, saying he wanted to get his stuff out the car and go somewhere and leave his mom. He threw his wallet out with his ID and Social Security card in the middle of the street. While I'm trying to chase down the flying SS card, he manages to sneak to the trunk of my car to grab somethings and disappear again. Chasing him down for the last time I finally was able to talk him into the car.

But before he did that, he took his anger out on one of the metal trash cans, removed the lid and threw it in the street barley missing an oncoming car.

Still having a 30-minute ride back into the city, Jahmel started cutting up again. I put his window on lock, so he couldn't roll it down to throw stuff at cars like he's done in the past or do something stupid again. We didn't make it too far before he started going crazy again. He kept yelling *"pull the f****** car over before I really spaz out. You thought back there was something put the car over right now. F***!"* Pleading with him to wait and hold on until we got to San Antonio instead of consistently stopping, we were maybe 20 minutes away from his hotel and he was not taking no for an answer. I took the next exit and pulled over on the side of the road. Jahmel jumps out the car and starts walking into the field that was next to us and started kicking the utility pole. I guess kicking it either hurt his foot or wasn't a good enough release for him because he came back to the car, banged on the trunk so I can open it and grabbed his baseball bat and went back to the pole. Yeah, you're thinking right. Jahmel started taking swings to the pole with his bat. Not just one swing big multiple swings. His mother and I yelling from the car.

"JAHEMEL! Seriously Bruh…IF YOU DON'T GET YOUR ASS BACK IN THE GOT DAMN CAR!!! LETS! GO!"

His mom so nonchalantly *"hmm, yeah! He's gonna go back to jail! JAHMEL! STOP IT!"* After he got his little "anger" out he then tossed the bat into the field and gets back into the car. His mom and I looking at him crazy and, in that moment, I thought out loud. I said *"hmmm… Are you done!?"* Man, the look he gave me, I thought he was going to swing off on me too; thank the Lord he didn't. That night ended with him getting his weed and a hotel room. After all that, he was chill and was acting like nothing ever happened.

While dealing with the many different personalities that Jahmel was showing, my Big Daddy's health was starting to decline more than it has been over the years. AH! I just love my Big Daddy so much. It was getting harder for him to walk and do daily activities. He had a provider during the day and my Uncle Mike (his son) at night; and on Sunday's, he was by himself. There are two things about my Big Daddy that he was passionate about: he did NOT like to be disturbed while eating, let alone disturbing others and he liked his sleep! Sunday's would be his sleep-in late days; so for me, it worked. I would come by after church to help him get out the bed, get him cleaned and changed so he can get to the den to eat his breakfast.

A weekend in late October, my mother and I agreed to stay with him, Uncle Mike can get a break and enjoy time to himself. I told Jahmel ahead of time that I will be with my Big Daddy and he needed to be sure his next few days were taken care of a head of time, because if the money ran short; I will not be able to spend my time Uber'n around the city to earn money for a room. Because it was Big Daddy and 'His Girl's' time. Praise the Lord, his mother's check came in and he was able to pick her up from the group home she was placed in and go cash it. She also gave him money, because even though she wasn't in his custody at the time, she knew the situation was still the same, me paying for everything and him not having a job or trying to help himself! So, I was finally financially free and would be able to enjoy and focus on my Big Daddy and spend some quality time with Mommy as well.

The day of our slumber party with my Big Daddy, I called my mom to let her know I was on my way and to see if she needed anything. She just told me to grab some ice cream for her and my Big Daddy's favorite "snack" it was H-E-B's *"Sock It to Me"* cake. He loved his sweets I tell you, so much so that his family gave the nickname "Sugar Pie."

My mommy knew how I was and felt when it came to my Big Daddy, so she warned me that he was having some difficulties eating and drinking. The nerves in his hand were bad, he kept dropping his fork and cup, which cause him to spill his drink on his clothes a few times and he was even slurring his words. It was the weekend, and he does tend to have a drink or two, but he never drank in front of my mommy because he knew she didn't drink, so I know alcohol wasn't a factor of his speech being slurred. Trying not to freak out, I ran into H-E-B super quick! In and out within 10 minutes so I can get to the house that was two minutes around the corner.

I made it to the house, and he's sitting in his chair in the den, as usual, I walked in and said, *"Hey Monkey!"* followed by a kiss on his cheek. With his eyes lit and a big grin on his face, he says, *"Hey Tiger!"* I don't know where that came from; but, since I was a little girl, that has always been the greeting! Once I got all the things in the house, I immediately went into action to be any assistance I can. I saw for myself the struggle he was having with his supper even though it was breaking my heart. I couldn't let him see me cry. We ended up having to feed him the rest of his meal, but when it came to the CAKE. He had NO PROBLEM eating that. HA! such a character.

He was having a lot of struggles more than normal that night; he would usually be able to get up and walk to his room with the help of his walker. This particular night it seemed like nothing wanted to work right for him. My Big Daddy is a very independent person, so these mishaps were frustrating to him; even more, so that we had to get him in the power chair for him to go to his room because his legs didn't want to work for him. The next morning, everything was fine. Mom had to go to the church picnic while I stayed back to make sure Big Daddy was awake and got everything to start the day. He was able to dress himself and do normal activities, although it took him a little longer than usual, but he got it done. Sometimes he loses his balance and falls from time to time, so I got him up, change his clothes, and get him all set for the day just like I did on Sunday's.

The day went on, my mom was back from the church picnic, and I were sitting in the den with Big Daddy watching 'The Golden Girls.' When he wants something, he won't come out and say it he would challenge you. That day, my own Big Daddy came for me...

Big Daddy: Sucking his teeth *"Hmm, y'all know what I want? But I bet y'all don't know how to make it right."*

Mom and I look at each other and smirk because we didn't know what he was about to say next. So, we both say back to him, *"What's that chile?"*

Big daddy: *"A good ole banana pudding!"*

As I side-eyed my mom, we both busted out into laughter, while Big Daddy sat there with the biggest but the sneaky-est smirk on his face.

Me: *"Really, Big Daddy? You know I make the best banana pudding!"*

Big Daddy: *"Naaw! I didn't know that."* Turning his head quickly at my mom saying *"Tonja can she really make some banana pudding?"*

Mommy: *"Shoots, yeah!"* As she said it like he would.

Me: *"Big Daddy, I just made you some a while ago; a big one too."*

Big Daddy: Laughing *"YOU DID!? I don't remember the baby.* (while sucking his teeth), *Big Daddy is so forgetful."* With a smile on his face.

The day went on and it was time to start getting ready for supper, I head to the store, so mom can cook and get the things I need for this banana pudding. I came back to the house to make it; once it was done, I took it out to the den to show him what it looked like.

Big Daddy: *"OOOOOOWEE, Azure (in his horse, raspy voice it sounded more like Aash-sha) mm, that looks mighty good. Scoop me up a little bit."*

Me: *"Right now? Big Daddy, you hadn't eaten supper yet."*

Big Daddy: *"Well, that's all right. I just eat a little and get some more after. It aint gone hurt nothing."*

I went and put some on a little saucer and brought it out to him so he can eat it.

Big Daddy: *"mmm-hmm."* (it was in that moment I knew I just got suckered into making banana pudding.) *Yep, you sure did make me some of this, this good baby, mmm hmmm."*

Me: siding eyeing my grandpa *"Yeah I know I did, you could have just asked me to make it for you again."*

Big Daddy: shaking his head while putting a spoon full in his mouth, *"I know I could."*

This is how I knew that he was feeling better; my Big Daddy has NO FILTER. He will say what he wants, how he feels and don't care about your feelings; he will just give it to you straight. The weekend with Big Daddy ended better than it started for sure and it was back to reality that night.

As the week went on. Jahmel and I were okay, not much fighting. He was actually in the process of getting an apartment, so his mother can get out of the group home she was in, because that within itself was a whole problem. That Friday, I would never forget it; all morning while

I was working, I kept thinking about my Big Daddy, I kept thinking about old memories, then that feeling became an uneased feeling. So while I was on my break, I check my messages and I see a text from my mommy saying, *"Hey sweetie, where are you?"* I immediately panicked because Jahmel had my car that day and I was at work. I wasn't sure if she saw my car in passing and wondered why I didn't stop or honk the horn at her like we'd normally do. In a panic I call her; she answers

"Hey Mom, I just saw your message."

Mommy: *"Yeah, where are you, honey?"* In her calm kind of scary voice."

Me: *"At work, I'm on break now."*

Mommy: *"Ok, what I'm getting ready to tell you, just know that everything is okay and under control, okay?"*

Me: *"Okaaaay? What's going on!?"*

Mommy: *"Big Daddy is in the hospital, BUT he is oh....!"*

Interrupting her, I say *"I knew it! I knew it, I knew it! He was soooo heavy in my spirit today while I was working. What happened? What hospital is he in? I'm about to leave!"*

Mommy: *"Calm down he is fine. You remember when we were with him last week, and he had a hard time getting up to walk? Well this morning he couldn't get out of bed and Uncle Mike or Mr. Steve* (his provider) *couldn't help him get out, so they had to call EMS. They came and got him out, took him to the ER and found out that he had pneumonia which explains the cough he's been having."*

I heard pneumonia and automatically panicked, a good friend of mine, his grandmother passed not long after she found out she had pneumonia.

"MOM, I'm on my way, just send me the address!"

Mom: *"Azure, just hang on, he still hadn't been transferred into a room yet; he's still in the triage."*

I didn't care! My Big Daddy was in the hospital, and I needed to get there! PERIOD!

I hung up and immediately reached out to Jahmel letting him know that my Big Daddy was admitted in the hospital, I give him the rundown of the story, and what took place, he quickly responds that he was on his way. He didn't get to me until a little after four o'clock, I clearly could have stayed to 6:00, but I just need to get to my Big Daddy. The plan was after Jahmel picked me up he was going to drive back to the hotel, and I was going to head to the hospital immediately after. I could tell he was feeling a way, but he knew I really wanted to get to my grandpa.

Sure enough, he wasn't going to let me leave without a fight. I can't remember what exactly happened, but it was probably over a message I had in my inbox from my old neighbor. Jahmal accused me of cheating and talking to other guys. The problem is, he would READ the messages; and nothing in there said ANYTHING about hooking up or doing anything inappropriate and if it was insinuated, it was from the other party and it immediately got curved; and to top it, he was doing the same thing to me when I was in my last relationship with Vince and he would talk so much mess about Vince at the time and everything time he did I shut him down and put him in his place. So why would it be any different?

When we pulled up to the motel, he got out the car and slammed my door HARD and I heard him throwing stuff in the room. I got out of the car doing the 'Angry Black Women walk' and decided *'Oh, NO; NOT TODAY, WE NOT DOING THIS! NOT TODAY."* I banged on the door, he swung it open and screamed *"WHAT!?!"* in that cringing stomach-turning tone like I described earlier (and literally to this day I cannot take a man saying "WHAT!?!" when talking to me. I just can't! it triggers a defense mechanism. I'm trying hard to overcome it, but triggers are something serious.) I asked him what his problem was and of course in good ole Jahmel fashion it turned in to a straight tantrum, talking about I can talk to whoever is in my inbox, since I'm cheating on him and he's been nothing but faithful to me. I stood there in complete awe; thinking he doesn't really give a hoot about me and doesn't care about nobody but himself. My grandfather, my heart, my EVERYTHING is in the hospital, and you want to pull one of your *"Houston We Have a Problem"* stunts??

He goes to my car and starts taking all his stuff out; his mothers' things that we still had, his things, basically his LIFE and started tossing them in the motel room and onto the ground. At this point, I was thinking cool, take all your stuff, and I can finally be done with you. He's still going off on me, cursing and making a big scene in front of another guest that was staying there. The man was looking like he was waiting on Jahmel to jump stupider and try to attack me so that he can handle it. He finally finished getting all his things from my car. As I'm sitting in the driver seat waiting for him to get done so I can go. He slams my door, then quickly opened it back up and said: *"OH, THAT PHONE, YOU'RE USING TO TALK TO THESE OTHER NIGGAS; GIMME MY PHONE BACK! Talking about your going to go see your grandpa, knowing got damn well you're going to go meet up with another nigga. I'm not stupid Azure."* I finally had a clap back that I felt will actually shut him up, and he won't turn it around on me and make me feel dumb…I say…

"Oh, no boo-boo, this is MY PHONE! Including the one, you have in your hand. I brought the phones and pay the bill. You haven't paid not ONE MONTH since we had them. The only thing that is "YOURS" is

the account. So, you wanna act like that, then RUN ME, **MY PHONE NIGGA! NOW! So I can do see my GRANPA!"** SILENCE. *"Yeah, that's what I thought."* I pulled off and headed towards the hospital. In my rearview I see him trying to chase after me and calling me a b**** while throwing rocks at my car.

I finally reach the hospital; now, I am not a fan of hospitals you would think I loved them as much I was there with Jahmel. Getting into the elevator to go up to the third floor I remember taking a deep breath and, on the exhale, I said *"whoooo,* (while holding my head down) *ok. Help me, Jesus!"* I approached the entrance of his room and took a second before I walked in because I didn't want him to see that I was worried, let alone I didn't know what I was getting ready to walk into. I walked in with a smile on my face, and with excitement in my voice, I let out a *"Heeey, Monkey!"* Big Daddy looks over and sees me and with a smirk on his face *"H..hh..heeey Tiger."* As I walked over to him to kiss his forehead, I ask him, *"what chu doin in here Big Daddy?"* I was nowhere ready for the response he gave me...

"Baby, I don't know what I'm doing in here, Big Daddy doesn't feel too hot, I know that much. I just want to get out of here."

I didn't know what to say, I wanted to cry, but I couldn't let him see me worried or break down. I told him that we were going to get him out soon. The nurses came in to check him and one thing about my Big Daddy; he doesn't like repeating himself, but the nurses kept asking him question about how he feels. He kept telling her he didn't know, but she kept picking. I was getting frustrated because I am thinking "lady you can't see he is a little confused on what's going on. He's 90 for heaven's sake." Mom and Fabio saw me getting a little irritated, and Fabio just calmly put his hand on my leg, so I wouldn't *NICELY* go off on the nurse. The nurse was getting ready to check his vitals and as well as the swelling in his feet. He couldn't understand what she wanted him to do, we're trying to explain to him what she is saying, and I could tell he was getting frustrated. So, I got up and went to stand by his bed side and rub his head. Big Daddy has NEVER been to the ER, let alone admitted, so this was all new to him and I knew he was scared.

As the nurse was checking him, she goes down to his feet where most of his pain was, and as she touches his foot, Big Daddy lets out a loud *"OOOOOO WE WE, just wait one minute!"* I immediately went into protective mode because she was going to be gentle with my grandpa. She apologized and explained that she needed to move him over, so she can test the swelling in his feet; when she did, he let out another yell that I couldn't handle. Next thing I know, I looked up at my parents and my Uncle Mike, with water filling my eyes, and my mouth curling up, I shook my head and said whispered *"I can't, I can't."* while turning around to walk out of the room.

As soon as I hit the threshold of the door, I lost it. There were uncontrollable tears; I mean a complete BREAKDOWN. I felt so lost, all I kept thinking was that I couldn't lose my Big Daddy. I was still trying to process the sudden passing of my Auntie Chelle, and the last thing I wanted was to lose my Big Daddy! (You know how you put some family members or celebrities in that "they can never die" category? Yeah, he's in that category for me.)

I was hit with tons of emotions, beating myself up for still being in a relationship with Jahmel, hurting for my Big Daddy because I knew he was miserable laying up in that bed limited from doing normal things that he would be doing at home. Another was the fact that he was in the hospital and had pneumonia. Lastly, knowing that his time was indeed going to come soon, and I was nowhere near prepared for it. I remember there was a year when we we're just losing people; I think it was 2014 or 2015. We lost some family members, close friends, longtime church members and then just losing my Auntie earlier in the year. I remember talking to my mom saying, *"I don't know who God is preparing me for but, I am not ready!"* As all of these emotions are rushing in I look up, and my Fabio was right behind me to console me along with my Uncle Mike, and at that moment I felt some relief, but I already felt like I had lost my Big Daddy.

After I gathered my emotions and tears, I was able to put the "S" on my chest that the women in my family passionately wear, and I walked back to that room like I wasn't just losing it a minute ago. First thing Big Daddy said when I walked back in *"Hmm, there she is!"*

Mom: *"He was looking for you. He was wondering where you went."*

Taking a deep breath and exhaling, *"I'm right here, Big Daddy."* He turns around and says, *"I'm not liking this here."* While sucking his teeth. It was in that moment I made up in my mind that I was staying, I wasn't about to leave my Big Daddy, I didn't want him to feel like we are abandoning him once we all left. Then one of the nurses came in to check his vitals again. I didn't like the way she was handling my grandpa. I look at my mama with that *'I'm about to get an attitude'* look and then said, *"YEP! I'm staying tonight!"* She just smiled and shook her head in agreement because she already knew.

I step outside to call Jahmel to let him know what my plans were, because he was blowing my phone up and texting and I was not responding. He seemed all concerned and cool when I was telling him. I told him my plan was to go home eat, shower; and that once I left I was going to stop by Big Daddy's house–drop off his clothes and stuff he was transported in the EMS with, grab Jahmel something to eat, because he was starving and was about to spas out because he was losing it, then head back to the hospital before it gets too dark so my grandpa wouldn't be by himself too long, especially since this was all new to him. Do you think he let me be great that night? NOPE!

While I was in the shower, he was apparently blowing my phone up. I was trying to get clothes together as well what I could change into for work the next morning. I checked my phone and saw a text…

Jahmel: *"Good Night! Have fun! You're free to do whatever. You don't have to bring anything, enjoy your night out. I'll need my stuff out the storage tomorrow, and we need to switch the phone to your name. Also, any paperwork with my name on it that you have I'm going to need that back asap."*

All of this because he was hungry and knew my focus was going to be on someone other than him, and I wasn't going to jump when he needed or wanted me. After I got myself together, dropped off the things at Big Daddy's house, pick up Jahmel's "stuff" aka weed. Jahmel kept texting me trying to see if I was still coming and he was giving me very specific instructions to follow; call me, so I'll know you're on the way, text me after you leave the gas station, etc. I guess he was trying to make me think he had another chick in the room or wanted me to pick a fight. Two things; I wasn't stunt'n him, because I knew his little antics and games and secondly, I was trying to hurry up to get back to Big Daddy.

When I got to the hotel, he was really short with me. You'd think after I went out of my way brought him weed and food he would be a little more appreciative; but hey! At that point I didn't really care, because my thought was *Okay, he got his weed, so he'll be high tonight and in a chill mood and he'll leave me alone while I tend to my grandfather.*

Finally, I made it back to the hospital, and when I tell you, Big Daddy was waiting for me. He was waiting for me. I was surprised he didn't call while I was on my way back. The nurse that was on his night shift was pretty nice, a lot better than the day shift nurse. She had pillows and a blanket on the couch ready for me because she knew I was coming back. I didn't sleep at all that night between the vitals and medicines around the clock. I didn't care though because I was with my Big Daddy, as long as he was a little comfortable knowing I was by his side, I was okay because I knew Starbucks was DEFINITELY going to be my friend the next morning.

I didn't want to leave him, but I had to go to work if I had time and didn't need money. I would have used it to stay with him. I found myself dragging to the time clock. Thank the Lord, Jahmel had an "upset stomach", so I didn't have to get him, because I wasn't going to be able to handle his little pissy attitude on top of my lack of sleep. Once I reached my floor, I remember my assistant manager looked at me and said: *"Blue, you look like s***."* I was so defeated because I was trying hard not to look like how I felt, but that didn't work. I finally got a chance to talk to Tre', and I told him that my grandfather was in the hospital and that I stayed over, and he was like *"yeaaah… You do have them bags under your eyes. You should have gone to sleep last night."* I just cut my heavy eyes at him and said, *"Really Tre'!!!? I just said I… "* taking a deep breath and rolled my eyes, shook my head and smiled. He could tell that I was really worried, and I wasn't myself. He asked me how old my grandfather was, and with my head hung down, I said, *"90."*

He responds… *"Wait a minute, Blue, 90!? He lived a good life! It is his time! Let me be 90 and still here; I'll be like whenever you're ready Lord I'm here! Yes, we want him here physically, but we can't be selfish, Blue. 90! You will have tons of memories that will last a lifetime. Let me ask you this, is he still here? Yes right! Okay then, why you acting like he went home already? He is still here, so enjoy this time with him. He's 90 Blue, he lived a good strong life and seen so much. You should be rejoicing in knowing that!"* One thing about Tre' is that he can easily distract me from whatever is going on for the moment and put everything in perspective for me.

It had been two days that Big Daddy has been in the hospital and I was hoping they would give him discharge papers, but instead he was moved to ICU. His heart rate kept going up; it should have been under 100, but it was coming in at 150. I wanted him home so bad; he was miserable in this place. I remember when I was living in Dallas, he was in a rehab place for about a month or two and he absolutely HATED IT!

I could only imagine he had the same feeling, but I am sure worse. I was fighting to have someone be there with him 24hrs, but that would have been impossible. This was his first time in a hospital, PERIOD; especially hooked up to machines and getting poked and pried. BUT the doctors know what is best; so they moved him to a nursing home that would help him regain strength so he can be able to go back home and resume his normal activities and for the record, he hated that place too.

Surprisingly Jahmel was very, "supportive" while my Big Daddy was in the hospital. He didn't bother me too much or throw any fits like he'd usually do; but I knew that our relationship was getting ready to take a turn when Jahmel made this comment while we were at church waiting for our evening service to start. The text said *"We're in the same room but so far apart. Sometimes I feel like your phone or other people are your main focus. We ride in the car in silence and when I talk, you barley listen* (I said to myself while reading, cause you be on that bulls***) *it's weird, maybe I'm just tripping."*

My exact response to him word for word:

"DISCLAIMER: I am not yelling, nor responding with an attitude. Are you referring to me making sure my Godmother was okay? (her best

friend passed away a few day prior.) *Or me going to check on my Grand-pa in between services? I offered to take you back to the room because I knew you didn't really too much care for my godmother and I was going to be doing a lot of running around today* (my typical Sunday) *YOU of all people should know I care about others, especially if I f*** with them."*

Regarding my phone after work, I like to get on my phone. I'll put it up to engage in convo with you more, but half the time and lately you haven't wanted to talk to me for some odd reason. Either it's "I'm good" or "I don't want to talk to you right now or look at you." Or just blah. So, yes. I will scroll through social media or emails if you do not want to talk or not "feeling well" Half the time when I try to talk and ask questions. You either think I won't understand or it's too much to explain…I'll do my part to do better. I hope you will as well. I appreciate you expressing how you are feeling. I will be more conscious of it."

Y'all do y'all know after all of that and trying to have an adult conversation and be open and transparent. I get an *"Alright Azure."* It seemed like no matter how hard I tried to take the adult approach about things with him, I was always left feeling dumb, stupid, or just flat out defeated. He asked what more did you want me to say? I just thought it would open up the conversation to see what the real issue was. He then tried to put it on lack of affection.

At that moment I didn't want to admit to him I wasn't really in the mood half the time. Especially after Harper; now I'm not going to lie, there were times where my flesh got weak and I tried to be affectionate or get in the mood, he would always shoot me down and say that he didn't want a hug, kiss, or to be touch. NOTHING. So yeah, over time if you're always getting shot down, you're going to start shutting down. I told him we really need to step back and refocus on US, because lately it's been consumed with how we were going to get through the day and how long I had to Uber to get enough money for a room for him for the night. We were so consumed with that, that the focus on our relationship was gone. I honestly thought that this revamping of the relationship would really help us. He was getting ready to move into his apartment, so I could stop Uber-ing my life away. But him moving into that apartment only made things worse and when I say worse... sh** hit the fan.

The apartment was looking good; there were some bumps and struggles that came with it. Remember when he got arrested and went to jail and they set a court date, and all that? Well the judge ended up dismissing the case because the baby mama never provided evidence. Okay well, that issue came back up when applying for the apartment. It was coming back that there was a felony on his record. Which I knew was a lie because the judge dropped it down to a misdemeanor. The leasing office threatened to deny him of the apartment and not return the $300 deposit that he put down (well, that his mom put down because he STILL HAD NO JOB!) and of course Jahmel was NOT happy. After digging and digging, we come to find out, that the initial charge was indeed a felony because the baby mama said the cost to fix her window would be $1,500.00. Now you and I know no car window, especially a passenger window on a Nissan won't cost $1500 to get replaced. Jahmel always had the thought that because she worked for the city at that time and she would always tell people how much a deadbeat he was that it was an inside job and she knew what to say for them to charge him with a felony. So, with all my digging, investigating, and going back and forth downtown with him and talking to the leasing manager. We came to find out that back then they didn't have a penal code to put in the system and that it was dropped down to a differed misdemeanor: and at the time all they had was the felony code, but they went back on the actual court documents and crossed out felony and put down deferred misdemeanor, but in the SYSTEM, it was definitely a felony!

They realized the "mistake" when they looked back on the original charge and docket and was able to fix it in the computer and updated his record so when the leasing office ran the background check again it would show as a misdemeanor instead of a felony and they would be able to approve him and he could continue the moving process.

While we were fighting with the court system and the leasing office. Adult Protective Services and the group home released his mom back into his custody. That was hell within itself. There were open investigation(s) on Jahmel and I. Yes, ME! His mom told APS when she first went in that WE steal her money and are always going out on trips, etc. WHOA THERE! I had my own job and did not need that lady's money.

Praise God, Jahmel did one thing right and cleared my name! He told them that if it weren't for me, they would be homeless and the reason they're surviving is because of me and the only involvement I had with her money is when the check comes to the mailbox every month. So, they dropped the case on me but still had his open. They didn't too much care about the money part because they knew his mother had dementia, they just wanted him to have a stable place for his mother.

November 14, 2017 was the day he got his keys to the apartment. I think I was the only one super excited because I knew what this meant. Having his OWN apartment meant that I could actually enjoy my off days because I didn't have to get up and go UBER to make sure we had enough money to get a room for the night. I could go to work and didn't have to go pick him up and most importantly I could keep my money for MYSELF and try to catch up on bills!

I agreed to give him some of m stuff I had in storage from my apartment, anything to get him in that apartment quick, I was for it! That even meant putting the electricity and cable in my name *face-palm! Stupid, I know. * He couldn't do it apparently because he had a balance with them…so the deal was would pay the rent, he'll give me the money to pay for the electricity and cable until it's switched to his name. I just wanted them in that apartment and slowly out of my pockets. I was so 'geeked' that I had my parents follow me after bible study to the apartment. I didn't care if it was furnished or not; I didn't even care about the little roaches that were having a party. I wanted them to see that he finally did something even though I did most of the work.

Mom and Dad came to see the apartment they even blessed the home and prayed that the roaches would vacate. Haha. As I was walking my parents down to their car, I reassured them that this wasn't Azure's new residence nor address! I think they were a little relieved to hear that because I was rejoicing and excited like it was my apartment. Before I went home, I did a Walmart run to go pick up a couple of air mattress, pillows, and some blankets for them. On my way there I called Erika to tell her the good news. I remember we had a conversation a few weeks after his mom attacked me. She was home visiting and spending time with her husband. I was telling her where I was with the relationship and that I was going to give him a few months to see if he gets his act together. He would always say he doesn't "like" that I have to UBER and that we have to pawn my stuff for him to be comfortable. I was telling Erika; *"but at what point do you have enough of your girl, your woman, the one you say you want to spend your life with taking care of you? It's getting to the point where I'm going to have to back out because it's looking like he like's being taken care of and I don't want to be taking care of a 31-year-old man. So, I will give him a few months to see if there are any improvements if not, I will have to leave."*

Erika: *"Are you scared to leave?"*

Me: *"My Mom asked me the same thing! I told her no, but in all honesty, YES, I am scared! Knowing how he acts when he gets mad, I would hate for something crazy or bad to happen to him because I left him, because I do care about him and I want to see him win and be successful."*

Erika: *"Well babe, you know whatever you decide. I support you because I am worried about you. You haven't been yourself, and you know I always want the best for you."*

Even though this conversation was months ago, the feelings and decisions were still the same. Jahmel was making improvements; the apartment was a big step, and he had a few jobs lined up, so it looked like things were finally looking up for him. I was still one foot in and the other out; this was just making it a little easier for me to leave; especially knowing that he was going to have a roof over his head.

When I got back from Walmart, we actually got into an argument because I still wasn't giving him my couch, washer and dryer. He felt like it was dumb sitting in storage when it could go to use. Now I did think about it; then I came to my senses. The couch I have is one of my dream couches as well as my washer and dryer. What if we did break up…that's a lost for me. He smokes, so then my couch will smell like weed. Or what if he gets mad and tries to destroy my couch and most importantly. BRUH! YOU GOT ROACHES!! All it takes is for one egg to be laid and I have an infested washer, dryer, and couch! Yeah, I think NOT! I shut that down quick. Only thing I was willing to give him was my pots, pans, kitchen utensils and little stuff, that type of stuff is replaceable! He wasn't happy that I wouldn't let him have it, but

I did not budge, and I finally stood my ground, and I was so proud of myself.

A few weeks had gone by, and he was settled into the new place, we spent Thanksgiving together again, and I am not going to lie. I was on eggshells praying that we wouldn't have a repeat of last year. Especially after he called a LYFT to take him home because he got mad that I had fallen asleep during the Cowboy game after we ate…TYPICAL THANKSGIVING, right? Plus, I had been working 60hr weeks, so I was super tired. Hey! At least I didn't have to take him home this time.

On one of my off days, we were trying to cash his mom's check, but we couldn't do anything until the first, even though the check was early; it was dated to process on the first of the month. He tried another Walmart for the last time to see if they would push it through. He and his mother got back in the car and Jahmel threw the envelope and pen down towards the floor on the passenger side and says *"It didn't work so don't even ask me what happen."*

Me: With a confused look on my face I look at him like did he just really throw this pen towards me I asked: *"…but did they say…"* Before I can even finish my question, he blows up…

*"SEE, YOU DON'T F****** LISTEN!*

My smart mouth said, *"Well, if you speak clearer, I wouldn't have to ask you to repeat yourself."*

Jahmel: *"I told you don't ask, and you still asked."* While groaning, holding his head and rocking back and forth in the driver's seat, I was looking at him like homie is crazy! He yells, *"I can't f****** take this s*** no more! I am tired of you; you always say stupid sh**! I'm done, with you and this relationship! MOM LETS GO! You can go talk to the niggas that be in your inbox."*

Me: *"Seriously, Jahmel, this is what we're doing today? I don't know how many times I have to tell you I am not talking to anyone other than you!"*

Jahmel: *"MOM, LET'S GO...Matter fact you can stay with that cheating b****!"*

I turned around and told his mom not to get out the car... she flops back in her seat like well do I stay or get out.

Me: *"How am I a cheating b****, the dudes in my inbox are my family!!! If you were smart and actually read the messages and stop jumping to conclusions you would see that it's nothing like you think.; but if anyone should be called cheating it should be you. I see your inbox and dm's I'm not stupid and the text messages! Of how you want to do this and that to her and so on. I'm NOT DUMB like you think. I just let you make it.*

Jahmel: *"Oh, so you are going through my phone now?"*

Me: *"Correction MY PHONES! When you sold your iPhone, I gave you my 210 phone so you can have something to use to make job moves and that phone you have now...I PAID FOR, AND I AM STILL PAYING ON IT! Don't try me bruh."*

Jahmel: *"Sure Azure whatever just keep lying. Mom come on, get your s*** and let's go."*

Me: *"Where you going?"*

Jahmel: *"Don't f****** worry about where I'm going. Mom! Come on."*

So, she then asked where they were going, and he says *"HOME!"*

Me: *"Jahmel, NO! You are not about to drag your 70-year-old mom down this highway to get home. No, you don't want to get in the car, fine, but at least let me drop her off at the house. Just give her the key so she can get in."*

Jahmel: *"No, Mom if you are staying with her, you might as well go home with her cause I'm through with both of y'all."*

So, Jahmel runs off mad and irate. His mom just told me to let him go and to hell with him while she's crying and screaming in my back seat. This all felt like a repeat of the day when he tried to fight me. I'm calling Jahmel, and he's sending me straight to voicemail. I'm thinking to myself I DON'T HAVE TIME FOR THIS. Better yet I AM TIRED of THIS! Like I could have went to work for extra time and they would have just had to wait to get this check! I texted Jahmel,

"She doesn't want to go with me, where are you so I can meet you."

Jahmel: *"F*** you!"*

Me: *"Where are you! I need to figure out where you are so I can meet you."*

No response so I message back *"Hello!!!"*

Jahmel: *"F*** you we not together anymore. I don't owe you no information."*

Me: *"Well, your mom wants to go with you, so…at least tell your mom where you are."*

Jahmel: *"Bout to go get some p****, so f*** you and her."*

Me: *"I didn't do anything to you but say speak clear."*

Jahmel: *"Since you want to cheat and act like a f****** hoe. I see why they*

(my ex's) *cheated multiple times. I should have too."*

Me: *"How am I cheating?? I have never cheated nor will…and you know that!"*

Jahmel: *"F*** you."*

Me: *"Jahmel, can you tell me where you are so your mom can get back with you; and you can do what you wanna do."*

Jahmel: *"Don't text or call my s*** ever again. Oh, and I will…and I did what I wanted to do last night."*

Sad part about this is, I knew he was just bluffin, he just wanting attention.

Me: *"You probably did. Can you just let your mom in the apartment or I'll just drop y'all off so you won't walk and we'll part ways after."*

Even though he was so nasty to me and everything, I still have a heart that I was even willing just to get them home.

Jahmel: *"F*** you. Lose my number do you want to do with my mom I don't care. Just leave her there."*

I didn't know what else to say but *"Okay."* He just told me to leave his mom in the parking lot. I don't know why I was acting so shocked, this is the same guy that would get arrested sometimes on purpose to get away from her, or catch a flight in the middle of the night without her right after she cashed her check take her money and dip or go to the ER so she could become someone else's responsibility. Like dude, she gave you life!!! I don't care how mad my parents make me; I could never do that to them. The Bible clearly states, "Honor your father and mother, that your days may be prolonged in the land which the Lord your God gives you." *(Exodus 20:12)*

Jahmel: *"Come get your cable box and all the other s*** too asap."*

Me: *"I work every day, and afterward I'm with you or at house; and lately I have barely been home because I've been with you. So, there is no possible way if I wanted to cheat that I would be cheating on you and you know that."*

Jahmel: *"I want all your s*** out my house tonight."*

Me: *"I don't have anything in your house."*

Jahmel: *"You're a cheater. You can't stop talking to niggas, that's what hoes do. The cable box and the dishes either you come to get it, or it will be on your doorstep within the hour."*

HOW SWAY!? You have NO CAR!!!

Me: *"I don't talk to anybody but you. When that whole s*** went down at the beginning of our relationship last year, I stopped it after you made it clear you didn't like it and we BOTH had an understanding.* (My first ever boyfriend reached out to me, wanting to talk and apologize for putting his hands on me. It only took him nine years to accept the fact he did what he did. Jahmel saw the messages and flipped, thinking I was trying to rekindle things with him, which was negative!) *LOOK! I know I am not a cheater but if that's how you feel, then that's how you feel. I know my truth.*

Jahmel: *"Bulls*** I told you to stop. You didn't so F*** YOU! It's plenty of loyal women out there, but you just had to be the hoe."*

Me: *"I did stop! I haven't talked to any of my TWO ex's .*

Jahmel: *"SMH f*** it and f*** you. Your too stupid to understand what I say so f*** it."*

Says that guy that said "Your" instead of "You're."

Me: *"How am I stupid? I do understand, that's why when I always ask you to clarify thing you never want to, so you can't blame a person for something they don't know they're doing."*

Jahmel: *"That's all you do is try to cover up s***. It's all good. I never cheated nor attempted to. So you played yourself."*

Me: *"How did I play myself? I never cheated; I'm covering nothing up. If I would have deleted the message and not have been so open with you using my phone. Unlike yourself."*

Jahmel: *"Have a good day. I'm tired of repeating myself. So I release you to do whatever you want to do, and I'll do the same."*

This back and forth went on for a few hours with me chasing him down trying to convince this guy that I wasn't not cheating nor have I cheated on him. He then tells me that he's going to Denver in the morning because the tickets are $25 and that he needed to get out of San Antonio for a day or two if not he will ruin everything that he worked hard for. (He should have said everything that I worked for.) I told him ok, and that whatever he felt was best I support it. After saying that he responded:

"Can't go anyway, the check is not cashed and no card to put the money on. F*** IT!"

HE SUCKERED ME IN, AND I FELL FOR THE BAIT!

Me: *"I have my card; what time the flight leaves?"*

Jahmel: *"Can't go."*

Me: *"Why?"*

Jahmel: *"No money, can't get to the bus stop either. If I had the check, I could go but f*** it. Can't cash it till tomorrow and the sale ends tonight on Skyscanner."*

Me: *"What time the flight leave tho!"*

Jahmel: *"2:35 pm"*

Me: *"You still have time tho. Cash the check and stuff. I can try my card and see if it works."*

Jahmel: *"The bus leaves at 6:30 can't do it."*

Me: *"That's the only time the bus runs? Really? Why not UBER."*

Jahmel: *"The flight is out of Dallas."*

So, I started to do some research to find another flight and cheaper flight options. Crazy me getting ready to reward this boy after the little stunt he pulled earlier. I ended up paying for his airfare charging it to one of my accounts that was already overdrawn. Jahmel got me in the habit of overdrawing my account by using the ATM to take out my withdrawal limit so that we could have cash on the go, some days I would have to UBER. Most days I really felt like he was my pimp and I was his hoe, but the downfall of that, if my account is overdrawn $300-$400 when my check hits, of course, it's going to eat that negative balance then I'd be back in the same situation. My car note was barely getting paid, and it was threats of them coming to get it. His whole reason for wanting to go was to get away, clear his head, meet up with his brothers, smoke of course and come back ready to grind and land a job; and if he didn't do it, he would end up catching a case. So, if him going to Denver will let me catch my breath as well and keep him out of "trouble" …GO, PLEASE GO!

After I sent him his lientery, booked his room (that he agreed to pay for when he arrived) I asked the *"Are we okay?"* question. This negro said, *"NO!"* I thought to myself, "I just brought you a plane ticket, so you can escape and getaway to clear your head and be better for us. Then I asked you if we're ok, you say, *"NO."* Like why did I even buy the ticket? He used and manipulated me yet again to get what Jahmel wants, no matter what or how he has to get it!

Friday, December 1, 2017, It was four days before my parents celebrated their 30th wedding anniversary. BJ and I were planning something really special for them, and truth be told, I felt like my parents and brother would be mourning the loss of their daughter/sister instead of enjoying the best part of their lives.

I woke up that morning and went about my daily routine, call Jahmel to make sure he's still going with me to work. If not, I would normally lay back down a few more minutes. He told me that he was, so it was still the normal routine. I made it to Jahmel; this particular day, his mom was coming on the ride. After they drop me off, he can go with her to cash her check. It was 7:25 AM and time for me to start my shift. I think I counted maybe five pods before I saw a lady from human resources at my station. She says, *"Azure? Did I say that, right? Sorry if I butchered it."* I giggle with her and say, *"Yeah, you said it right."* After the pleasantries were out the way I saw her face get serious. I thought LORD, being fired is THE LAST thing I need right now. She says with a face of uncertainty, *"Your husband?"* I corrected her quick, shook my head and said...

"No, he's my boyfriend. Everything okay?"

HR: *"He came into the main office and said it was a family emergency and that you needed to go. We already contacted your manager, Tre', right? So just go clock out; I hope everything is okay."*

I automatically went into panic mode, thinking it was my Big Daddy. I would usually leave my phone in the car, (especially when he UBER'S for me, but for him. Totally not right but hey; we had to make it work) so I'm thinking how did they get a message to him? Maybe my mom texted me saying get to the nursing home. I was trying to process that in the back of my mind, BUT in the forefront. I was praying that God didn't take my Big Daddy.

I get around the corner a little shaky; I needed to find Tre'. Yeah, HR said they took care of it, but I had to make sure this was legit or not. I saw him, and I began fumbling with my stuff and trying to get my words out *"H..H.HR said..."*

Tre': *"I already know. GO!"*

Me: *"But Tre', I can't, I can't what if…"*

Tre': *"You won't know standing here, GO! GET OUT MY FACE! Yo' "husband" waiting."* He says with a smirk.

I cut my eyes at him and gave him my infamous side-eye; while he pointed towards the front, basically telling me to GO!

Now, my job is about the size of nine football fields: that's PREEEEETY HUGE! So imagine my little 4'9 self, coming from the back of the fourth floor, running and jumping down stairs (so not safe) to get to the front so I can figure out what's going on. I finally got to security, and as I walked out, I saw Jahmel sitting there with my phone in his hand. I felt my fast "FC walk" get slow. I walk over to him.

"What going on? Is it my Big Daddy?" my voice raised a little bit higher

"Is my BIG DADDY OKAY!??"

Jahmel: With an attitude Jahmel says *"Yeah, he's fine."*

Confused and much calmer I look at him and say *"Okay, so what's going on? Your mom, okay?"*

Jahmel: *"Yeah, let's just got! I just ETR'd you. It popped up on your phone. So I took it for you."*

ETR is excuse time request, where if I'm needing to leave for whatever reason I can put in a request for approval. Most times, it's a random thing that's offered.

I went from panic and concern to "piss-atatied" Pissed and Irritated at the same time. While snatching my phone out of his hand I said, *"SERIOUSLY JAHMEL!?"* I think he felt like I was going to make an issue, so he just wrapped his arm around my back and forced me toward the door. I think if security weren't watching, he probably would have snatched me up and dragged me out the door. We got to the car, and I am just overly confused, so I asked: *"Jahmel, where are we going?"* He responded with that 'you're annoying me' tone; *"HOME AZURE!"* He then orders me to call my god-mommy. The plan for when I got OFF work, at SIX. Was to go get her truck so that we can get the TV my Dad was giving to Jahmel for the apartment. I knew something was up because he had this look, very familiar look. I just thought it was from the mess that happened the day before. He also wanted to go cash his mother's check so that he can get to Dallas. His motive was to get out of San Antonio.

Still sitting in the passenger's seat, mad cause I could totally be making money right now; he could have cashed his mom's check without me. As we're approaching the exit to get to the apartment. He yells, *"MOM! ARE YOU HUNGRY!?"* Timid and scared she clears her throat and answers *"Y..Y...Yes Jahmel."* he whips into the Jack In A Box and pulls in the drive-through— *"MOM WHAT DO YOU WANT!?"* After Jahmel orders the food, we're waiting behind a few cars, and it's just an awkward vibe and silence. So, his mom breaks it. She sounded like she was hesitant to ask what she asked, but she did anyway *"Um...Jahmel?"* he looks up at her through the rear-view mirror like he wanted to snap her neck. *"WHAT!"* he says.

His mom: *"Um, since I cashed my check, will I be able to get my medicine?"*

Ladies and gentlemen; THAT! Was the cherry on top for him; he lets out a yell of frustration while banging his head on the headrest. I looked over at him like "Here we go!"

Jahmel: *"WHY DO YOU CONTINUE TO ASK STUPID F***ING QUESTIONS!? YES, YES, YES! YOU'RE GETTING YOUR F***ING MEDICINE."*

In my opinion, she should have just left it like that, but she kept on…

His mom: In a swirly defensive voice, *"Well, Jahmel! I just asked because I haven't gotten my medicine. You keep saying when the check comes, so I just wanted to make sure, because I need my medicine."*

Next, the thing I know the driver's door opens and I prayed he's not trying to put her out the car and throw her stuff on the street… AGAIN! (yeah, it's happened before; more than once.) He got out of the car, slams the door, puts his hood on his head and walks towards the apartment. By now I just let him go, I didn't even try to chase him, I didn't have the energy too. I climbed over to the driver's side. He's mom asked, *"Was I wrong for asking? I just want my medicine."* I told her – *"no, you wasn't wrong and either way it went, you were going to get your refills, whether I paid for it or if ya'll did; BUT you already knew he was mad, you just pushed his buttons more."*

She then tells me she's tired and fed up, he's her son, but he has some problems. I said under my breath but loud enough for her to hear me, *"oh, you got a problems too!"* I expressed to her that I couldn't continue to live like this; it's like you never know what you're going to get with Jahmel. She agreed and told me that I deserve to be happy and she wouldn't blame me if I broke up with him. She also thanked me of ALL that I do and have done for them. That made me feel good, at least she saw how kind and giving I was especially when I didn't have too. While we were talking, waiting for our turn in the drive-through to get our food. My phone goes off, YUP you guessed it; it's Jahmel.

"Bring me my phone. Now!"

Me: *"What phone? Again, I paid for the phone, it's just in your name."*

Jahmel: *"Give me my sh**, or it's on."*

Me: *"Jahmel, it's just in your name! I put the money up to get the phones, and I have paid the bills. The only phone that is indeed yours is the one you just brought for your mother."*

He never responded, and by that time we have already reached the house. We get in; I start distributing the food amongst us three. Hoping that he would eat and relax a little bit. I can't remember what question was asked or what was said, all I know things escalated QUICKLY! I hear him tell his mom, *"...You hate it so much here, then leave."* Her petty response was... *"I have the money; it's not like you can pay the rent for this place."* Next he rushes towards her room going in between her and me to get there, almost knocking us down. While he is going to her room, he's talking to himself. *"OKAY, OKAY, YOU WANT TO BE LIKE THAT! GET THE F*** OUT OF MY HOUSE! I DON'T NEED YOU! YOU'VE NEVER BEEN THERE FOR ME, I'VE BEEN ON MY OWN SINCE 10, YOU'VE NEVER DID SH** FOR ME. GET YOUR SH** AND GET OUT."*

By this time, he had deflated her bed and was packing up the stuff in her bathroom putting it in one of that bags she had when she came back from the group home. Jahmel takes the first bag, opens the front door, and throws it over the balcony (they lived on the second floor.) We both yell out. *"JAHMEL!"* I continued saying, *"JAHMEL STOP IT."* While standing in front of him grabbing his arms, so he won't throw anything else out. Yeah, that didn't work he just walked over me.

He then goes back to her room, but now he is in the closet. His mother started crying, *"just stop Jahmel."* He looks at her with that look of rage and says, *"well, are you going to get your sh** and get out?"* His mom then starts to put stuff in the bag slowly, (kind of like a kid who just got in trouble and has to pick up all their toys) yeah she was moving too slow for him, so he did it for her. He then grabbed her bras, panties, and some clothes and threw them over as well. I stood there, shocked and wondered if this was really happening. He comes back in and says, *"mom let's go!"* guiding her towards the door forcing her to go outside.

I look over the banister to see his 70-year-old mother, picking up her stuff off the ground. Bras and jeans stuck in the tree, one shoe missing, and toothbrush buried in the dirt. At that moment, I had a glimpse of what my life could be like, and I made up in my mind this is was not going to be me! I went and helped her pick up what we could off the ground, but he's steadily throwing stuff out. I told her to let me talk to him and to stay where she was. I went back upstairs to speak to him.

"JAHMEL! What is your problem? You need to go apologize because she has nowhere to go and she can't come with me."

"F*** YOU!" While I'm pleading with him to come to his senses, I heard him make a ruckus in the kitchen. He rushes out with a knife coming towards me. With my hands up while moving out of his way, I utter *"Whoa, WHOA, WHOA! What are you doing?"* Walking out of the door, he says, *"I'm going to kill that B****!"*

Me: *"Who, the manager?"*

Jahmel: *"NO! THAT B**** THAT SAYS SHE'S MY MOM!"*

Once it sunk in that he was serious, I tried to run down the stairs and past him to warn his mom. I was again, putting myself in danger to protect one of them. He got to the corner of the building before I did and sure enough she was walking towards his direction, not knowing what he had in his hands and pockets. I yell out to her, *"GO, GO! Get help!"* he says, *"NO, somebody calls the EMS cause I'm about to kill this B****!"* He throws one knife at her and Praise God; he missed. That only made him madder, he then charges at her with the bigger knife! I grab his arm and shake the knife out of his hand while I told his mom to run and get in my car. I stood on the knife so that he couldn't get to it, and I told him to leave and got back upstairs. He yells out, *"f*** y'all!"* and goes back upstairs.

I kicked the knife under a car and ran to get in the mine. I asked his mom if she okay, and like anyone, she was hysterical, crying and shaken up. I asked her where she wanted to go. I mean she still had her money; she never gave it to Jahmel or myself like she normally does. So, she finally had her ticket out and was free to go like she's wanted to do so many times and at this point, I was going to help her get away from him. I drove her up to the Jack In The Box; the plan was for me to go back to the house alone gather more of her things and try to see what I can straighten out. I asked her if she had her phone with her, so I can call and text her or she could do the same if need be. She then tells me that she has it, but Jahmel shattered the screen on it. She pulled it out, and sure enough, it looked like he took a hammer to it.

Driving back down to the house, I call Auntie London to tell her what was going on; she didn't answer. I reached the apartment; I bang on the door like I am the police, and when he opens the door I push it open! Fussing… *"what was all of that about? Like one question led to you trying to kill your mom and throwing her things out REALLY JAHMEL!?"* I could see he was getting angrier as I was talking. He kept pacing back and forth in the living room, so I told him that he needed to calm down. His response was a kicking the door to his room, which caused the whole frame to be destroyed. I ran to the door as if to rescue or hug it. (a lot of work went into getting this apartment) He then goes and punches the closet door; he thought it just made a dent. NO! It went all the way through.

I stood by the corner of the door and said to him, "*c' mon, I really need you to calm down.*" (trying not to be too close to him especially if he starts swinging) He looked at me "*you, can get the f*** out my house too. I don't want to see you. I told you it was over, and I'm done! Leave and don't ever come back.*" He's directing me to go out the door, and I'm like Jahmel "*no, we nee...*" he says "*NO? OKAY.*" He then takes me by the hood of my purple Nike hoodie and drags me out the door saying, "*Don't f***ing come back here!*" while slamming the door in my face. As I stood there shaken up looking at a closed blue door, I felt my face getting wet from the tears that were streaming down. I turn around to start walking down the stairs, to head to my car, while thinking to myself. What did I do wrong? How did we get to this point? All I wanted to do was help him and see him win.

I checked my phone to see if my Auntie London responded, she hadn't. So, I ended up going through my contacts, trying to figure something out. While I was trying to conjure up a game plan, I hear a distant voice... "*Didn't I tell your ass to leave!?*" I quickly look up, and I see his scruffy face, dirty black shirt and grey sweatpants charging my way. While I see him coming, I try not to make any sudden movements, but I slide my hand towards the button to make sure indeed my doors were locked. There was no telling what he could have done, probably drag me out of the car and try to hurt me too. More frighten because I couldn't tell if he had another knife or weapon on him.

"*OPEN THE DOOR!*" he yells while approaching my door. He tries to open it and when it didn't open, he got mad and hit my window and the top of the car. He walks around the back of the car, I'm thinking to check to see if the passenger was open, so I put my car in reverse so when he passes the trunk I can pull off; but he stands behind the trunk. I said to myself, "*OH You trying to get hit-hit.*" I looked in my rearview to see what he's doing; he then bangs on my trunk yelling

"OPEN THE F***ING TRUNK SO I CAN GET MY S***!" I see him grab one of the black trash bags that had his clothes and other things along with some laundry detergent.

He finishes getting stuff out the trunk, he comes and stands in front of my car asking *"where that b*** at? You need to go where she's at. You cheating ass funky b****! Or go to your man you cheating on me with! You dumb ass hoe! I got something for yo' ass!"* I notice while he's doing this ranting he's opening up the detergent, it all happened so fast, but he's starts pouring it on the hood of my car; then leans into the car to get the windshield! Then lastly, he throws the bottle and cap at my windshield. HARD. Like he was trying to break it. He says, *"Take that you cheating ass b***"* and walks away.

*So now for those who always wondered how that little crack in my windshield grew across and started to curve around. Yeah! This is how it happened. *

He poured it so well on the windshield that I could barely see. So, I now had to drive with this crap on my car, not fully thinking because I was filled with emotions. I tried to get it off with my wipers and while doing that, yelled out, *"it's soap AZURE! It's F***ING SOAP! UUUUGH!"*! I sped out the apartment so fast I didn't care about his mom sitting at Jack in the Box at that point. I wanted to get this s*** off my car and hope I didn't get a ticket in the process. I drove to the nearest Exxon to go through the car wash. While I was waiting in line with uncontrollable tears, I grabbed my phone to call my auntie YET AGAIN. She didn't answer. I said eff it, imma calling her office phone; it stopped ringing, and I heard *"this is Tri…"* I know it was hard for her to understand me with the crying I exclaimed *"AUNTIE, AUNTIE, AUNTIE! I can't, I can't, I can't."*

Auntie London: *"Azure? Calm down, baby, hold on.* (I click over because she was calling me from her cell) *okay, what happened, what's going on?*

I was crying like I was in "BOOKED," probably worse. I told her all that happened and that I was now at the car wash getting the soap off my car. I remember saying over and over... *"I want to call my daddy; Imma call my daddy! I'm DONE, I'M DONE! I'm telling my Daddy, Auntie, I can't do this anymore! I can't live like this anymore. I don't want this life! I feel like if I stay...* (trying to catch my breath because the tears are getting worse) *If I stay...Aun...tie. If I stay he will K..k...ki..kil..kill meeeeeeeeeee!"*

I knew she was pissed, and if she could leave work, she would be on IH-10 in a hurry to get to here. She says, *"OOOOH LAAAAAAAWD! Okay, Azzie I need you to listen to me okay?"*

Me: sniffling and snorting *"ye...yes ma'am."*

Auntie London: *"Don't call your Dad yet and I only say that because. I want you to calm down first. You're upset and thinking out of emotions... and if you call your Dad for one crying like this and you tell him what happened, that's going to be the end of it...and what you don't want is another "Light em Up" situation and y'all end up back together, and it blows over. Take a couple of hours or day to cool off. I'm only saying this because I've been there and it only gets worse. You say you're done and I believe you and if your feelings are the same tomorrow then go for it! When I was younger going through a similar situation your Granny would always tell me that I'll know when I have had enough, and she was right. So, baby you'll know."*

I didn't know what to do at that point, or where to go. I honestly thought about going back to work. I tried to get a message to Tre' through a friend that I was in trouble. I thought going back to work would be best because it was far away from him, it would be hard for him to get to me without a car and two I felt safe in knowing I had Tre' there. He was the second-best thing to a father figure other than my Dad. I couldn't call my brothers; BJ (623 miles away) and Marcus (my older brother all the way in freaking CHINA.) That message never got to Tre'. He probably couldn't do anything physically anyways because he was at work himself, where I wished I was at that moment; but I knew there was two things he could do very well, calm me down while talking sense into my head and most importantly PRAY!

While Auntie and I were talking…Jahmel was blowing my phone UP and the conversation we were having I could tell he has literally lost it!

Jahmel: *"Going to jail, so it don't fucking matter."*

Me: *"How?"*

Jahmel: *"So, you blocked me? Okay, it's on!"*

Me: *"How did I block you?"* he was calling me and sending it straight to voicemail as he would do me, so I guess that's how he thought I blocked him. I don't know.

Jahmel: *"Y'all both wanna play with me when I told you I was at my breaking point. I'm going to kill one of these police so goodbye."*

I'm still on the phone with Auntie London while I'm telling her what he's saying; she says, *"LORD! Here we go again with this bluffing sh**!"*

Me: *"What police?"*

Jahmel: *"Oh, they coming, and I'm going to kill them or myself. Have a nice life."*

Me: *"I didn't call the police."*

Jahmel: *"My mom did. I'm going to kill her before they take me. I'm done with life."*

Me: *"HOW? She doesn't have her phone. She said you shamed it."*

Jahmel: *"I should have spit in her f***ing face."*

Me: *"Idk, where she is."*

Jahmel: *"She ran to a neighbor's house by the liquor store apt 14 or 15. I saw her ass at the bus stop and was trying to give her, her debit cards, and she started screaming saying I was hitting her. So the lady came out. So, F*** her."*

Me: *"Wow"*

Jahmel: *"F*** it I'm done with life."*

"Goodbye for good this time."

"Tell Ja'Nay I love her."

Fed up and done! I still didn't want him to do anything stupid or lose his life, so I went into my psychiatrist mode.

"Why you done? You can change everything."

Jahmel: *"F*** all that. I'm killing myself last message."*

Me: *"Don't do that!"*

Auntie London says *"AWW, HELL NAH, Azure don't go back over there. He talking like that!? I don't feel comfortable with you over there alone with him. We don't know if this is a bluff or if he really is serious. How far are you away from the house? Matter of fact, I rather you be around family. I'm calling Jeff!"*

Jahmel: *"You don't give a f***, so why should I?"*

I really wanted to reply, *"You're right, I don't."* Given past history, that wouldn't be the best thing to say to hommie at that point, I wasn't petty and responded with *"How don't I?"*

Jahmel: *"You ain't here, you probably setting up your new dude apartment."*

"But I was the dumb one. Should have killed myself a long time ago."

Me: *"You told me to get the f*** out of your house and never come back. So I'm doing what you said."*

Jahmel: *"I bet you are."*

"Police at my door. I'm about to make them shoot me."

I didn't respond right off the back, because one I knew he was bluffing. Auntie London got my cousin Jeff on the line, and she told him what was going on. The first thing he said was, *"DID HE PUT HIS HANDS ON YOU!?"* Now, my cousin looks like Shug Knight but bigger so you can kind of imagine the tone he had. I told him *"No."* my sweet Auntie London; *"BULLS***! He grabbed her by her hoodie and drugged her out the door. Hell yeah he put his hand on her!"*

Jeff: *"Aw, f*** no!"* (boy I tell you they like this F word. GOODNESS!)

Cousin where you at? Just make your way here; I'm outside.

Auntie London stayed on the phone with me while I drove to Jeff's. He asked me if I ate breakfast or anything yet. Crazy thing about all of this; it wasn't even noon yet! While on the way to get food, my text messages went off, and it was Jahmel.

"You really don't give a f***. Glad I know."

Me: *"How don't I give a f*** Jahmel? When I was trying to calm you down and stuff. You grabbed me and pretty much threw me out of your house and then threw detergent on my car...like really, I didn't do anything to you. I'm not cheating on you nor have I."*

Jahmel: *"You not coming, so it don't matter."*

Me: *"Never said I wasn't...I went to check on my grandpa. He said he needed his charger so that's what I'm doing."* Just lying, because I knew if I told him I was with Jeff, he was going to flip and try to come over and fight and he probably would have DIED!

Jahmel: *"I'm about to kill someone." "It's all over for me. I love you."*

Me: *"You're choosing to make it all over when you don't have too."*

"You didn't do anything so why fight...you said that makes you look guilty."

Jahmel: *"I'm killing them if they come up here. So if I don't answer, just know I'm dead."*

Rolling my eyes to his message *"That's what I'm saying...why kill someone especially if you didn't do anything wrong. Stop talking like that; I already told you that you could change all of this."*

Jahmel: *"Can't change sh**. It's already done."*

Me: *"You can change what you want to. Now if you chose not to then, that's on you."*

Jahmel: *"F*** that. It's already done."*

Me: *"What's already done?"*

Jahmel: *"It's over now. Just about to slit my wrist and end this sh**."*

"These bitches at my door again."

Me: *"Who?"*

Jahmel: *"See how f***ed up a b**** can make the day go to s***."*

"The police."

"I'm going to kill her when I see her."

"Now, they banging on the door. F*** it I'm going out with the Knife. I'll make them shoot me."

Me: *"For what?"*

Jahmel: *"I WANT TO DIE!""Is that clear enough?"*

Going back and forth with this dude while I'm sitting at the Mexican restaurant with my cousin. It felt like I was on autopilot messaging him. I didn't mean half the stuff I said. I was really done with him and the situation. Jeff sitting there looking at me, I know he was concerned, but more than likely pissed off. I ignored his messages for a while, so that I may have time to myself and eat before I got sick. I was already feeling nauseous after what I just experienced…and all that kept going through my head was Tre"s words *"You have no idea what life would have been like for you and that child."* What if I had Harper with me and he was acting like this. It would have been a whole different story.

I look at my phone to read his newest messages

"You're not coming, so it's no point in living. The three women in my life have all left me, so it is what it is." He says.

I knew he was trying to guilt-trip me, but it wasn't working.

I'm thinking your daughter didn't leave you. He was probably acting like this, which forced her mother to act the way she acts when it comes to you having or seeing her. I was finally starting to see her side of it all and maybe just maybe she's not as evil as he makes her out to be. Her first job as a mother is to protect her child, at ALL COST! Now your mother, he would abandon HER because he didn't want to deal with her. Now me; *"Nah, I didn't leave you. You left me and told me never to come back."*

Jahmel: *"Ok, Azure. Like I said. Have fun doing what you're doing. I wish you the best in your life and future."*

Me: *"It is what it is. You were supposed to be getting away for the weekend, and you still can. If you don't do anything stupid."* I was hoping that he would remember that he has a flight the next day and that it would calm him down. When he leaves, that would be an easy way out for me. I can change my number block him, etc. Yeah, not quite.

Jahmel: *"I can't do sh**. I ain't sh** and never will be sh**. So why go."*

"You said you were just dropping off his charger. But I guess your plans changed."

"Have a good day Azure, that's more important than me. So do what you gotta do. I'll see you on the other side. You think I'm playing."

His antics went on for a while, and I was letting him. I wasn't going to stop what I was doing to go save his ass yet again. NOPE, and YES, my grandfather *is* more important than him. ABSOLUTELY! Did I want to help Jahmel, yes, I did; but not to the point where it's going to cost me my life. Jahmel, was to the point of no return. The conversations were getting worse and worse. Everything ticked him off, and he was complaining that I left him and was not there for him and everyone always turns their back on him. Me responding to his BS text messages should have shown him that I cared about him, wasn't in love with him, but I did care.

I eventually went to see my Big Daddy; I wanted to crawl in the bed with him and just lay there. While we consoled each other, he didn't want to be in there, and I was scared as HELL. Jahmel was still blowing up my phone saying, *"If you're not here in the next 30 minutes, forget I ever existed."* I kept having to explain to him that I wasn't going just to drop what I was doing and get to him. Over time while my grandfather was in the nursing home, it had gotten harder for him to pick things up, so eating and drinking got hard. I wasn't about to say *"Okay, Big Daddy I can't feed you, I have to go now. I'll see you tomorrow."* Hell no! He was barely eating as it was, and when my mother told me how he felt about Jahmel, I wasn't leaving my Big Daddy. He told them one night that he wasn't worth sh**. Big Daddy never held back his thoughts or feelings about someone, he would be blunt about it. So, to hear that those words came from him. It shook me a little because now, my Big Daddy is seeing through him.

The messages are still coming, and it was getting to the point where I was running out of things to say.

Jahmel: *"When I need people, they are never there. It's all good, maybe the devil or whoever can keep me company in hell."*

Me: *"I'm always there and have been there. Plenty of people want to see your win, but you push them away. Your Dad is always calling. People do actually care about you."*

Jahmel: *"I was and still is mad. You don't see that. You don't see that something is wrong with me, but it's all good. I'll be a loser and an asshole for my last few minutes on earth. If you're not here in 20 minutes, just know it was all your fault."*

Me: *"I'm not going to make it there in 20 minutes, Jahmel."*

Jahmel: *"Any other man would have beat your ass. Hell, they did in the past. All I did was grab your jacket to move you out the way.*

Me: *"REALLY?"*

Jahmel: *"Guess I'm not important enough. You're not coming, so stop talking."*

Me: *"I never said I wasn't"*

Jahmel: *"You choosing to sit with him when you can go back anytime, but I'm in a crisis, so I guess I gotta wait."*

Me: *"I'm feeding him Jahmel, OMG! He is having a rough time. Chill bruh."*

Jahmel: *"F*** life. You don't understand. Time to die, you don't care your still there. Obviously, you don't care enough. When I find that b**** I'm going to kill her."*

Me: *"I'm almost done here, Jahmel; just hold on."*

Jahmel: *"My blood will look good on this carpet. Deep blood."* This comment here really concerned me. I didn't know what I was going to get when I walked through that door, with his talking like this.

Me: *"Stop talking like that!"*

Jahmel: *"Blood on the walls."*

Me: *"I'm trying to help you. But you have to help me and stop talking like that seriously Jahmel. It's not going to solve anything."*

Jahmel: *"I can't calm down or sit down. Just pacing waiting for the right moment and right way to spill this blood."*

"I want to die."

Me: *"No, you don't."*

Jahmel: *"I want to die."*

"I want to die."

"I want to die."

"I want to die."

"I want to die."

"Life is not fun anymore."

"Never has been"

"I want to die."

The *"I want to die"* and *"I don't want to live"* text messages kept coming. I finally make it over to his apartment after taking my time. I walked in the house, no blood anywhere, just a few plates and broken glass from when he threw them at the wall earlier that morning. After all of that, he was still trying to figure out if I had talked to my God-mother, so we can get the TV from my house. I told him that the TV was the furthest thing from my mind at the time. Jahmel insisted on going down to the other apartments where the lady called the police.

The story he tells me is that he went down the street to go try to find his mom, so that he can give her, her debit card and identification card and that he found her at the bus stop. (didn't I tell her to stay at Jack in the Box!!?) She didn't want to talk to him and made a big scene and flinched every time he came near her. To the point where it drew the attention of the neighbor and the trash collection man because she was screaming. Jahmel said the trash guy pulled over and was telling him not to talk to his mother like that and not to pull on her. Jahmel, said he explained that she had dementia and she ran off, and he was trying to get her home. That's when dude backed off, but the neighbor wasn't buying it. She called out to his mom, and that's when she ran over to her for safety.

Well, I did what Jahmel asked and went to the lady's apartment. I parked to where she could see the car but wouldn't be able to see the passenger side with him in it. I knocked on the door a couple of times, and there was no answer. I started to walk away until I heard the latched on the door unlocking and the door opening. I say, *"Hello, I was told you might know about my boyfriends' mother."*

Lady: She says, *"Yes, she isn't here, though."*

Me: *"Okay, do you know where she may be or what happened. I told her to stay at the Jack in the Box; I went back she was gone."*

Lady: Looking around out in the parking lot, and on to the street, she asked, *"What's your name again?"*

Me: *"Azure"*

Lady: *"Okay, Ms. E said you would try to come looking for her,* (looking towards my car) *yeah with the sliver car are you, okay sweetheart?"*

Me: *"Yes, ma'am **I'm fine**. I'm just trying to make sure she's okay and figure out what happened. If she's by herself, I want to make sure she okay because she does have dementia."*

Lady: *"Yeah, she's not here; the police came and ended up taking her. I'm pretty sure to APS; I work for them, so I know how that works. But her son is very disrespectful. I was sitting here watching TV while my husband got ready for work and I hear a woman screaming and a guy cursing. It was a lot of commotion, so I look outside, and he has her pinned up against the fence by her neck. The side of her face was smashed in the fence. I opened my door and yell out to him, get off of her and let her go. He told me to "mind your f***ing business b****"* (I'm thinking, yeah what she's saying definitely fit his persona and is telling the truth.) *Some random guy tries to stop him, but he's not listening. While they're arguing, I call out to her to run over her so that she can get away from him. He runs over cursing me out, and my husband told him that he needed to leave before he calls the cops. He ends up leaving, but my husband told me that if he comes back, to shoot and asked questions later. So, if he comes back, I am ready. I gave my report to the police, and they took her with them."*

Now her story seemed legit, up until the police took her. Why would they take her? She didn't commit a crime. I honestly think she was in the lady's house waiting on APS to come and pick her up. In my head, she was safe because she wasn't on the street and she had money to go wherever she wanted to go. So that situation is good. I get back in the car and say, *"Jahmel, you had her pinned to the fence by her NECK!??"*

Jahmel: *"What? Did that b**** say that? OOOH, I promise imma come back and kill that hoe. No, she pushed herself on the fence screaming and hollering, I was trying to give her – her cards."*

I honestly believed the lady more than I believed him after I saw him try to kill her by throwing knives. I definitely would not put that past him. Jahmel is now trying to call the lady we were in contact with while his mother was in APS custody the first time and he was reaching a dead end. So, he actually called the office, and the lady at the front desk was kind of rude, that I'll admit, but Jahmel, cursing at her didn't make it better. After about the third time of him calling the lady, he got fed up, and he started punching my dashboard multiple times (a few days later I notice my airbag light was on and some of the features were weird. So, I googled it, and I found out that if your car has been in an accident or the airbag location has had any impact the car will think that it was in an accident and if and when you get in an accident the airbags may not deploy. I could either replace it at $6,000 or reset the light. That's when I remembered him punching the area where my airbag is.) and started screaming, hyperventilating and banging his head on the headrest. He then starts ripping his clothes. I'm sitting there so annoyed and over it while he's going through the motions. It lasted for about a good 3 minutes, and I made him stop because he was going to make himself sick and drive me crazier.

We went back to the house first, so he can change his torn-up clothes because he wanted to head to APS to try to get some answers. I thought the worst of him trying to kill someone was over until he turned on me. I think the fact of seeing his mom's room trigged some of his anger. He goes and starts cutting the rest of her clothes that were in her closet. He grabbed the mop in glow out of the kitchen and poured it on everything in her room and closet, and takes out his lighter and says, *"I'm bout to burn this b****."* I quickly grabbed the lighter out of his hand. *"you burn the closet you burn the whole APARTMENT!"*

"OOO, THIS! This will hurt her feelings really bad! Yeah!" he said as he grabbed the only funeral program, his mom had of her sister that

passed away a few months prior. He tore it in pieces and stomped on it. While he was stomping and spitting on her stuff, I grabbed his arm and pulled him out of the closet and dragged him by his shirt out of the room and swung him on to the wall and pinned him against it. Yes, little ole me, had this big dude up on the wall. He is fussing for me to let him go; I told him I wouldn't until he calmed down. He calmed down enough for me to let him go.

I should have known something was up when he went in to the kitchen, and I heard him rumbling in the drawers again. He came back out more frustrated and empty-handed; and while my back was turned towards him, I hear him say, *"Is this what you want?* (the real creepy part about it was, he was laughing.) *Imma just do it now, since you're here."*

I turned around to see him holding a butcher knife up to his neck. I dropped my phone and automatically put my hands up calmly saying *"Jahmel, put the knife down!"* He puts the knife closer to his neck while walking towards me. Still pleading with him to drop it. He moves it down to his wrist, *"hmm, maybe I should go here and finish it."* Putting the knife back up to his neck I ran over to him, grabbing his arms and pushed his back against the wall like I did while I had him pinned. I'm pleading with him to drop the knife; he was pushing the tip closer to his neck while I'm using all my strength, pulling it away from him. *He says "you'll get to see me die; I'll bleed faster this way."* Next thing I know he turns it around on me. One of his heads is wrapped around my neck, gripping my shirt with it, while the knife is in the other hand, pointing at my face trying to drop to my neck. Both of my hands were on his arms, trying to push the knife away from me. While this is happening, he's saying *"why shouldn't I just kill your cheating ass too! You're only going to leave me and if I can't have you know one else should, because you'll cheat on them too."*

I'm looking at him with tears rolling down my face saying *"Jahmel, please don't do this. Please put the knife down."* His grip got tighter, and all I could do was call on JESUS. *"Oh, God, help me please, please Jesus, help me."* He says, *"Yeah, you better call him to help you, or can he?"* I keep calling on HIM; I saw my life flash before my eyes. I thought he was really going to kill me. I started to feel his grip loosen, and the hand with the knife starts to get lower. That's when I put my karate move my Fabio taught me to use; I'm pretty sure I did it wrong. It worked cause I'm telling the story. The knife fell to the ground and so did Jahmel. He was looking up at the ceiling laughing more like crazy laughter. I picked up the knife and put it in my purse and went to grab the rest of the knives, well, what was left and put them in my purse as well.

Eye's full of tears I told him I was leaving, and that I couldn't stay there longer. He told me that he understood, but I should at least help him find where his mother was. Stupidly I agreed, I was afraid of saying no, he probably would have choked me to death. But first, he wanted to go get some weed, so of course, I hit up the weed man and tell him that Jahmel wanted an eighth. I wanted him to smoke at this point because if this was going to calm him down…PLEASE DO IT, he rolled up and smoked, and honestly after almost losing my life I should have rolled one up myself; but I wanted a drink instead and go home. After he had a few puffs we headed over to APS. I didn't want to go in because I didn't want to be mixed up in it like I was last time. I wanted no parts! So at that point, there is no definite answer on where his mom really was. I was finally able to get in touch with my god-mommy, and we meet her at her job so that we can switch cars so that he can get this TV he been hollering about all day. He felt that watching TV that night would take his mind off of all that happened as well as his suicidal ideations. After doing all the moves and car switching.

I finally made it back home. I started getting ready for work the next day; I get in the shower and thank the Lord for sparing my life, and I just cried, cried, and cried. Before I went to bed, I told my parents I loved them and to have fun on their pre-anniversary vacation, and I would see them once they came back. My parents not knowing ANYTHING that took place hours before, let alone that I had a knife pointed at my face. I got in bed and cried again. He could have indeed killed me that night, but it was only by the Grace of God and the prayers of the righteous that avails much that I am here today to tell the story. As I'm preparing to pretty much cry myself to sleep, I get a text message from Jahmel saying…

"I'll probably die tonight for everything I did today. I swear I didn't hit my mom all I was trying to do was give her the card back and that's it. She jumped on the fence and damn near fell, and I grabbed her. You know if I would have hit her, they could have kicked down my door and did all that. The lady wasn't even out there until she heard my mom yell. So, if I die, I die."

Me: *Jahmel, don't think like that.*

Jahmel: *"I'm serious. I lost it today for real. It's like all that sh** came out at once. Thirty-one years of repressed memories and let downs. Not being loved or even cared for. It's like my pops just gave up on me and was like when he's older he will reach out…. HOW if we have no relationship. Yeah, my mom may have messed me up but that don't have sh** to do with me and you* (talking about his dad). *My mom, bruh it's like she antagonized me to a level of where she knows I'll go off and it always comes when she gets money in her hands. It may have seemed like a simple question she asked, but I got asked that same question 10 times that same morning that's why I was in a rush to get to San Antonio to get her check cashed and get her medicine, but she kept at me that's why I got out the car and walked* *home. Soon as she got inside, I'm an ungrateful nigga who steals her money and does all this foul sh** too. HOW? I busted my ass to get this apartment so that she was as comfortable as possible. So I know I was wrong, but I'm not 100% to blame for this. Sorry for the long text."*

My response was, *"It needed to come out, so you can start to heal. The way it came out was not right. I didn't know she asked the question before then. I would have just answered it for you and took care of it. I knew you got out so that you could walk it off and I told her that. I wasn't even mad, nor did I try to stop you. Yes, you busted your ass, we both did so she can be comfortable, safe, and finally get what she has been waiting. As far as the blame, both of you all are to blame. You all know each other's buttons and y'all like to test them quite frequently."*

I was over it and him, did I really want to respond? NO! I literally just escaped death and being terrified of what he could do to himself or me…I told him what I felt he wanted to hear.

The next day at work, after our huddle, I went up to Tre', and he asked, *"how's Grandpa?"* I looked at him with such disappointment and said, *"BRUH, it wasn't even HIM! This dude excused the rest of my day for me. HIS SELF! Had me thinking that something was wrong with my Big Daddy."* Tre' was HOT! He looked at me and said, *"WHAT!? He ETR'd you!? Explain Blue!!"* I told him how he went about ETR'ing me and the whole mess that I encountered.

His response was a response of a concerned father, uncle, and big brother. *"I want you to listen to me and HEAR ME! When my people come to me with their problems and situations, I take their word for it. If they need to leave, I'll let them go. Now, once I feel like it's being taken advantage of that's where I draw the line. Don't ever get to the point where you cross me. PLEASE, understand I am not mad at YOU, nowhere near mad at you. But I need you to understand that.* Deep inside I was mad that he was disappointed, like Jahmel didn't know of the conversation Tre' and I had about him and how he was helping me cope and work towards getting out of this situation and that one little stunt could have ended a good working relationship.

NOW! About this situation…Blue, when are you gonna get tired of the same ole same ole??? YOU CAN'T HELP EVERYBODY! You take on entirely too much. You're going to get to the point where you snap, right now your bent so far that you're one day, one argument away from snapping and once you snap! It's going be hard to try to fix yourself back. Trust me, I know. You gotta stop trying to play GOD! Once you stop playing God and let go and give everything over to him, things will start to turn around! I'm proof of it! How far are you willing to bend before you break?

You have not been yourself. When you come in for work, I use to see you walk this long mile, and I would see that glow and a bright smile. Now, you're just here unhappy. You're not happy, Blue. Your joy is gone, and you need to get that back. Because this guy is robbing you of that. Feeling convicted because of everything he's saying and just full of emotions I start balling, I mean the "ugly cry." *Why are you crying? You're crying because there's no other outlet…did crying fix your problem? Others cry because they are lost. Tell me something, Are these tears worth it??"*

Confused as to what he was saying… *"If you can look at me straight in the eyes and tell me the tears that are rolling down your face, and this that you have going on right now is WORTH IT. I will say okay Blue; you see that in the end, your tears that you cried on this day would be worth it. I would be okay with that. So, are sure they're worth it Blue?"*

Looking him in the eyes trying to force myself to say these tears are worth it, I find myself making the "ugly cry" worse. While shaking my head uncontrollably saying *"NO."* Tre' continues, *"Okay then stop it! You think your Father (God) likes seeing his daughter cry? I don't like seeing you like this. You have to let it go Blue! LET HIM GO!"*

A few days after Jahmel's psychotic break, he gets mad at me yet again, because I did not call him on my last break. In the midst of him arguing with me and doing the same ole same ole, he ends one of his arguments with... *"Enjoy your night, do you. Oh, and I have to be out by Monday. I'm getting evicted"* with a smiley face emoji.

I was trying to figure out why he was getting evicted it hadn't been three months with nonpayment. It was just a few weeks. Apparently, they can evict someone at any time. I told him to go back and check his lease because something still didn't seem right. His response

"It don't matter, and I give up. Got a warrant for my arrest too—Battery with body injury's."

Me: *"Hooooooooooow!?"*

Jahmel: *"They (APS) filled charges so f*** it. That's why I was calling you. It's all good like I said I give up. My anger is at an all-time high I'm really about to spaz out again. My mom told them that I used hard drugs too. Like crack and cocaine and that I've hit you, but you won't press charges. She didn't want to leave the group home, but we forced her to leave, and that we have both been banned from the street and if I go, it's an immediate arrest."*

Me: *"Whoa, whoa, How did we force her to leave when she kept saying she didn't want to stay there, and she told APS she didn't want to stay as well, so what the f*** are they talking about?"*

Jahmel: *"APS opened another case for assault, theft, elderly abuse, and bank fraud. So it's over for me. Whether it's true or not, it matters to no one."*

Just when I thought things couldn't get worse, they did! I was definitely getting ready to hit my ***BREAKING POINT!***

The Breaking Point

Erika finally made the move back home to San Antonio officially, and she wanted me to help her unpack ALL her stuff especially since it was the last day her little sister and nephew would be in town before flying back to Alabama. She was basically using us for FREE LABOR!!! So, I wanted to go hang out with my cousins and be there for her. I texted Jahmel to know the tentative plan for the next day.

"Hey, a tentative plan for tomorrow. Take me to work...you'll go drive. I ETR if they have it. Drop me off at Erika's, and you can go drive again."

Jahmel: *"Okay, sounds good."*

Sounds simple right? Of course, Jahmel made it more complicated than it should have been. I got up that morning, picked him up, and we head out to my job. We got there around 6:45. At seven o'clock, ETR popped up, so I took it. I was going to take it anyways, so why not hop on this opportunity early.

"OHH.ETR!" I excitingly said to Jahmel. *"C' mon babe, let's go."*

Jahmel lets out a long, frustrating sigh *"Seriously Azure, why would you do that. I was supposed to drive!*

Me: *You can still drive Jahmel, nothing has changed. I just took ETR earlier. You can still drive...we'll just head back home now, maybe get breakfast; if Erika isn't awake, she can just get me from your house, while you're driving. No big deal."*

Yeah, he wasn't too happy with that choice, and at that point, I didn't care. It's my car, and I wanted it to take me back to San Antonio. On the way back, I gave Erika a call; I knew she wasn't up yet, being that she doesn't wake up till around 11 or noon; just like my Nanny used to do. But he still could have easily dropped me off and went on and drove. Now one part I didn't factor in, was that I wouldn't have a cell phone to call since he was using mine to UBER; and most times he needed his incase he gets that call for "that job."

The majority of the ride was silent until he got road rage. I thought I had bad road rage; I'll just honk my horn, flash my lights, or slow down if…okay, well I guess my road rage is pretty bad. But he's rage would make the *60 Minute* segment. Jahmel was trying to get over into another lane because a car in front of him was driving slow and of course Jahmel was speeding, which caused him to have the hit the brakes. He also had to wait for the car in the right lane to pass so he would be able to get over to pass the slow car. Once that happened Jahmel gets over in the lane, and upon passing the car up, he reaches for the open Sprite bottle in the cup holder then rolls down the window. Realizing he's getting ready to throw a bottle at another car, let alone an OPEN one. I immediately go into action!

Reaching for his arm so it won't raise high enough to throw it I'm yelling at him *"Jahmel, the bottle is open, you'll be doing more damage to my car than HIS!! The soda is going to spill all in here, bro. Think and calm down for a change, OMG!"* Just as I thought, I was right…while he was throwing an open soda bottle out of a car going at least 65miles an hour since he had to slow down to meet up with the car. He makes eye contact with the car and yells *"LEARN HOW TO F***ING DRIVE YOU STUPID F***."* Then throws the bottle at the car, of course, it missed cause the wind took it, and the contents of the bottle were now all on the dashboard, window, steering wheel, door jams and hood on my car.

"REALLY JAHMEL, ARE YOU SERIOUS RIGHT NOW. Like I

*Have **HAD IT!** I don't know what your problem is. YOU don't think before you react, you always talking about me being stupid and not thinking before I speak. Did you really think that soda was going to impact that car at all? NO, now I have to get my car washed and detailed, which cost a good coin! You mad about this ETR and stuff acting like I said let's go back to San Antonio, and I'm going to take my car, and you stay home! LIKE GET OVER YOURSELF…seriously and QUICK, cause, THIS. I can't do it."*

"Don't put this on me!" Jahmel yells out. *"So, tell me Azure; what was the whole point of driving all the way out there if you were going to take ETR!? I don't mind you taking ETR, but you didn't even make it into the building. You wonder why you hadn't moved up yet because you always take ETR. Managers look at that stuff; I'm surprised they hadn't fired your ass yet. You get fired then what? You can't rely on your so-called graphics business. Your barley doing anything with it, a project here a project there."*

Me: *"I'm not trying to argue with you today, but you don't know when to stop. I take so much ETR because of you! If I don't have to leave early to come to your stupid rescues or diffuse a fight between you and your mom or go chase one of y'all over San Antonio and lastly YOU ETR'n me for me! I can't do any designs because of you! Please tell me! When do I have time to design anything? Between UBER'n on my OFF DAYS, running around the city with and for you and lastly, when I'm not doing that I'm trying to work 10 hours a day."*

The arguing continues all the way until we hit his house; both giving each other the silent treatment we walk into the house. He's in there long enough to use the bathroom and drink some juice. He said to lock the door on his way out and slams the door behind him. Like whoa, dude, where are you going...IN MY CAR. While I felt the vibrations of the slammed door, my heart sunk, I just hoped he went to get some food or to UBER.

I didn't want to take my shoes off, put my purse on the counter or sit on the floor because he still had a few unwanted guests around and I did NOT want to bring those jokers home with me and yeah, no furniture in the house yet. So, I just walked around and paced back and forth, I tried to call him, but then I remembered that he had my phone and his. So, I was really stuck. I opened the door to his mother's room to see what more damaged he done and surprisingly it was just how I remembered it on the 1st of December.

I felt this heavy urge to pray I wasn't sure why I was being led to pray, but I was obedient. I don't know what to pray for, but I knew where to start. With a heavy heart, I let out a deep sigh and followed it with

"Father God, in the Name of Jesus! I come before you now God. You see my heart and my struggles. You see what I'm going through daily. God, please touch my heart and touch my mind, God, give me peace in this situation that I'm going through. I ask that you touch Jahmel God. God, I ask that you soften his heart, wherever he is right now. God wrap your loving arms of protection around him right now God. Let your Angels encamp around him. God as I pray, I asked that you work on him; that he may be able to gain peace. God, I ask that you comfort his mother. God, protect her from all hurt, harm, and danger where she is Lord, that she will find peace in her situation she is in right now. God thank you for never leaving my side. Thank you for life, health, and strength; thank you for saving me the other day. God that was nobody but your Grace and Mercy that kept me that night. God, it was you that stopped that knife for going into my

neck or my body. God I just, (with tears flowing down my face and my hands raise to HIM.) *GOD, I THANK YOU! THANK YOU, GOD, for sparing my life JESUS! God, I'm tired, I'm tired I...I can't do this anymore though God help me to be strong to walk away from this. God, I want to be happy. God, I wanna be happy, I wanna be happy. God, I wanna be so happy, so I don't have to continue to go through this and worry about if I will make it through the day. I know how a man should treat me. I have that blueprint at home. God, I just ask if it is your will, send me that man that will treat me right. Like my Dad treats my Mom, how my Uncles treat my Aunties. I know I am not perfect, but I know you have someone designed for me. God place him in my life in your timing though, because this is not what I deserve. I know I am worth more than this Jesus, I'm worth more than this guy and how he acts and treats me.*

God, I lay everything at your feet God like Tre' said I give it all to you— like I can't do this anymore. I don't wanna continue to get to the point where I'm slowly breaking. I...I don't wanna snap or be so far gone that it'll be hard for me to come back. God get me back to you, I'm running back to you God, I know your arms are open wide and I don't have to cry any more, I'm tired of fear; I don't want to be in pain anymore; I'm tired of the headaches— Imma give it all to you God. Have your way in this relationship; have your way in my job and in my life. I just I give it all to you God so you can have your way and that you will be able to move how your gonna move. I give you total control over my life; I no longer wanna drive. I'll let you have it God and also whatever you decide to do help me be OK with your decision. Help me be OK with whatever happens next whether it's removing him out of the situation or myself.

Allow me and help me to be OK with and accept what you have worked out, and God when that decision is made, God guide me to where I won't fall backwards. I don't want to go backwards. I don't want to go running to him or to his rescue as I have always done. God, thank you for allowing Tre' to talk some truth into me. I can plant the seed, but I am not obligated to put all my time into it while it grows. Help me walk away from things that are not your will; and if this is your will God, show me, so I will know it is your best for me. God, I just wanna be happy, and I can't do this on my own anymore. I'm done trying to be you, and I'm done trying to fix people I just want to be happy. I wanna have Azure back; I wanna enjoy the things that I am used to enjoying. I wanna have my money back! I just thank you for your Grace and Mercy God I thank you for your healing power. I thank you for being God and God alone. Thank you for never giving up on me. God I just thank you for always being there in the midst of every situation; for sparing my life when there were many times God where my life was hanging in the balance and should have ended. Thank you, God, for your protection and the prayers of my loved ones. I thank you God, I wash my hands to it God, I dust it off God, and I lay all my troubles, God I lay it on the alter and release it all to you, Lord. Jesus takes the wheel in my life…GOD, I THANK YOU! GOD. I THANK YOU! GOD! I THANK YOU!"

While I was thanking God for his love and protection, the Holy Ghost took over. For those who may not know what the Holy Ghost is; It is the visitation of the power of God upon a sanctified believer; the in-filling of God's Spirit and power in us with the initial evidence of speaking in other tongues/language.

While I was speaking in my heavenly language, I began to walk through every inch on the apartment pleading the Blood of Jesus over everything and asking God to remove everything that is not like him out of the house…then what I was done speaking in my heavenly language I end my prayer with *"These things I ask, In Jesus Name…Amen."* When I tell you, I felt this peace come over me; and all the heaviness I was feeling was gone. It felt like I just prayed all the *HELL* out of my life and it was replaced with a hug. I felt so light, and I had an instant smile on my face, and at that moment, I knew that God had heard my prayers, and he was already working things out for my good.

About ten minutes after I prayed, Jahmel came banging on the door. He walked in…no greeting or anything, but I was perfectly fine. I just prayed, and nothing was going to take me out of that vein. *"Call you, cousin!"* he say's handing me my phone with an attitude.

Me: *"Did she call me?"*

Jahmel: *"DID I SAY SHE CALLED? Just call her to see if she up so I can take you over there so I can get back to UBER'n!"*

He dropped me off at Erika's house, and she could tell that I have been crying, but didn't want to ask. I followed behind her to her bathroom and said, *"Erika? Can I have a hug?"* She quickly stopped what she was doing looked at me *"Yes, babe, of course, you can."* While I hugged her, I noticed it was the same hug I felt after I prayed… I just cried on her shoulder. She looked at me, wiped my tears *"Everything is going to be okay. Okay? Now let's unpack these boxes! Mmmkay!?"* We both laughed and started unpacking and decorating the house.

The Break Up

I tell you, not even 24 hours God already started moving and shifting things. I was on my last break when I saw a missed call from my Uncle Mike; my Big Daddy's only living son. I was trying to figure out why he called me. I checked the rest of my missed calls to make sure my mom didn't call around the same time. When I saw that he was the only missed call from that time, I decided to call him back. The conversation that we had automatically put me in-game mode, and it was time to make the winning shot to end the game.

"Hey, Azure. How is it, goin?"

Me: *"O, nothing much, at work."*

Uncle Mike: *"Well, okay, I won't keep you long. I just wanted to ask you, had you been over to the house and take a pistol out of my drawer?"*

In a shocked and confused tone, *"No!?!?"*

Uncle Mike: *"Well then, I can't put my hands on that pistol for nothing. That's the only place I kept it at."*

Me: *"No, I didn't even know you had a gun in the drawer."*

Uncle Mike: *"Yeah, that's what I said too, that nobody knows. The only reason why I'm asking you and your mama…"*

Finishing his sentence *"…Cause we both have keys."* I knew I hadn't been to the house in a while, as well as my mom. The only person that came to mind was. JAHMEL! I had the rush of anger come over me! I tried not to let Uncle Mike know I had an idea who might have taken it; although he probably had the same idea I had. My legs started shaking because I was ready to hurt JAHMEL.

Uncle Mike: *"…yeah, y'all have key's, and it shows no sign of anybody breaking in. So, somebody else knows."*

Me: *"Yeah and HAS A KEY!"*

Uncle Mike: *"Exactly! 'has a key.' Well, I was just checking, I want to make a police report, but I want to do some more digging first."*

After we hung up, I immediately called Jahmel, and the tone of his voice and how defensive he got gave me my answer.

"Hello," Jahmel says, answering the phone.

Trying so hard not to let any attitude come through my voice and not wanting to ask that question straight off the back, we were talking about my day and the Chris Brown documentary he was watching about Chris and Rihanna and also looking at cheap unlocked iPhone. I was trying to get my iPhone back as my Christmas gift. There was the awkward silence and I felt like that was my cue.

Me: *"Hey, have you gone over to my grandpa's house?"* That awkward silence lingered for a few more seconds.

"Huh…why?" Jahmel asks

Me: *"Just asking a question Jahmel."*

Jahmel: *"Nah un, the last time I was there was…. the day…the day…. You went over there to get the money for your grandpa. They got one for $99."* While trying to change the subject. He kept talking about the iPhone's and how *e*Bay had one for $99

Me: *"…I don't trust eBay."*

Jahmel: *"But, what's going on at your grandpa's house?"*

Me: *"Oh, nothing. Uncle Mike called me and said that he was over there the other day and noticed that some stuff was out of place..."*

Jahmel cutting me off *"... like what!?"*

Me: *"He didn't say what it was, it was just some stuff out of place, and he wanted to ask my mama and me because we're the only ones that have a key. He's looking for something, and he can't find it..."*

Jahmel: *".... Um, so, so you just ask me?"*

Me: *"What?"* trying to play it cool

Jahmel: *"So you just, you just decided to ask me."*

Me: *"You have access to the keys too."*

Jahmel: *"WHAT! WHAT KEY! I DON'T HAVE ACCESS TO YOUR GRANDPA'S KEY'S"*

Smiling, shaking my head, thinking "GOT EM" that was the response I was waiting for. In a soft tone *"man why you getting all...I just asked a question."* He tries to match my tone, *"I'm not; I'm just saying, I don't have access to your grandpa's keys though."*

Me: *"But they're in my purse. You could have been in the area and needed to use the restroom. I don't know Jahmel, it's just a question."*

Jahmel: *"Whaa..."* he scuffs and sighs *okay? Yeah, yeah, let's just end this before it goes any further."*

...and that's exactly what he did. Changed the subject and I went along with it because I didn't want him to know I knew something that I wasn't telling him, but that was all I needed to hear. I was beyond mad. I was LIVIT, and that's to degrees passed pissed! Like, how do you have the audacity to go and steal something from my family, let alone my BIG DADDY'S HOUSE?? Knowing his situation and how much he means to me you go and do that! Yeah, I was completely done, if he had the gun a few weeks ago, he could have shot all three of us.

Now, going back into work I was in fight mode and trying to figure out where this gun is. I probably picked like a 400 because I was so mad. When I got home, that night, Fabio calls me in to the room, and he had that look on his face; and all I could think was, what did I do now? Well my neighbor, reached out to Fabio and asked him how he felt about Jahmel. Dad told him he couldn't stand the fella. My neighbor didn't want to say anything bad if my dad indeed liked Jahmel. Fabio came to find out, the night we were picking up the TV from the house when he and his family was leaving, and he came over to greet me and Jahmel, but when I walked away. My neighbor said that he told Jahmel he was getting ready to look at some trees for the kiddos. Jahmel pulled out "his trees" and wanted to know if he wanted to buy some. But my neighbor was talking about CHRISTMAS TREES.

He felt like he needed to tell my dad, due to the high level of respect he has for him and our family. So not only did he use my key to walk through my Big Daddy's house and stole a gun and God knows what else, he asked my neighbor who we're closed too and thought that he was trying to hook up with me if he wanted to buy some weed! Yeah, that was enough for me! Fabio made it clear that he no longer wanted him on the property. After the fight we had outside, Dad didn't want him in the house unless he approved. Now, he didn't want him on the street; and I was perfectly okay with that.

A few days went by, and it is now Friday, December 15, 2017. I was headed out to work as usual, and I always go and let my parents know I'm leaving. Fabio prays over me, and I kiss Mommy on the way out, this is a typical morning. While I gave my mommy kiss, and before I could pull away, she grabs my wrist. Her grab triggered some emotions, and I felt myself want to get defensive and wanted snatch away, but I realize that I was okay, because it was mommy. She asked, *"Azure, do you be picking up Jahmel? Does he have your car when you're at work?"* Trying not to get defensive I say *"sometimes"*— she sits up and I see her big green eyes, and she says *"be careful honey. I don't know what this is, but I don't feel right about that, I have this knot in my stomach Azure."* When she said that I immediately got that knot in my throat like something isn't right, or something is getting ready to happen, then I remember one of the posts I saw on IG; it was a picture of a car shot up with the caption saying *"Ladies, stop letting you man drive your car while you are working and he out her beef'n and causing issues with other people. They're not going to check to see if it's him in the car before they start shooting."* When I saw that that it hit home with me because Jahmel had a bad mouth and was very hot-tempered.

So, while getting in the car, I was trying to shake this feeling, but I couldn't. I pulled out my phone to call Jahmel to tell him I wasn't coming. I got a text from him saying to go ahead and without him. I gave him a call anyways to tell him how I was feeling. He said he had a weird feeling as well; he thought that he may get pulled over. I was thinking on the line of an accident. So, for once we were on the same page, and I was happy that I listened to my mommy and didn't take it as if I was being attacked.

I came out to my car to check my phone and called Jahmel like I normally do for lunch and my last break. Our conversation for lunch was short because he was asleep. Apparently, when we got off the phone, he texted me and asked if I could order him a pizza; but I had already gone back inside. When I came out on my last break, I was greeted with an angry text from Jahmel with him going completely off!

"I know you saw that message…kinda f***ed up. I sent it less than two minutes after we got off the phone. Like I said it's tension coming from somewhere. So I'll let you do your thing tonight. Don't worry about food or calling. Do you. And yes, I'm quite pissed off. Just FYI."

After reading his text messages, I rolled my eyes and called him anyway. He was going off on me because he thought that I read the text message about the pizza, but I hadn't because as soon as I got off the phone, I turned my car off and got out. He was not having it though and thought I was lying and that I was full of s***.

He assumed I was lying about going to hang out with my mom, and felt that ever since Erika came back home, I had been acting differently. He felt like she got in my ear and was telling me a whole bunch of mess about him and persuading me to leave him. He also blamed it on my mom. He felt like since she asked about him driving me to work, she was being negative and getting in my head and that over the last couple of days she was the cause of my attitude changing towards him. He kept saying he knew why my attitude and mood had changed but he would never say what it was. I'm thinking, yeah, it did change. After finding out he went into my grandfather's house; YES, I looked at him completely different, it's really hard for me to be fake so I'm sure that was coming out a little in our conversations and interactions.

Before we hung up, he said, *"Look, I'm tired, you're tired. You send me something to eat cool if you don't, I don't care. You come over here when you get off before you go hang with your "mom" and it's going to be the end of it probably."* I shrug my shoulders and say, *"Okay!"*

"OKAY!?" He said surprisingly, because I didn't try to fight for our relationship. *"Yeah, OKAY!"* I said snappishly. After I said it I felt confident and didn't plan on taking it back.

He hangs up and sends me a threating message saying that I will regret my decision then calls me right after, in complete threat mood.

"Imma say this, and you can take it however you want to, whatever moves and decisions you make, I can do the same just know that."

Me: responding emotionless *"...as far as what sweetheart? What are you referring to?"*

Jahmel: *"I'm, not referring to anything, I'm just making a statement... just know what you do. Just.... Just... just be careful."*

Me: *"Oh, so you're threatening me now?"*

Jahmel: *"I'm not threating anybody I don't have time to threaten you, all I said was be careful in the actions and decisions that you make. It's just you're pulling away from me."*

The gist of the conversation was that I was pulling away from him and that we didn't do anything anymore; and that I rather spend time with Erika and my other family. HECK YES, I want to spend time with Erika and my family— one of my little cousins just had her second child, and I wasn't going to miss that. Erika and I had been separated since our freshmen year in high school and it was important to me to catch up on lost time. Jahmel didn't understand that. In that conversation, I was starting to see clearly the hold on me, and how so consumed with him. I began to realize that because he was miserable, he wanted me to be miserable with him. But I wasn't settling for that anymore, I just told the Lord I wanted to be happy, and that's what I was going to be.

We pretty much ended on him saying it's basically over and me agreeing. Usually, I would be "oh, baby wait. Let's fix it." Or "No, let's fix it and talk about it." Nope, not this time. I was like "okay, BET!", hung up the phone and walked back into work feeling FREE! I was so excited. I was looking for Tre' to tell him I finally did it! I broke up with Jahmel. BUT, in the back of my head, I still needed to find this gun! I asked the Lord to reveal the location of the gun to me. I thought of two places; My storage unit and the TV box that was sitting in his living room.

I got off an hour early, and I called my mom to tell her I was going to run by Jahmel's for a second then I would be on my way to come pick her up for our date. One the way to his house I call Erika to tell her what I was up to; she says, *"Hey babe, what's up?"*

Me: *"Oh nothing, just got off work. On my way to break up with Jahmel."*

Erika: *"Wait! Like right now, right now?"*

Me: *"Yes, right now, right now!"*

Erika: with her Eddie Murphy laugh *"Well shit, alright then, go girl! Haha!"* I swear, I love her silly self. She was shocked and happy I was finally getting it over with and so was I.

When I arrived to the apartment, I walked in to secretly look for the gun and finalize the break up. None of those things happened, because he was too concerned with the cluster of baby roaches that was having a party in the corner of his empty dining room; as much as I wanted to look for that gun I wasn't about to put my hand in a deep cardboard box; one, not knowing if their cousin's was in there having a party. I just wanted to throw up, run home, and take a shower. I. Don't. Do. Bugs, NOPE! We tried talking about us, but he was not focused at all. So, I used that opportunity to suck it up and look in the box. I took the flashlight on my phone, and while he turned around, I shinned the light in the box quickly but I didn't see anything. Defeated I say…

"Okay Jahmel, I have to go. The nail shop is getting ready to close soon. I gotta go so me and my mom can make it on time."

He walked me out to my car, and before I drove off, he says, "don't worry about ever coming back over here. You didn't even help me in there!" (I gave him that stink face look like; nigga you darn right I wasn't.) "Don't even bother calling me tonight. Go have fun with whoever you're getting ready to meet." Not having time for his tantrum, I pull off and call my mother to tell her I was on my way and that I would call her when I got to the gate so she could be outside.

I call Erika back to tell her how the "break-up" went. While I was trying to talk to her. Jahmel calls I answer the phone saying "yes Jahmel?" He says" I feel like I'm alone in this thing. Yeah, you give me money, but it's emotional support I need."

Me: "How can I give you emotional support when you always shut me down?"

Jahmel: "We need a break, so I'd rather leave or take a break than to cheat."

Me: "I agree! I don't want it to get to the point to where we start hating each other."

Jahmel: "Cool, so you do you like you've been doing, and I'll do what I need to do. You've been distant, and I don't know why. I never said you were cheating but you definitely doing something, and somebody has been in your ear. I can't do anything for you emotionally, financially, and sexually that's fine. You go and have fun with your mom even though I know that's not where you're going. As I said, it's your attitude that has change man."

I got tired of going back and forth with him, so I just came out and told him why my "attitude" towards him changed. "OKAY, FINE! You want to know why my attitude has changed? Well HERE YOU GO! My *dad approached me and told me that somebody came up to him and told him that you were trying to sell him weed."*

"WHAT! Did I try to sell him weed? Or did I show? I'm a grown-ass f***ing man! If your Dad has an issue with me talking about how I'm selling somebody weed, why can't he just come to me? And why the f*** is your neighbor snitching? When I come over there, that nigga better be ready and ready to go. I don't give a f*** who he is, I don't give a f*** about none of that s***. So if that's what y'all niggas wanna do, y'all wanna sit up there and play like I'm selling weed and all that bulls*** bruh, then he's a whole b*** ass nigga. So I ain't gon' be cool next time. I'm TURNING UP! So, I'm about to call your f***ing Dad right now and see what the f*** is going on with this mutha f***ing issue. Now I'm selling weed? I'm selling weed now? When have I ever sold weed to anybody? Imma beat that nigga ass, on everything I love, if I see that nigga we gone have a problem. You know I don't f***ing care. Imma beat his ass. Imma 31-year-old man, if I have weed on me so what. But you going around snitching and stuff that's what literally get muthaf***as killed! So like I said I'm getting ready to call your Dad right now."

Me: *"For what?? I wouldn't do that if I were you."*

Jahmel: *"What you mean, niggas out here saying I'm selling weed, I need to clear my name cause that aint cool."*

Here's the thing, if you didn't try to sell this man weed, why, WHY are you getting so mad about it and wanting to fight him and say that's he's "snitching"!? I was just letting him bury himself deeper and deeper. In my mind, we were no longer together, and I was a single woman. As I was approaching the gate to my parents subdivision; I text my mom *"GATE!"* with a smiley face. She replied back

"Come inside." Rolling my eyes. because I already knew what was happening in the house. I respond back... *"Jahmel?"*

Mommy replied: *"Yup, on the phone with your Dad."*

I whipped my car in the driveway so quick, and angrily put my car in park. I don't think I even grabbed my purse or locked my door. I just knew I was hot! Like dude, you just couldn't let me be great so that I can have this time with my mommy! Like bruh! Just because I'm going to spend time with my mama, you think I'm cheating because I'm not in your face? I just wanted to hang with my mommy. I get in the house and run up the stairs; BJ is standing there waiting on me with the annoyed look on his face like; this isn't going to end well or like here we go again. When I get to my parent's room, I hear my dad going back and forth with Jahmel on the phone; and mom standing there listening.

All I hear from Jahmel to my Dad, because the phone was on speaker… *"If you have an ought with your brother you go to him, right? Right?"* I noticed that whenever it was an argument or an issue he had with my parents, he would start quoting scriptures or get really biblical to help his argument. My Dad laughs, *"Don't quote scriptures to me, man."* Jahmel, then called my dad a *"Hypocrite"* and that he was a *"B***"* rather than coming to him. That was all I needed. I yelled *"Bruh, who the hell you think you talking to yo?…* (y'all I promise, deep down inside, I think I'm hood. Haha!) …*Dad let me talk to him, give me the phone.*

My mom is telling me *"stop, sweetie, let THAT NIGGA GO! Let him go!"* Looking at her with excitement but determined to go of on Jahmel for coming at my dad sideways I say

"Mom, I did. I did mama, BUT what he (Jahmel) *not gone do is, talk to HIM* (Fabio) *CRAZY!"* Reaching for the phone, *"Dad, let me see."* BJ came over and pulled me away. While I'm fussing at my mama, I want to tell Jahmel, that he was out of line and that it was over. Mom says, *"WATCH IT! I'm still your mama. Watch your tone, girl."* But my family

thought I was reacting the way I was because I was being defensive behind Jahmel and was trying to save him. NO, I was on their side, I just wanted to tell that nigga it was over. Jahmel and my Dad was going back and forth still in the background…until my dad said, *"I'm tired of this clown!"* and hung up the phone.

Jahmel then calls me; I look down to answer it, and my mom just goes HAM!! *"NOOOOOOOO! NOOOOOOO! YOU'RE NOT GOING BACK TO HIM! NOOOOOOO! ENOUGH I PUT MY FOOT DOWN EEEENNNNOOOUUUUUGH AZURE…* (breaking down in tears grabbing on to me) *ENOUGH AZURE. WE HAVE HAD ENOUGH!!!!!!"*

At first, I didn't know what happened…her eyes we're all big, and all 32 of her pearly whites were showing, spit and snot flying, It was a different side of my mother that I, let alone my Dad and brother have seen; but when I saw all the hurt and pain that she had bottled up from seeing me in such a toxic relationship come out that way; it confirmed that I made the right decision. How I could I let my three hearts get to this point? I couldn't continue to have their hearts break for me; their daughter and sister, because of the continuous stupid decisions I was making.

My Dad reaches for my mom to hold and console her, Critter and I join in and wrap our arms around her as she just breaks down in tears. My Fabio then says to us in his serious voice, *"I'm tired of that clown Azure. When it affects your Mom like this, we have a problem. ENOUGH IS ENOUGH!"* While BJ and I continue to hold our mommy. This dummy decides to call my dad back. BJ and I looked at each other like "THHHHIIIIS NIGGA" (in Kevin Hart's voice) Dad answers the phone *"What!?"*

"YO! Mr. G., I just wanted to let you know! I will be at your house in 20 minutes! I'm bringing Azure's TV and the little stuff she had over here

and I'm going to knock on your neighbor's door, and it is going to be what it is."

Fabio: *"Jahmel, I'm warning you, sir! Don't bring yourself over here."*

Jahmel: *"Oh, so you threating me now. Look. It is what it is; I'm not coming over to be peaceful, that nigga wanna be a b**** and snitch. He's gonna have to get his and if you want some, you can get it too. It's not going to be like it was when I was in front of your house. If you gotta get it to then oh f***ing well! That's not a THREAT either that's a F***ING PROMISE!"* and hangs up.

Jahmel, then calls my phone, Mom intercepted it… *"Jahmel, I need you to listen to me. Do not come by this house; do not call my husband's phone nor my daughters' phone. This family is done with you. DO YOU UNDERSTAND. DON'T YOU CALL THIS PHONE AGAIN!"*

Jahmel: *"Yes, ma'am."*

While mom was talking to Jahmel, my Dad called our neighbor to let him know what happened and what could potentially go down. My neighbor said, *"I wish he would knock on my door; he's going to wish he didn't!"* Mom then calls the police, to let them know that I just broke up with my abusive boyfriend, and he has been calling and threating to show up at the house. The dispatcher said she would send an officer out. While Mom is on the phone with the dispatcher. I called my cousin to let her know what happened and to let her husband be aware in case he tried to pop up at her house or do something stupid. I press on her name to call her, and I heard, *"To place this call, you will need to activate your service."* I exclaimed, *"OH NO HE DIDN'T! HE CUT MY PHONE OFF!"* I then told BJ to text Auntie London to let her know what happened and that Jahmel cut my phone off.

While we're trying to prepare for war, my mom asked *"AZURE, what do you have over there? Is that apartment in your name!? This is the time for you to be straight up and honest with us, so we can help you. Okay?"*

I take a deep sigh *"No ma'am the apartment is not in my name, it's all in his name, and I'm not on the lease at all. The only thing that I have over there is my work shirt, some toiletries, a house dress and I think some sweats oh and the TV that I brought. I could care less about all the other stuff I just want my work shirt cause I worked really hard for it."*

Mommy: *"Okay. Is there anything else over there? Is there anything in your name? C'mon Azure, you need to be honest."*

With my head hung down in defeat and shame, *"Yes ma'am, the cable and electricity are in my name."*

Mom then says okay, *"Where is that information? We're cutting that off; He wants to cut your phone off, two can play that game."* She asked where all the paperwork was; I told her that it was in my car. BJ and my Dad walked outside with me so that I can get her the stuff. While I'm trying to change my passwords to my social media accounts, and emails. While my Dad and BJ headed downstairs, my mom asked in a serious tone *"Azure? Where's the gun!?"*

With my eyes widely opened, I look up at her, because I didn't know she knew I knew and that I thought it was Jahmel, *"Mom, I wish I knew. I was praying that I would find it at the house. That was also one of the reasons I went over there earlier; to break up with him and look for the gun. The only other place I could think of is my storage."* Mom shakes her head *"JESUS, well Azure, I'm glad that the breakup didn't work over there, because if that gun is indeed there who knows how things would have turned out. OOOOOOH JESUS! Thank you, Jesus!"*

Mom gets on the phone with the cable and electricity company and arranges for the services to be disconnected. The cable was automatic, and the electricity would take a few days for it to go into action.

They gave me (my mom, because she called in as me) the final balance. My parents made it clear that I needed to pay that off ASAP, so it won't affect my credit or count against me when I decided to move out and get my own place.

While we all are handling the cable issue the doorbell rings and I think to myself this nigga is really crazy. Dad goes to open the door with BJ following right behind him while my mom and I look down from upstairs. Once we realized it was the police officer, we knew it was safe. It was weird seeing a police officer at my front door; as I said before, my neighborhood is pretty quiet and safe, especially my street. So to see a squad car parked in front of the house and a uniformed officer standing at our front door was a not so pleasant experience.

My dad tells the officer what transpired; that I went over to my now ex-boyfriend's house to break up with him and look for a stolen gun that he had taken from a family member's house and that when I left things escalated quickly and that he was threatening to come over to fight my dad and our neighbor. The officer quickly asked if Jahmel hit me or was there was any sign of abuse. I told him, *"No."* He also said, *"ma'am I just want to say that I am glad you were able to get out of this relationship. We know that it is not easy, but I do commend you."* He looked at my parents, Crit and myself and said, *"Now there is nothing more I can really do. He didn't hit her, so I can't put out an arrest warrant for him, but I will make this police report and give you a copy of it; and if he does come over call us right back. Be safe and have a good night."*

Everything died down, after a while he was messaging me on Facebook, but I did not respond to his messages.

After all of that, I still had to get ready for work for the next morning. We figured out what the plan for Saturday would be. So, the plan was that my parents and BJ would go to the gym to work out and blow off this steam, go to the phone company to put a phone on my main phone account, my line was still open because it was on my parents account. Jahmel just ended up breaking it, and it disappeared and it ain't no telling what he did with that phone. My mom had her old Galaxy Note II that I would be able to add so I can have some type of communication, then lastly, they were going to go to my storage and search for the gun. I wasn't to enthuse with the old phone; I couldn't be picky or go into brat mode. Because my parents didn't have to keep that line open when I ended up getting my own iPhone in my name. They could have easily said, "welp you just got paid, figure it out yourself." My Dad once told me after he paid 3 months of my car note so they wouldn't repo my car *"I got you; better than B.E.T got you!"* and this moment was the evidence of it.

Saturday came, and it was time to go to work. Dad and BJ walked me outside and told me to be aware of my surroundings. They would do this every morning to make sure I was safe Especially because I didn't have a phone so that I would be winging it. The drive-in was a little uneased; I cried a bit. I really didn't want it to end as it did, I wanted to be adults and end things amicably, but that would be impossible to do with a person like Jahmel. While I was on my way in, I panicked. *"SNAP! MY BANK ACCOUNT!"* I opened my old bank account back up, and I was pretty sure he didn't have my card information. Even though I would leave my purse in the car while I was at work, I would take my driver's license and debit cards out. I didn't trust him; especially after some money went missing from my wallet at the beginning of our relationship and coming across a blank check from one of my accounts folded up in his wallet, when he went to jail. I couldn't check my account because I HAD NO PHONE! All I could do was pray that my money was safe.

I got to work, and I stood behind after our team huddle to talk to Tre' to tell him what popped off the night before. Reaching up for a highfive I say *"Tre'! I DID IT! I officially broke up with him!"*

Tre': *"Good Girl, you okay?"*

I told him I was okay and where we were at; and that the only concern now was my safety. I told him that he threated to come to my house to fight my Dad, (I noticed his eyebrow raised) he cut my cell phone off, and we still can't find the gun he stole from my grandpa's house. *"YOU DIDN'T TELL ME THAT BLUE!!"* He says sternly. I put my head down and said, *"yup; dude is crazy."* As I was telling him what my parents plan of action for the day was, I saw him grab paper and wrote something down. I thought he made a note of everything for security or something. I told him I wanted to put a hold on my account and change my card just in case he copied my debit card or account number.

Tre': *"So, you're basically telling me you're not working today, right?"*

Me: *"No! I'm here, imma work."*

Tre': *"SO YOU TELLING ME YOU'RE NOT WORKING TODAY, RIGHT!?"* hands me the piece of paper he was writing on. I grabbed it to notice it was a number on it. *"That's my number, use it if you need to. But I need you to go take care of that."*

Me: *"Tre', I can work! I'm okay."*

Tre': *"Blue, why you still standing here? Go!"*

Me: confused and trying to understand if he is telling me to go clock out or what *"Sooo, do I go to my station?"*

Tre': "GIRL, GET OUT MY FACE!! Go take care of that, be careful please!!!! "

I smirked put my head down because I really did want to work and try to get it off my mind; BUT in the back of my head I wanted to be with my family IN CASE he decided to be stupid and pop up. Standing there a few seconds to see if he was serious or not but he gave me that look and pointed towards the front— that's when I knew I needed to "get out of his face". Haha. You know how you see a bratty kid get something and they hug their parents or whomever. Yeah, that's how I felt. Since I didn't have a phone, I called my mom from the job phone and told her Tre' told me to go handle my business. Mom, on the other end, *"Okay, well we're still at the gym, you know how to get here?"*

She gave me directions to the gym; I was a little intimidated. I didn't have a phone, so if I got lost, I couldn't look it up, and I didn't have a pen to write anything down. She was giving me street names, exit's numbers and with my dyslexia, I tend to get things backwards at times. But I took my time, didn't get lost, and made it to the gym. The person at the front was expecting me, so I was able to go straight back to the locker room where my mom was. Now, Fabio and BJ didn't know I was there, so when I walked out with my mom and they saw me they instantly and I mean INSTANTLY went into the *"WHAT HAPPENED? WHERE HE AT?"* mode. Their faces were EPIC; Mom quickly had to calm them down *"She's fine, she fine* (as she walks towards them like "I come in peace") *she was granted time off to take care of her business."*

BJ: *"OH. OH OKAY, I was bout to say! WHAT. NOW!?"*

We all laughed and went on about the day. We decided to drop my car off at home and leave it in the garage. We got the phone situation fixed and then head to the storage to look for the gun only come up empty-handed. At that point, we informed Uncle Mike so he could file a police report because we had no clue where it could have been. Once I had all the important contacts locked into my phone, I sent a text to my best friend Bianca, Auntie London and Erika letting them know I was safe and everything was taken care of. I also told Marcus what happened, his responded was *"SIS, if I wasn't in China, I promise, I'd be going to jail. When I come home, and I see that nigga, ON SITE, SIS ON SITE!"*

Sunday came around, and we felt it was only right to let our Pastor know what was up, he was aware of the issues and problems we had with him and being that the gun was missing and the recent church shooting, we just wanted to have all basis covered. Our head of security works with the SAPD, and we made him aware as well. Now, my Aunt Danielle serves with Pastor, and she had no clue what was going on, I didn't really tell her anything, because I knew she didn't care for Jahmel from the beginning, so I filled her in real quick, and all she could say was *"Ok...ok...ok...mmm...ok, Jesus... mmm. Wee wee wee...mmmm* (reaching for a hug) *I'm glad you're okay though, but Jesus."*

After church on the way home, my Dad notices that he has a missed call from an unknown number. When I looked to see the number, I realized that it was Jahmel. Mom says, *"he just doesn't listen. I told him not to call this phone again."* Fabio interjects *"I rather he calls me, but when he calls her, it's a problem."* Jahmel, calls back while and my Dad answers, *"How can I help you, sir!"* Jahmel wanted my Dad to come bring his stuff from my storage over to his house in exchange for my belongings. My dad said *"NO!"* and that if Jahmel wanted to get his things, it would be on my dad's terms. We weren't going to alter our schedule as we would normally do to accommodate him, that was just out of the question. If he wanted to get his things, we would meet him at the police station closest to our home.

He finally tried reaching out to me; he called my original number. When I recognized his number, I sent it to voicemail and automatically blocked him. About 3 minutes later a voicemail pops up. I was standing next to my Mommy, so I nudged her and told her he left me a voicemail, we both listened.

"Wow, so you blocked me for what reason? Like, what the f*** did I do to you seriously? What did I do to you to have you block me? All because of your f***ing parents. You're 27 years old and can't function without your f***ing parents. It's sad bruh, really sad. You need to come get your stuff before it goes in the trash; that's all I'm trying to have you do. Somebody come over here and pick up your stuff; I'm not going to no muthf***ing substation that's fifteen miles away, when there's one right by my house. But he wants to be f***ing difficult, so if y'all wanna make it difficult we can make it difficult. Your choice."

My mom and I both look at each other and started glancing around the store for my dad and brother. We let them listen to the voicemail, and my dad says you tell him to call me! You can tell my dad was getting frustrated and was tired of going back and forth with this guy. So I did what my Dad said and told Jahmel if he wanted his stuff, he needs to call my dad to arrange it. So Jahmel calls him, but my dad sends him to voicemail; surprisingly, it was very mature and adult-like "Hey, Mr. Gabriel, this is Jahmel. Azure told me to give you a call so we can schedule to pick up my things and so she can get her things. Give me a call back. Thank you." But when my Dad didn't respond quick enough for him, the Jahmel we all know came out in another voicemail.

"You have until 3 o'clock to respond; or is gonna go to a place that I don't want it to go to and you don't wanna go to. So like I said so be

an adult and let's handle this amicably (boy trying to use big words). *I can come over there and get my things; I can meet you guys at the storage. She can take her things, or if you just want to leave them here I can trash them, it does not matter to me. I don't care about the relationship I don't care about anything else I just care about my things and let's amicably end this. You're 59 years old; an adult so handle your business. BE AN ADULT, be an adult!! Before it goes somewhere that you can't come down from. Yeah, I don't give a f*** if you take it as a threat or not. It's whatever, if you wanna be disrespectful I can be disrespectful too!"*

After about an hour, my dad finally responds back to Jahmel with the time to meet at the substation. Jahmel confirmed that he would be there. My mom didn't want me in the car during the time of the transaction, so we decided that I got into the police station and wait. She didn't want him trying to talk to me or touch me. Before our arrival, my dad texted him and told him we were on our way, and we would be there in 15 minutes he never responded. While we were waiting on him we asked the police officer there if someone came in and made a police report about a missing gun he said: *"yes, are you are related right?"* My mom told him the story, and the officer said that it matches what Uncle Mike had told him and that he was expecting us. He said, *"Ma'am, I looked up the gentlemen in our system and he has a loooong record; mischief and some assault charges, I'm so glad you got out of that relationship, dear."*

Ten – twenty minutes went by, and no Jahmel or phone call. We were approaching an hour and at this point it looked like he was going to be a no-show, so we decided we were not going to stick around any longer and he pretty much wasted our time. Jahmel put up that big fuss, curse my dad out and even threatened my dad; over a broken suitcase (which was mine) full of dirty clothes and a beat-up pair of red shoes and still didn't show up.

A few days went by, and I hadn't heard from him. One day after work, I had a missed call and a text message from Jahmel stating that he just wanted to talk and get some closure; he just wanted to hear it from my mouth to be for sure that I no longer wanted to be with him. Even though I had already told him that my decision was final. I called him hoping that this would be the last conversation that we would have and hoping that him hearing *"no, I don't wanna be with you anymore or we're not together"* would finally put an end to him calling and messaging me.

At the beginning of the conversation, he was very cordial asking how my day was and how I had been. Then he started his sob story of how he has no lights in the apartment and how it's cold because I cut off the electricity and didn't give him a heads up. I told him, *"WELL, you didn't give me a heads up when you disconnected my phone!"* He claims he asked them to put it on a different account. BRUH! That's basically saying cut it off, especially if I'm not present to open a new account. He started crying and kept asking me to please order him some food, because he has no money and hadn't ate. I told him I didn't have any money and that I couldn't. I obviously lied, but it felt GOOD! Amid his pleading his 'cry' got louder, he says, *"You left me at a time when I need you the most. Guess what news I got yesterday, GUESS?"* I say, with little to no emotion in my voice, *"What, Jahmel?"* *"My mama, man, my mama is gone. She's dead!"*

Trying so hard not to laugh in this boy's ear; I'm thinking, did this boy really pulled the *"my mama dead"* card. This dude is full of it!

"Your mom is dead; you say…" I responded, trying to hold back laughter, praying that it wasn't true. Jahmel sniffles *"See, man. I knew you wouldn't believe me; you don't even care. Now I gotta figure out how imma put my mama in the ground. I officially have nobody, the three people I cared about and loved all left me, I can't see my daughter, you left me, now my mama dead."*

All I could do was shake my head; he was trying so hard for me to fall for his antics. I thank God for the prayer that I prayed, asking him to help me be strong when these instances came up, that I wouldn't be weak and fall for his schemes and tactics. My mama always says prayer will do one or two things, it will change you or it will change the situation. There was a song that one of the mothers in the church would sing during praise and testimony services when I was a little girl says I know prayer changes things everybody ought to pray and never faint I know prayer changes things. I my situation I know prayer changed my AND it changed my situation. The devil comes in many forms. That's why it's so important that we stay covered and prayed up, so we will be able to detect the tricks of the enemy. It only takes one small crack, that's all the devil needs to get in to our head and whisper deceitful things.

Once Jahmel realized I wasn't falling for it, he backed off and ended the conversation. But a few days before Christmas, getting off work, I have a text message from Jahmel…before I open it, I was able to read a little bit of the message *"Somebody is going to die!"* Trying to figure out what this dude is talking about, I open the message to see several pictures of his mom; the only thing is…her face is beat up! Knots on her forehead, face black, blue and purple. The rest of the message read *"…They beat up my mama. I'm pissed! Somebody is dead!"* I kept saying, *"HE DID THAT, OMG, HE DID THAT! It has his name all over it."*

It was 6:04 pm, so of course, he knew I was off work, so he called… I answered, *"WHAT!?"*

"YO, you get my message man? The lady at the group home put her hands on my mama… Azure, say something, I need help?"

Me being petty, *"Well,l first of all, I'm glad to see that your mom has risen from the dead!"* that ticked him off of course, but I didn't care. How did you go from calling me a few days ago crying because your mom is dead to her, now being in the hospital with a busted face? BOY BYE!

He was hoping that I would come to their rescue. According to him, they were trying to discharge her with her face still swollen and her blood pressure still extremely high. First of all, no hospital is going to release a patient who appears to be a victim of a domestic violence or assault without involving the police or Adult Protective Services (APS). Aint no way! He wanted me to pick him and his mother up from the hospital to take her to another hospital where he felt like she would get the proper care.

I told him no and that I had other things planned that were more important. (Just telling stories like my big daddy says.) I was just getting Christmas cards and candy for my co-workers) He wasn't buying it, and honestly, I didn't care. He was no longer my problem, issue, or concern. Now if that was indeed true about his mom, my heart went out to her. I said a prayer of healing and restoration; but that was all I was obligated to do and all I was GOING TO DO. He kept begging me to come to their rescue; it got to the point where I just hung up in his face. He then sends a message along with a picture of another female stating how a "friend" could come from Austin to be there for him, and she was going to do this and that, but I live 25 minutes away, and I couldn't come. Well, boo, if she is coming from Austin why you are calling me!? After he realized I was going to keep sending him to voicemail and was no longer responding to his text messages, his final message was a *"F*** YOU! "*and he left me alone.

And that ladies and gentlemen, was the END of Azure and Jahmel. At least so I thought!!!

"Seriously Bruh!?"

I never thought I would find myself walking into a police station to file multiple police reports on someone I once loved and cared about. I felt like I was reenacting a scene from Love & Hip-Hop Atlanta or something. Ha! Y'all remember that episode when Tommie was turning herself in from that Josline mess, and Stevie was standing at the gate watching her walk-in? Then you hear her interview in the background saying, *"I never thought I'd be in this type of situation,"* while everything is in slow motion and slow or somber music is playing.

That's exactly how I was feeling; I even caught myself looking around for camera crews and Mona Scott-Young yelling "CUT!"

I walked in and up to the window; the female officer took my info and said, *"have a seat, and an officer will be out to take your statement."* I waited about a good ten minutes, and no one came out to greet me, nor did the lady at the desk give me a courtesy update. As I'm sitting there alone, I started to think is it was even worth it?? I don't belong there. 'what is going to come out of me making this report?' I thought to myself. 'He's going to find a way to get out of it like he always does.'

See, the thing about Jahmel is, he's smart and if you haven't figured it out by now a MASTER MANIPULATOR. He could "talk" his way out of anything when his anger didn't take over or convince you do things you would otherwise not do. At that moment, it was clear as day that because I didn't belong in there and I needed to go through with this. I needed to take a stand, whether anything came out of it or not.

I knew this was the right thing to do, and like my mom always told me *"DOCUMENT EVERYTHING"*, a paper trail was now started.

It's approaching an hour of me sitting and waiting. SO, I nicely go up to the window and ask,

"Um, excuse me, but do you know how much longer the wait is going to be? I mean…"

She cuts me off … *"no, I don't. They're in the middle of a shift change and are doing roll call right now. I'm sure once they're done, they will send an officer out to take your statement."*

Now my mama would say, *"Azure, is patience with you!?"* She was with me all the way up until she gave me that bogus response. So of course, Porsha started to come out and I almost said, with an attitude neck roll and all…

"Um, don't you think that's something you should have told me first-hand??? I have been sitting here for a whole HOUR! Like, you knew shift change was getting ready to take place as soon as I walked in! You could have at least said Yes, sure thing, they're getting ready to do shift change, I'm not sure how long it will take, but you're more than welcome to wait or come back. A little common courtesy, eh? No wonder why they say eff the police, cause you in here on the BUUUULLLL!"

But I remembered quickly where I was and why I was there; it probably wouldn't be in my best interest to pop off on the lovely officer. I could just imagine my Moms face; while shaking her head and laying her hand on my forehead saying, "LOOOORRRRD, AZURE! Touch my child, Lord."

I kept battling back and forth in my mind, whether to stay or come back or just do it another day. I know myself though, there was no coming back after I left. So, Porsha and Patience had a conversation.

Patience: *"Girl you ain't got nothing to do."*

Porsha: *"I can do a lot, I can go see Big Daddy, and or cousin, since they're both up to the street then come back on the way home. Or just go home."*

Patience: *"... or you can just sit your tail down and relax! You don't have anything to do, Jahmel is not in the picture you are no longer on his "schedule" SO CHILL I SAY!*

Porsha: *"ugh, sad to say. You're right; I ain't gonna do nothing but go home and watch TV or go to sleep."*

After the going back in forth in my head, I sat my tail down and waited. I waited so long I lost track of how long I was there. Finally, an officer came to take my statement. That day I filed two police reports, and updated one report that was previously filed two-days before by another family member. You're probably wondering how in the world did you get to the point of filing police reports for this guy. Well go ahead and buckle your seat belt, this roller coaster is about to take a drop.

It had been three weeks since "***The Break-Up.***" I was in a better place mentally, emotionally and spiritually. I was also enjoying the freedom of hanging out with my family and not having my time split or fully consumed by Jahmel. One major way I knew Jahmel was surely out of the picture was when after paying *MY* bills, I still had money left! Things were already starting to look better just by that! Haha! I was excited because the amazing mentorship program I signed up for called *'SistHER™* by Kierra Sheard was getting ready to start which I knew would help me get back on track spiritually and the wisdom that would be shared will help me become and be mold me into the woman I know God has called me to be, I was looking forward to being Azure again.

It was January 2, 2018; only the second day of the new year. When Fabio comes home, he always yells *"Mail Call"* when he's bringing us mail. This time he just comes in my room; (BJ and I can always tell when our Dad is upset, irritated, mad, or shoot all of the above). He looked annoyed, and with a stern voice, he said, *"I have a bone to pick with you!"* with his eyebrows raised while throwing junk mail onto my bed. So, I'm confused as to why he had a bone to pick with me. I started thinking; I'm not with Jahmel anymore so it can't be nothing he did. I didn't leave anything out on the table. Did I? I was really trying to figure out what I did wrong. I hate being in trouble, especially with my Daddy.

I was walking towards his room replaying my past events and movements to figure out why he wanted to pick this bone. As I am approaching the door, I let out a sigh followed by *"What I do now? Whatever it is I ain't do it, man."*

Fabio: *"Right, you didn't do it that's the problem!"* while slapping his hand on a yellow postcard that was laying on the bed.

With a confused look, I felt my eyebrow go up (those who know me know about this infamous raising of the eyebrow.) as I read the big black bold words;

Me: *"A **WARRANT**!?? HUH, how do I have a warrant!?"*

My mind started racing back to all the shenanigans I was in with Jahmel. Now there were some things I did on his behalf that could have DEFINITELY been warrant-worthy. (I asked the Lord for forgiveness so y'all don't come for me.) I kept reading and finally got the common sense to look up the citation. It was from a speeding ticket I got while I was with him from a time when he had me on the other side of San Antonio trying to get to the shooting range.

Fabio: *"So, what you going to do? I thought you took care of that."*

Me: *"This was something he was supposed to be giving me money for, so I could do the defensive driving, but I totally forgot and lost the original ticket. I found it the day after the date I was supposed to appear in court. I was telling Auntie London about it because I was on the phone with her when I found it and she told me to call anyways. They told me all I could do at that point was to pay the full amount of the ticket. That was my plan, and I had started saving to pay the amount. I didn't think I was gonna get a WARRANT FOR IT THO!"*

Fabio: *"Well, it needs to be taken care of..."*

Me: *"Yeah, I'm going to have to miss work tomorrow so I can take care of it."*

Fabio: *"YES, you drive a long way to work, and if you get pulled over, you're going to jail, and you'd be in real trouble. You gonna tell your mother!?"*

In my head, I was thinking HEEEECCCCK naw I ain't telling her.

"Yeah, I'll tell her."

Mom comes home; I told her and BJ the news, she wasn't happy AT ALL. BJ had that same look when I dropped the "I'm pregnant" bomb. She told me I needed to handle it quickly and that she'll take me to court tomorrow to get it taken care of! Dad interjected and said, *"I could meet y'all, so you can get to your meeting* (referring to my mom) *I'll stay with her and get her back home."*

I was upset with Jahmel, but more so myself. The ticket was on me and not him, although he said he'd pay for it so that I could do the defensive driving; my dumb behind believed and trusted him as he asked me to do. I couldn't believe I let things get to this point. We were already broken up, but things that took place while with him were still affecting me; even still until this day! The next morning, Mom and I made our way to the court, and as we were pulling in, I saw Fabio come in the right behind us. Talk about time management, well, that's all Fabio and me; BJ and Mom struggle with it. She would always commend me for getting to work an hour early, then she'd follow up with: *"You got that from your Daddy's side, cause I KNOW you don't get it from my side."*

I had a rush of emotions as we were walking through the door. I've been on this side with Jahmel, sad to say. I mean I've had my share of speeding tickets, and often found myself in a precinct/court paying tickets but never for WARRANT! I'm so glad I wasn't by myself; I just knew I was going to jail! Because that was always the case with him, you missed a court date, they will issue a warrant, and when you do go to court, they run your name next thing you know; you're in cuffs! Praise the Lord that wasn't my case (no pun intended) it was only for people who were on active probation. I tell ya, you date one convicted felon, and you feel like you have degree in Criminal Justice. Ha!

The clerk called me up to the window and asked how he could help me. I gave him the postcard, and he started plugging things into the system. He says, *"Ms. Gabriel, we sent out three letters before any warrant is issued, did you get them?"* I look puzzled and said, *"no sir, I didn't get anything thing in the mail prior. This postcard was the first I've received on this matter."* I also told him the story of how I lost the initial ticket and what the lady suggested I do to take care of it.

He asked for my drivers' license, took a look at my ID and then the computer… *"Ms. Gabriel, is Markville Dr. still your place of residence?"*

Me: *"No, sir."*

Clerk: *"Okay, that explains why you didn't receive any correspondence. So, is the address on the postcard your current residence?"*

Me: *"Yes, sir."*

Clerk: *"... and how long have you've been here?"*

Me: I responded quickly, *"About a month, I just moved from Dallas not too long ago."*

I felt my Dad give me that, "yeah, good cover." nudged, because I was clearly lying. I had been back in San Antonio for about two years at this point, and you're supposed to change your address within 30days of moving. I found that out the hard way when I went to visit Jahmel when they transferred him from Harris County to Bexar County back in *"BOOKED."*

Clerk: *"Ok, not a problem, this will suffice as your proof of residence. I am going to give you a number. Once your number is called, you will go in to speak with the judge. Once he gives you a judgment you will come back to this window, and we'll get everything squared away."*

Fabio and I: *"Cool, thank you!"*

Fabio: *"So you're getting ready to see the judge now? That's good; so you won't have to come back."*

As Fabio and I were sitting in the back of the courtroom, listening to all the other cases, I was taken back once again. I never thought I'd be sitting in the courtroom for ME! Not that I wanted to be in the courtroom with him either; but hey, it happened. I was so nervous I didn't know what the judge was going to say let alone what his ruling would be. Everyone else seemed to be getting a warning, cased dismissed or defensive driving.

Clerk 2: *"Case of Bexar County vs. Azure Gabriel? Please approach the bench."* Yes, y'all it wasn't a game, it felt like a scene straight out of Judge Faith, Judge Joe Brown or better yet Providence Court.

Judge: *"Hello, Ms. Gabriel. Let's see why we're here today!"* Speeding?

Me: *"Yes, your honor."*

Judge: *"Tell me what happened, where we're you?"*

Me: *"Well your honor for one I was lost, I was on the side of town I wasn't familiar with, I was pulling out of Walmart and realized I was going the wrong way while going down a hill..."*

Judge: *"... ahh, yes, those hills will get you. Well, speeding is a bad habit, the only way we can break a habit is not to do them and discipline, do you think you can break the habit? I don't want to see you in here again."*

Me: *"Yes, sir."*

Judge: *"If you're in an unsure area, make sure you are aware of the speed limit, even if it's a familiar area. Okay?"*

Me: *"Yes, sir!"*

So, he broke down the original cost of the ticket (he dismissed it which was $360) the court fee (I can't remember the original amount, but I had only to pay $60 in court fees.) He also knocked down other fees which included, adding and removing me from the database for warrants and something else. So, all I had to pay was about $160 plus take the defensive driving course. The price was less than what I was going to pay from the beginning to take the defensive driving course and less than the actual ticket.

I walked out that courtroom so quick! I didn't want him to come back and change his mind. Fabio and I walked back up to the first clerk and he asked if I would be paying the fee that day and how much. I quickly told him I was going to pay the full amount; he looked up at me, shocked. I guess people usually do the payment plan. My thinking was "naaw doc, let me knock this out NOW!" I went to the ATM withdrew the amount and STILL HAD MONEY LEFT! I took it back to the clerk; he said to allow 24 hours for everything to update on the system. I was going to go into work, but I didn't want to take the chance of someone running my plates, and it hadn't updated in the system, and I'd be going to jail. This was a true example of God's grace, mercy, and favor over my life. Because if you think about it, they were sending all the correspondence to my Dallas address. Why not send the warrant notice there as well? You can't tell me that wasn't GOD!

I was now almost free and clear of all things 345; we didn't want to hear his name around the house, so we came up with 345. It was that Saturday after we broke up, I was feeling petty in my spirit. Everyone was in the car waiting for me; with a little pep in my step, I jump in the car, exhaled saying

"WHEEEW! I feel 100lbs lighter! A weight has been lifted off of me."

BJ gave me a petty look and said, *"You, childish!"*

Mom: confused, laughing *"huh, I missed it. What did she say!?"*

Dad looked in the rear-view mirror and then to my mom, looking confused! BJ told them what I said. Then BJ said, *"Well technically, you lost more. How much did he weigh?"*

Me: *"Uh? I don't remember."*

I think I was just a 'petty day' because my mom's response was the 'pettiest' of them all!

"Aww c' mon! what you mean you don't remember, as much as he went to the hospital!"

BJ and I had the big bug eyes with our hands over our shocked open mouths. While Dad chuckled and told her.

"You cold man!"

Me: *"I don't know; I know he lost some weight. I don't know why I want to say he was 290 something."*

Dad: *"Please, he was at least three something!"*

BJ chimed in *"Yeah, easily a good 300! Azure, how much weight you gain with him?"*

Thinking how much I weighed when we got together to what I weighed at the moment *"About 20lbs."* I responded back.

"Well we'll just say 345lbs," Says BJ

Everyone else… *"YEAH, 345! That's his new name!"*

I was enjoying my freedom to do what I wanted, go where I wanted, buy, and eat what I wanted. I was used to a certain standard and lifestyle because of how I was raised. How I treated myself and how I lived while I was in Dallas I could finally get back to. Plus, I had Erika to do girl things with and run around the city getting into cousinly shenanigans. I was even staying my entire shift at work.

January 17th; that was a great Wednesday, BJ just went back to Wichita after being home for winter break, and it was the first day of my work week. My mind was clear I had a little pep in my walk, and that smile was starting to come back again. Next thing I knew it was 5:57 PM, time to start walking to the time clock. My work buddy and I would always walk out together. As we were walking out the door, laughing at somebody, I said to her

"Girl, that looks like my ex!" I was referring to the guy that was standing with arms folded next to my car.

Co-worker: *"Blue-Blue, that can't be him."* While we're still walking closer, I look and say with an annoyed tone.

"UGH, omg YES IT IS!" I still wasn't sure, because "the guy" had on a nice light grey hoodie and I mean it was nice, so nice that it didn't look like something he'd have on. As we were pretty much up on my, car, I nudged her , *"It's him!"* Walking passed him

to get to my car, I calmly say *"My job bruh? That's what we doing? MY JOB!?"*

345: *"Where's my sh**? You have my clothes in your trunk?"*

Thinking to myself; does he really think I'd ride around with his nasty smelly clothes in my truck?

Me: reaching in my car to grab my phone to call my dad while trying to stay calm but shaking *"I don't have your stuff bruh, we tried to give you your things literally a month ago!"*

He interrupts me, *"yeah, he (my dad) wanted me to meet at a police station, knowing I didn't have a car!"*

Listening but not listening to him, he starts to make a scene and starts cursing, TYPICAL JAHMEL! I tell my work buddy, "GO GET TRE'! CALL TRE'!" I figured Tre', was the closest thing I had to my Dad at that moment, plus he knew the recent history of this dude. I finally get my dad on the phone

"FAAWB! GUESS WHOS UP HERE BRUH!"

Fabio: *"Azure, who? Please don't tell me that knucklehead!"* I heard his New York accent come out too.

Me: *"YES! Asking if I have his clothes!"*

I saw my colleagues walking by looking at me crazy. One lady told him, *"YOU NEED TO LEAVE!"* He went off on her *"B****. I AINT GOING NO G** DAMN WHERE!"*

All the while, Dad was in my ear, and I heard him say, *"Your mother is almost home, then we're on the way!"* I told him there was no point driving forty-five minutes down and that he would be gone before they arrive. They just had a fear of him following me home or doing something stupid on the highway which wouldn't be a shock due to all his antics he's pulled in the past.

I saw and heard my work buddy say *"Yes, please."* to another co-worker who parked in front of me and saw what was going on he ended up going to get security.

345: *"I don't care if you calling your little daddy, he a b**** anyways, he didn't do nothing when I was about to beat his ass the first time. I just want my s***! Matter of fact, I'm about to be at your house. It's cool, its cool! Tell him I'm coming."*

Fabio: *"Tell him to come on! I'll be waiting for him."* 345 was talking so loud my Dad heard him.

By this time security made it out there and my work buddy explained what was going on.

My Dad asked me how Jahmel got there.

"He's in somebodies' car!" I said.

I couldn't see if there was anyone in the passenger seat because the windows were tinted pretty good. I wouldn't be surprised if it was a chick. He did the same to his baby mama while we were together, he'd pop up at her job or house. I ignored that sign because a child was involved. I'd do the same if someone were keeping me from my child. I told my Dad, that it's okay and that security was there and he's going off on them. Before I hung up, I gave him the make, model, color, and license plate number of the car he was in.

While he's going off on security, I wasn't even scared; I was more embarrassed and pissed! My job is a pretty quiet place, especially during a shift change, it's either too early, and people are sleepy and trying to wake up or vice versa

Security finally got him to leave. However, he got in the car, backed out and blocked me in, so I couldn't leave if I wanted to. He then got out to yell at me *"REALLY AZURE; YOU CALL SECURITY, YOU A B***, YOU CAN'T EVER FIGHT YOUR OWN F***'N BATTLES OR MAKE YOUR OWN DECISIONS IT'S ALWAYS MOMMY AND DADDY OR SOMEONE ELSE WHO HAS NO BUSINESS TALKING! IT'S COOL, IM ON MY WAY TO YOUR HOUSE TO GET MY S*** AND IT AINT GON BE NO TALKING IF YOUR POPS COME AT ME SIDEWAYS, I'M KNOCKING HIS ASS OUT! THAT'S NOT A THREAT EITHER!"*

In a tone of warning, I say, *"You might not want to do that!"*

"OH, he got a little gun now? I ain't scared of no bullet! I'll see you in a minute!" he says. Security is yelling at him to leave, they walk up to him and Jahmel say's *"Don't touch me bruh, I'll beat yo ass."* As he got in the car to leave, the co-worker that told him he needed to leave drove by, but he was blocking the oncoming traffic. She rolled her window down and said, *"get you're a** out the way, BOY!"* looked at me, winked and drove off!

While Jahmel pulled off behind her, security asked if I was okay and if he was my husband. I quickly say, *"NO, he's my ex-boyfriend."* They tell me that I needed to come in and give a statement and my work buddy can as well if she'd like. I walked back into the building and saw my PA Andy, looking at us confused because we should have been gone. All of the process assistants and managers come in before and leave after the associates. I just looked at him while shaking my head and told him, "I'll tell you in the morning." While giving my statement the security guard told me that he didn't strike him as the type to leave, he felt like he'd be waiting on me; and I felt the same. After the statements were given, they escorted me outside, I got in my car, and I was trying to decide whether I should take the back-road home. He didn't know that route, but it was also a dark road too. I felt safer going the normal way home. That way if he were hanging out at the nearby hotel waiting for me to pass, I would be able to spot him easier than on a dark road. I called my parents back, and they said they're en-route to my job! I told them to turn around, because he was now gone and it wasn't that serious, Dad wasn't have it!

"I rather, follow you home or ride in the car with you in case he does something stupid."

Me: *"I'm fine, I'm almost to New Braunfels now, and I don't see any sign of him. So, I am okay."*

Mom: *"Well, we're gonna still keep driving in your direction, and we'll just meet you at the H-E-B at 3009!"*

I hung up and called my Erika, she answered, and I say, "BRUH, TELL ME WHY!"

"OH, HELL, hold on. I know it's something because the way you said bruh," she responds.

I told her what just happened to put her on alert and to let her know I'll call her when I get home. I don't know, after the break up; I had a habit of alerting my friends and family he knew, especially if he knew where they lived. I didn't want him popping up on them, but I also wanted them to be aware, because I knew what he's capable of as well as what he always "said" he was capable of. The last thing I need was him targeting my family because he couldn't get to me, especially with Big Daddy's gun still missing.

I made it to 3009; I pulled up beside my parents, they were able to see my face and see that I was really okay. Dad directs me to go ahead and head home and that they'll be right behind me, but if I reached the house before them, pull over to the side before turning on our street so they can do a perimeter check to make sure he's just not hanging out waiting on me. Everything was clear, and we all got in safely. Before we sat down to eat, I pulled out some water from the fridge and turned around to put it on the counter all to see my dad's gun with the clip laying right next to it. It scared the mess out of me because I wasn't expecting it to be there, but at that moment I knew he wasn't playing and Fawb WAS READY! OKKUURRT!

The next day, I told Tre' what happened. He gave me that look like "that nigga crazy!" He says, *"So are you staying?"*

Me: *"Yeah, Imma leave after lunch, so I can go try to file a restraining order; that's what security and LP suggested. I also have to pick up a copy of their statement before I leave to take with me."*

Tre': *"Good job. Just get it taken care of and let me know."*

Lunch times came, and I head out shortly after. I called Erika because she said she wanted to roll with me for support while I filed the order. We got there, and I was only able to do half of the restraining order process, which was fill out the paperwork and the next step was to talk to the DA (District Attorney) and provide the evidence that would help my case. It was close to the end of the day, so I had to come back within seven days to complete the process. Knowing that I had a few off days coming up, I was going to take that time to get all the threating voicemails, text, DM's, the two police reports that were filed and other stuff together.

I had a whole file of stuff, from the texts he sent threatening to kill us, cursing my dad out, you name it, I HAD IT. Recorded phone calls and everything. I even had the pictures of his mother's beat up, swollen and bruised face. After she magically rose from the dead when he told me she got into it with the lady APS placed her with. Naaawww, I have a good feeling he did that. I even went online and pulled up his record, printed out the previous restraining orders he had, from his baby mama and ex-wife. I presented all of that information to the DA; I even left work early to do so, only for her to say it wasn't enough evidence for a restraining order. "EXCUSE ME, WHAT? What you mean it's not enough? So y'all basically want me dead!? Like I even told you how he said he was going to come into the house and kill one of us, and THAT'S NOT ENOUGH! He even has previous orders filed basically for the SAME THING, and it's NOT ENOUGH?"

DA: *"No, ma'am that's not enough, we suggest you keep filing police reports if he does continue to make contact or pops up again at your job don't make any communication with him; but we'll keep everything on file. Are there any questions?"*

I hung up in that lady's face because what I just heard was straight BS. I was mad that I wasted all my time and took off from work to have NOTHING come out of it. Yeah, I was hurt—after I told the people that knew of the situation, they were confused as well as to why it wasn't enough evidence. My Auntie London said… *"Girl, you should have gone in there crying!"* I honestly thought about it; I felt if I walked in there with everything organized and my ducks in a row it would show that it was a serious issue. I guess I needed to come in there with a busted face, but even then; men and women walk in there looking jacked up, and they tell them the same thing. They literally want to see you dead; our system needs to get better. Thinking back on it, I don't regret I did it; because if I didn't do it, the approval of a protective order was going to be an automatic NO. Then I got mad all over again, thinking about how uncomfortable I felt making that police report for the stolen gun from my Big Daddy's house.

I wasn't able to get the TV I purchased along with the equipment for the cable back. The cable company recommended I make a police report. They also wrote down in their notes that it was no longer safe for me to go back to the apartment due to it being domestic violence. That way with the report, I won't be held liable for the equipment, and they could just write it off, and all I would be responsible for was the bill.

Plus, they said doing all of that would possibly help my restraining order that I did NOT get. It really messed with me mentally. YES! Mentally I began to get fearful; because Jahmel was so sneaky and knowing how he would pop up on his baby mama. I became paranoid. Leaving the house in the morning I would fear that he would be waiting for me outside or would somehow, some way be in my car. It seemed like every month Jahmel would reach out and contact me, one month, in particular, I'll never forget it, I was at church, and Mommy happened to be preaching that Sunday. While I was looking at my phone following a scripture she was reading, I got a text message that read "Jahmel Edwards-Oneal" at DeSoto County Jail would like to connect…" It gave me a web link to visit for more info.

My heart sunk, and I wanted to get up and shout so bad. Haha. All I could think was yup; God was going to get him sooner or later. I did click on the link, to see what this boy had to say but it wanted me to sign up and make an account and all of that stuff. I wasn't about to give him any MORE of my time, just for him to asked me to bail him out of jail and or curse me out when I said *"NO!"* Of course you know I took a screenshot and sent it to my petty Auntie London; and we both tapped into our inner inspector gadget trying to figure out what he did NOW!

After all of the running around downtown, back and forth to the courthouse, fighting with the apartment people trying to get the "mistaken felony" off his record. *THIS* dummy goes and actually picks up one! We were able to find the docket information and found that he was in Contempt of Court on ONE of his charges; FELONY TAKING OF MOTOR VEHICLE! My first thought was that; this boy rented a car and never turned it in; just like he almost did with mine and another car he rented shortly after he got fired. OH, there's more! He was originally picked up in Texas for Assault and Battery, sound familiar? Then was extradited to Desoto, Mississippi. I tell you the internet is a beautiful thing.

With knowing that he was behind bars, I was at peace; I was no longer paranoid walking to my car in the mornings and coming home late because I knew he couldn't get to me. I found myself going back to look after his scheduled court date to see what the verdict was only to find out he was no longer in the system. Freaked out, I called the jail. Yes, I did and made up a story about trying to find my cousin. When the lady said *"Ma'am, uh he's been released…like two weeks ago."* In total shock, I dropped my phone, sat back in my chair and in an instant that fear, anxiety, and paranoia came rushing back. It was bad; I notice that I wasn't performing my best at work. I had headaches again and was not my normal self. One day I was leaving work early so I can meet my deadline to submit my book; I ran into to Tre' on the way out. I asked him while he's in prayer to pray for me and my mind. He asked me what was going on, and I gave him the rundown.

I was in the process of moving church homes, going back to The Rock, but knowing that he was out. My mind started overthinking and these questions started going through my mind.

"Well, what if I go back to "The Rock," and he comes to the church with a gun looking for me or for a fight?" What if something happens to my parents, BJ, my pastor or an innocent church member." "What if I move out, and he indeed hires people to come in the house and take me out, but

they can't find me, so they take my brother?" My mind was just going... Tre' didn't even let me finish my statement and yet again...he threw down some knowledge

"Why are you afraid? Jesus wasn't afraid, do you know how many times 'fear not' appears in the Bible??? OVER 365 times Blue. So, you know what that means EVERY SINGLE DAY OF YOUR LIFE you should FEAR NOT! Get out of your head sister...NOW GO HOME AND WRITE!"

I stood there with my mind BLOWN, Like whoa! GOD IS SOOO DOPE. I was also reminded of a call I had with Kierra and my SistHER's about staying in our minds and it was complete confirmation. As soon as I got in my car, I get a random text message from my mentor, knowing it was going to be a quote, scripture and or song I was scared to open it. Sure enough it was a song; and it TORE ME UP; I was doing the ugly cry, snot-nosed and everything! "Trust in You" by Anthony Brown and Group Therapy; the words simply say

"You did not create me to worry.

You did not create me to fear.

But you created me to worship, daily

So I'ma leave it all right here...

...I will trust in you, Lord...

...I will put my trust in you."

At that moment, I heard the Lord say, *"I GOT YOU, No, fear my child."* So whenever we begin to show signs of fear like worry, anxiety and stress we must remember that God did not CREATE us to Fear! For God hath not given us the spirit of fear but of love and of a sound mind. 2 Timothy 1:17 FEAR is False Evidence Appearing Real.

My friend, if you are currently in a toxic relationship, I would encourage you to pray, pray and pray some more. What is Prayer? Prayer is simply talking to God. It is not as complicated as some people think. Just like we talk to people through varies methods and tools we talk to God through Prayer like a person to person conversation.

Here are some examples:

Matthew 6:9-13 (ESV)

9 Pray then like this: "Our Father in heaven, hallowed be your name.

10 Your kingdom come, your will be done, on earth as it is in heaven.

11 Give us this day our daily bread,

12 and forgive us our debts, as we also have forgiven our debtors.

13 And lead us not into temptation, but deliver us from evil.

Psalm 23:1-6 (KJV)

The LORD *is* my shepherd; I shall not want.

2 He maketh me to lie down in green pastures: he leadeth me beside the still waters.

3 He restoreth my soul: he leadeth me in the paths of righteousness for his name's sake.

4 Yea, though I walk through the valley of the shadow of death, I will fear no evil: for thou *art* with me; thy rod and thy staff they comfort me.

5 Thou preparest a table before me in the presence of mine enemies: thou anointest my head with oil; my cup runneth over.

6 Surely goodness and mercy shall follow me all the days of my life: and I will dwell in the house of the LORD forever.

You may be thinking that you can handle it on your own. You may be thinking that you can fix the situation. You may be thinking that if you do this or that things will get better. You may even be thinking that the reason you are going through what you are going through is because of something you did or did not do. My friend believe me, I understand what you are going through but there is nothing you can say or do to "fix" or deal with the "hell" you experience in a toxic relationship accept Get the Hell Out of it. How do you do this? Pray and ask God for deliverance. He will give you the strength to walk away. If He did it for me, I know He can do it for you. There is nothing too hard for God. Believe me He already knows what you are going through He is just waiting for you to stop trying to fix it and surrender your will to His and He will come to your rescue.

Proverbs 3:5-7 (MSG)

5 Trust GOD from the bottom of your heart; don't try to figure out everything on your own.

6 Listen for GOD's voice in everything you do, everywhere you go; he's the one who will keep you on track.

7 Don't assume that you know it all. Run to GOD! Run from evil!

GETTING THE HELL OUT!! It will be the best thing you can do. The future you will thank you later. TRUST ME.

"Big Daddy"

Big Daddy had to be transferred back to the hospital because of some complications he was having. The nursing home was nervous to transfer him because they didn't think he would survive the trip over, BUT he did. The doctors were saying he wouldn't make it through the night, not even the week. Big Daddy is very independent so I knew he wasn't too happy he couldn't vocally respond to us, other than blinking his eyes, squeezing hands or smiling.

I got a phone call from my mommy saying that he wasn't getting better, his breathing started to get shallow and the break between each breath was getting longer. She suggested I should come up and see him. I was just getting over the flu and normally I would be up there every day, but I did not want to chance him getting sicker because of me. When I hung up the phone with her my legs got week, my hand became clammy and the tears started to flow while I paced back and forth in the house. I called Erika for support and to see if she could go with me to see Big Daddy. Of course, she said yes and came to pick me up.

I was uneasy walking into the hospital which happen to be the same exact hospital Jahmel had his award-winning show in *"Oh What A Night."* I had on heels that day, so my mom heard me coming down the hall and told Big Daddy she thinks she hears me coming and she said he made some movements. When I walked through the threshold of the door moms says excitingly "YEP, That's her! Azure is here Big Daddy." When I reached his beside and held his hand, I noticed his eyes got big; he knew I was there. As leaned over to kiss him, he instantly squeezed my hand back.

My mommy went downstairs to get some coffee and left Erika and I to have time with Big Daddy. Lost for words I didn't know what to do or say, Erika suggested I talk to him and let him know I'm there and that I am okay. But I wasn't ready yet, I needed a minute. Later that night I swung back by the hospital to bring my mom something to eat and spend some more time with my big daddy. We knew, aside from a miracle, it was just a matter time before the Lord would call him home.

Sitting at his bed side, holding his hand, I hear Erika in my head saying *"Just talk to him, he would love to hear what's going on, tell him about your book. He'd love the hear about that."* So I take a deep breath and say *"Hey Big Daddy, I just want to let you know I am okay! I am safe! I broke up with that boy, I know he wasn't worth anything. I just want you to know your baby girl is okay. I'm okay. Okay?"* I felt his grip get tighter and with tears in my eyes. I continued to pour out my heart telling my him how I am grateful for everything his has done for me and how he has always been there for me. While I was beginning to sing his favorite song, I was interrupted with a knock on the door, it was the nurse coming to give him his medicine and check on him. I had to let his hand go, who knew that that would be the last time I would hold my Big Daddy's hand.

Later that night. February 2, 2018 my word was shook. It would be a day I will never forget. I was talking to my best friend about our day. I hear my dad's phone ring in the distance and a few minutes later I hear a knock at my door and my heart sunk! Not knowing what I was getting ready to hear I say "Come In." Fabio walks in and tells me we have to head to the hospital. Hanging up the phone, I felt everything going in slow motion. As I approach my parents' room, I say *"I'm ready, is Big Daddy okay?"*, looking at my Dad & BJ's sad face. Dad shakes his head no and just grabs me and I broke down and crying. In that moment I felt so lost, I still feel lost at times. I regret that in his last days when I could have been spending time with him, talking to him, joking and laughing with him, I was literally fighting for my life and ended up with the flu. Do I feel like Jahmel robbed me of some of that? ABSOLUTELY!!!! But never again.

I never understood when people would say that *"As time goes by is gets a little easier to deal with the loss of a love but the pain/void his still there."* Yes, I've lost loved ones dear to me but this one by far is the hardest! Just sharing this part with you all has been difficult. But I am grateful to have all the great memories of my Big Daddy.

Please cherish your family and friends, you never know when the Lord will call them home.

Lessons Learned

YOU MADE IT TO THE END! That was a rough one, wasn't it? Now, I'm going to help you, **"Get the HELL Out!"** Now let's break down each chapter; you'll get how I was feeling, some tough love, what I thought, quotes & references, and most importantly Biblical backing. You ready?

Mr. Right & I'm Not as Think as You Dumb I Am.

Always, always, always follow your spirit, gut and instincts! A women intuition is NEVER wrong. So many red flags at the beginning that were right there in my FACE! I was too concerned about settling down and not being alone that I ignored every last one. Jahmel showed me that he had a problem the 1st hospital incident in Dallas. Now thinking back was all that a bluff? I don't know, but I definitely wouldn't be surprised if it was. Another lesson I learned. NEVER! If a man/women still hasn't produced the things they say they have then maybe just maybe they are living a complete lie. To this day, I don't know where his Tahoe is. It probably got repo'd. Like how can you pull up a picture of a house off google and pass it along as your own. My mama didn't by it when he showed a goggle image of his so-called house he had in Atlanta. Trying to cover for a man/woman so they will appear to be all together knowing something is off and not right. Don't do it, is pointless and you'll probably end up having a story like mine if not worse.

BOOKED:

OH, Goodness! One thing I will tell you is that I was SCARED and very naïve, to think that this was really God's will for my life! To even think that him getting arrested and going through the whole jail process was the ultimate test of our relationship to see how we were going to overcome it. No boo! That was just stupid to think that God would put me in this type of situation in order to test me. That was definitely not God's will for my life.

I honestly feel that God was sending me several outs! I believe God was looking down on me saying *"okay girl, how many more red flags do I need to send you for you to see that HE AINT THE ONE!? I sent you a sign when y'all first started dating. Remember the rental car? The one he couldn't put in his name, so you put it in your name? And remember when it was time for you to turn it he flaked on you. Remember how the same exact car magically popped back up on a Dallas trip, EXACTLY how you left it from the original trip. And remember how you started getting phone calls from the company saying they we're going to report the car stolen if it's not turned back in by 5 pm." Yeah, you remember that red flags Azure?"* *"Yes Lord, I remember."*

Never, ever put anything in your name for him or her, If he/she wants to rent a car, you let them rent the car on their own. If they can't then it is not meant for it to happen. If I had never went to that apartment and saw that truck sitting there and turned it back in—I would have been in the same boat as Jahmel, with a grand theft auto charge and probably in jail. Sad to say I still owe the rental company for that darn truck. Please never allow yourself to be in a situation to where you are taken advantage of. Never lower your standards or values by living outside of your means to impress a man. It is not worth it! Trust Me!

"Do not be deceived: Bad company corrupts good morals." 1 Corinthians 15:33 NASB Every day in this relationship I was being corrupted. I was so focused on this being my *LAST* relationship and Jahmel was indeed my husband that I forgot all of the values, morals, teaching, and principles that were instilled in me at an early age. Don't lose your focus.

I will say this, if a relationship, is taken you away from you being you and your character you shouldn't want it. Never let someone else come in and cause you to lose yourself. God was constantly giving me an OUT! He showed me many red flags before this day. Jahmel going off on me in a hospital room trying to sling his IV stand towards me was a definite sign that hommie was full of "hell" and had the potential to become violent. It was definitely time for me to get the "hell" out.

The great Mya Angelou said, *"When someone shows you who they are, believe them."* or like another great woman told me after reading "ENOUGH"; *"Azure, if a nigga shows you his true colors, you pay attention and GET THE HELL OUT!"Mommy*

I have a commitment to myself that I will continue to seek God's face more and get that fire back for God. I don't ever want to have to question God and his purpose for my life. I Thank God for His grace and mercy

HOUSTON WE HAVE A PROBLEM:

I can just shake my head at this whole chapter! You have to have something seriously wrong to do what he did. Bluffing on 1000, you hear me! The fact that he KNEW what he was doing; I am almost certain that he was in the hotel room watching TV and just chilling. Now I'm pretty sure he was indeed upset and thought about giving up; but once it got to the police scene and he threw his phone to a random guy...

Yeah right. Then then me ending up texting with the police. C'mon bruh. You would think. I would leave after this…Nope, my dumb tail stayed because I felt like I could fix him. He's dating a Christian woman, with deep Godly roots. We were going to pray him up out of his mess, and God was going to do a GREAT thing in him. Nope! Not saying God couldn't do it; He of course, can do anything but fail. I realize now I was trying to change someone who didn't must want to change. This was not my responsibility Like Tre' always said; I can't be God.

Don't ever let someone play mind games with you like the way he did with me whether you're married, in a relationship or even just a friendship. Family also; If a person makes you feel crazy/guilty for addressing them when they are wrong, stay away from them. That is manipulation and teeters on abuse and you, my friend, are a dealing with a manipulator. They make you responsible for their emotions and feelings. The worst part of being manipulated in a relationship is that most of the time you don't even know it's happened. Others can see the manipulation before you can. You see a manipulator will twist your thoughts, actions, wants and desires into something that benefits and serves them. They make you feel guilty – spoiler alert—Guilt is not love. Manipulators (Jahmel) would not accept blame or responsibility for his actions but always tried to place the blame on me. Even when I did nothing wrong. He knew how to turn things around to accuse me of not caring. Manipulators (Jahmel) spent a lot of time talking about how I couldn't think for myself but then turned around and tried to make me responsible for his emotions and feelings. If he was sad, or angry it was because of something I did or didn't do for him. As much as he complained that I was incapable of making my own decisions it is interesting to now think how he expected me to be responsible for how he felt. Twisted. I truly believe that Jahmel was suffering from some type of mental health condition.

I'm reminded of a messaged my mother preached called "Spiritual Anti-Depressant" she preached this shortly after the suicides we had in Hollywood. Her message was saying that it is okay to be a Christian and need outside help or medication. Yes, we have medicines that can help people cope with mental health conditions such as: ADHD, ADD, bipolar disorder, schizophrenia, depression, anxiety, and so much more. But when those don't work or when you run out, you can lean on your "Spiritual Anti-Depressant." JESUS. That's what I needed to do to be delivered from the hell I was going through with Jahmel. When you call on Jesus, he will answer prayer.

No one should put anyone through something like that, not saying you can have a relationship with someone who has a mental disorder… there are plenty folk out there who do, but when it starts to become toxic, mentally draining for you or abusive in ANY way; you should Get The Hell Out!

LIGHT EM UP:

I wish my dad would have lit him up! I was so disappointed in myself that I let ALL that transpire, and still went with him! I still wanted to bring out the best in him and us. Let me tell you something! Y'all better stop believing these Facebook quizzes over GOD! "When Will You Get Married?" "What year will you have a baby!" Facebook quizzes are not GOD! I'm not saying I don't do them, but don't take that as God speaking to you through a computer-generated quiz.

I will admit I have been guilty of doing so; one said 2017, will be my year to get married. So, when Jahmel came along, I knew he was "from the Lord", so that is why I felt that everything we went through was ordained by GOD! Not so!

"Don't look for shortcuts to God. The market is flooded with surefire, easygoing formulas for a successful life that can be practiced in your spare time. Don't fall for that stuff, even though crowds of people do. The way to life--to God! ---is vigorous and requires total attention. Be wary of false preachers who smile a lot, dripping with practiced sincerity. Chances are they are out to rip you off some way or other. Don't be impressed with charisma; look for character…genuine leader will never exploit your emotions or your pocketbook…" Matthew 7:13-20 MSG

When Jahmel would reach out to me, before we got together, he would always comment, *"Man, dude trippin. If you were mine, I would have put a ring on your finger!"* Even when we started dating, he made it known that the end goal was marriage. That was something he told me and announced because he knew that was what I wanted to hear. There was a time when we were in a heated o argument, and he said *"…please, I was never going to marry you!"*

One day, one of my older cousin's spoke some real TRUTH, she doesn't know it, but the statement she made was a real eye-opener to me and made me evaluate somethings.

"A man who makes many promises but never keeps them is a man who knows how to pacify… A man who has to apologize for not being consistent, is a man who will devour your happiness and steal your joy… A man who does the minimum to get by is a man to flee from. Therefore, we should pick wisely, or you could be blinded by all that he is NOT."

Others would tell me things similar to this, and it may not have seemed like I was listening, but I was. I was soaking all the negative comments, tough love and bluntness from others and putting them into my ammo bank to build up enough strength and confidence to end the relationship and not be fearful of his response or the outcome.

OH, WHAT A NIGHT A NIGHT:

THIS! I DON'T EVEN KNOW WHERE TO START! So much happened in this chapter. I saw the movie "The Hate U Give," and that whole movie reminded me of this chapter and *'Booked.'* All of the police interactions I had been in with Jahmel and the many times we got pulled over, it could have been him reaching for a brush and getting shot. Then I thought about me, and how I probably would have reacted; my first thought would have been to get out of the car to run to see if he was okay, but my actions could have ended my life. In BOOKED when he wanted me to get out to ask the officer what was taken to long.

I also realized that when you become more focus on someone else's life, you will begin to lose sight of you! You're not focused nor paying attention to your surroundings. That happened to me around this time. This was one of the seasons where he was INDEED "showing me who he was."

One day Jahmel was mad that his plan he had failed and we had no money. He wanted to go to the men's shelter but threw a big fit about it in downtown San Antonio, just minutes away from my mom's job. He got out of the car, broke some of my CD's in the process because I was annoying him by trying to calm him down. He started walking, and I followed right behind him and ended up parking in an empty business lot, to wait for him to pass the street hoping that by the time he reached where I was, he would have calmed down.

Once he got to the corner, he saw my car and turned around. I decided to follow him but, I was too busy looking at where he was going that accidently drove over the huge concrete parking block and pretty much took out my front bumper. Later that day, his anger escalated which resulted in him throwing his cell phone at my window, (I honestly think he was trying to break it) and then my door which made a dent. While all this was going on, my phone magically called my mom, and she heard EVERYTHING! I knew that was God. She walked me through that whole incident. I was embarrassed that she had insight on what I was going through sometimes on a daily basis. NEVER, NEVER, NEVER stay in a relationship where your vision is so blurred you can't see yourself, and you start to put yourself in danger for some-body's ignorance or issues! That curb was high up, if I freaked out and accelerated instead of putting the car in reverse I could have gone off the little cliff, and it would have been my fault, I would have had a totaled car and no transportation to get to work. I felt like because he didn't have anything, he wanted me not to have anything either.

If your boyfriend, prefers for you sell or pawn your things rather than getting his tail up and getting a job or finding a clean and honest hustle! DROP HIM! He pawned EVERYTHING! Two pairs of my Jordan's, some of my Coach and Donny Burke bags, my Bose speaker, BOTH of my iPads and Lastly my mother's RING! The one she gave me when I moved to Dallas and made me promise to never take it off until someone replaces it. Every-thing I pawned I lost, EXCEPT my mom's ring! After Jahmel and I broke up, I came across the slip that had the last day I could come and buy it back. It was going on the 2nd week after the agreement expired. Driving home one day I happened to pass the pawn shop; I whipped my car in that parking lot so quick. My heart was racing so fast walked through that door; praying I would see it sitting in the case. In the back of my mind I had a feeling it would be there, because it was a diamond ring with a cross engraved on both sides. Thinking to myself, no one wants that. As I calmly and slowly scanned that case…my eyes LOCKED and to my surprise my mom's ring was sitting there. I waited 30 minutes until someone helped me. I told the lady that I wanted to buy this ring. She said okay ma'am it will be $190." That was more than what they actually gave me for it. She suggested I do the layaway pay-ment plan; and I did just that. March 5th, I got the ring out! Now it never leaves my sight. Don't get manipulated into giving up the things you work hard for to make sure someone else is taken care of.

"Don't you remember the rule we had when we lived with you? "If you don't work you don't eat!" **2 Thessalonians 3-10 MSG**

SHOCK THE WORLD & BLOOD SWEAT & TEARS:

The ultimate hurt and let down: first, my baby brother was going away to college, and he wouldn't be able to be apart of the pregnancy of his niece or nephew. Then I lose my baby; then the fight with his mother, when all I wanted was to do the right thing as a Christian woman.

Then they BOTH bit the hand that fed them. Literally. I still think what if I would have fought this lady' how would that had turned out.? Or what If I never went to their rescue? What would have happened? All I can say is be aware of the signs and seek help for them.

WHO ARE YOU:

This was just a true testament that God had me this whole time. When we ask God to place us where he wants us, he does just that. Did I really want to work for the largest online retailers? HECK NO! But God knew I needed to be there. Because he knew the lives I would impact and the one (s) who would impact my life.

If I never applied, Tre' would have never entered my life; help and push me as well as challenge me in my walk with Christ. Yeah, I have parents in ministry, but it is always different hearing things from other people who have gone through similar challenges.

What he said after the stunt Jahmel faked a family emergency to get me out of work. Tre' pretty much read my life like a book!!! (He still does.) It was hard to digest, but it was the TRUTH! This was really tough love. I'm reminded of a quote, *"God is sending you people who have the anointing to pour into you like you do everyone else."* -@tyspeaks

ENOUGH:

Do we really need to dissect this one? Enough was me Getting the HELL out for sure! Prayer changes things, I prayed the HELL out of my situation and less than 24hours God started to shift things in the atmosphere and as well in the physical. HALLELUJAH. Growing up this was and STILL is my favorite scripture. I always love to hear sermons about Paul & Silas. Not knowing that years down the line I would have to pray like Paul and Silas. *"AND AT MIDNIGHT! Paul and Silas prayed and sang praises unto God, and the prisoners heard them. And suddenly there was a great earthquake, so that the foundation of the prison doors were shaken: and immediately all the doors were open and everyone's bands were loosed. And the keeper of the prison awaked out of his sleep, and seeing the prison doors open, he drew out his sword, and would have killed himself supposing that the prisoners had been fled. But Paul cried out with a loud voice, saying, Do thyself no harm for we are all here. Then he called for a light, and sprang in, and came trembling and fell down before Paul and Silas, and brought them out, and said Sirs, what must I do to be saved?"* Acts 16: 25-30 God is ready and willing to shake some things up in your life BUT, YOU have to pray that prayer!—and those very things, situations and or relationships that were keeping you bound will turn around and want to know the God you serve.

Go ahead and pass the collection plate. I'm done preaching, now

SERIOUSLY BRUH:

I found myself putting things in my name for him. He would always play the guilt trip (manipulation) card, and it worked for a while I ain't going to lie. But in the breaking point stage right before he got the keys to the apartment, he was hungry and wanted to smoke. I didn't have the money, so instead of going over right after I was done with my family, I told him I was going to go Uber to get at least 25 dollars. $10 would be for the weed, and the other $15 could be for food for him.

Jahmel didn't like that because he wanted it NOW and knew it could be a minute since I was Uber'n. He said that I didn't have to worry about Uber'n he was going to turn his phone off, go walk in the rain and pray he catches the flu again and get to stay in the hospital. That's how he would run away from his problems and more so abandon his mom. This is NOT the type of man I wanted, and neither should you desire for yourself. He has to be able to make something shake and bake for himself! Say if we did get married and I lost my job again or couldn't work for whatever reason,

I needed and wanted to be confident that he would pick up the slack and not hop on the first flight to Colorado to get high "to clear his head and regroup." No negro, work, get your tail out there and hustle. Get on your knees, ask God to help you and guide you to provide for yourself and your family. In other words, a man that don't work don't eat. 2 Thessalonians 3:10

The Importance of Prayer & Having a Relationship with God

Although I was "born on the pew" I still have a lot of growing to do. I often feel like if my relationship with the Lord were more solid wouldn't I have gone through what I went through. That I will never know, or maybe I would have gotten out faster. Still. I'll never know. One thing I do know is that HE knows every plan for me, the roads I am going to take. HE even knows the number of strands of hair I have on my head. He's not blind to the fact that the devil has set up snares and tares, …. He even knows my un-canning knack of simply fowling up the simplest things in my life. But He says to me and he says to you I know who you are. I have called you by name and you have found favor in sight. I can truly say this journey has brought me closer to God. Do I know it all? Nope. Can I still grow and be groomed? ABSOLUTELY.

As a believer, you must be mindful of the powerful secret weapon of prayer that is available to you no matter where you are or what circumstance surrounds you right now – this weapon can stand against the forces of hell to effectively change the atmosphere and spiritual climate of an entire nation, world and indeed your situation.

At the start of the book, I mentioned a scripture, Mark 9:29; "… *this kind can come out only by prayer."* There are some situations you can ONLY change by prayer, asking God to intervene and have his way. BUT there are steps:

Step 1: **Acknowledge**that you can't fix it like you're used to or normally would.

Step 2: **Recognize "It's Above Me Now"** come to grips with the you can't always be the hero.

Step 3: **Ask for HELP & Pray!** read this part out loud. *"I can't fix this by myself; I need help."*

Now let's break down these steps; These steps are just not just for a toxic relationship, but for anything we face in our lives that is just too much for us to bare on our own.

Acknowledge – When you stop putting on that persona that you have it all together, "I'm Fine" but at the same time you feel like you're about to break, THAT'S when you acknowledge that you can no longer do it on your own, you CAN'T BE GOD so give it over to Him.

It's Above Me Now – If you try to fix it yourself, you'll fall deeper and deeper and could possibly find yourself in a hole so deep you can't dig your way out. You may very well end up dying in your own MESS. The same SPENDING habits, the same JOB habits; (not everyone at your job is the problem, it could fairly well be you) the same kind of friendships, the same kind of boyfriends – you left one thug and went to another thug. You left one gold digger and ended up "falling in love" with another gold digger. THAT'S MESS, and you wonder why you keep going through the same HELL over and over and over again. You keep trying to figure out what's wrong with you, why you can't change, make better choices or discern the voice of God and hear the Lord clearly.

It is because you haven't acknowledged your MESS! Those who know me know I always I refer to myself as a "G" not so much a G as in a Gabriel…even through my parents told my brother and I growing up "ACT LIKE A GABRIEL," but a "G" as in a Gangsta. If something comes up or someone tries me, family, and or friends. My response would always be *"WHAT!? I'm about to handle this.* (while getting up or walking towards the problem) *watch out Imma G!"* NOT God is the ultimate "G" that can fix those problems way quicker, and smoother than we can.

HELP – Some of you may have heard the song 'Help' by Erica Campbell. In this song, she cries out to God for help. When she felt like she was going to lose her mind after she lost her father. This step doesn't necessarily mean you have to reach out to people for help but to the One *who can do anything but fail.* You may find yourself crying out for help like I did, standing in that empty apartment asking fully surrendered asking God to have his way and fully surrender. You may find yourself at your wit's end and may need to seek counseling/guidance or just the support family member or friend. All of these ways are great, and it's okay if you have to get help more than one way. Some of you may be prideful like I was and may take some time to get to this step. BUT I promise you if you keep Acknowledging that the Situation is Above You. Pray and Trust God, Help will come. TRUST ME.

So when you find yourself faced with the challenges of this life, there is one thing that will guarantee your success, and that is PRAYER. The Bible tells us in James 5:15 tells us that "the effectual fervent prayers of the righteous avails much." USE YOUR WEAPON – PRAY! When things go wrong – PRAY. When life is good – PRAY! When life gets you down – PRAY! Prayer is the key that unlocks and reveals faith. Effective prayer needs both an attitude of complete dependence and the action of asking. (The 3 Steps) Prayer demonstrates complete reliance on God. There is no substitute for prayer, especially in situations that seem impossible. Often these disciples would face difficult situations that could be resolved only through prayer. Their humiliation made this a painful lesson to learn.

Quick story, while my relationship with Jahmel was in the last phases; I noticed I would randomly kneel at my bed or at the couch in my mother's office. While I was writing this book, I noticed I was doing it more often. I would skip the whole chair next to the bed or and would kneel, I'd be typing, writing, on the phone, surfing the net, even watching TV on my knees. One day my Fabio came into the room and knelt next to me, closed his hands together, closed his eyes, and looked like he was in deep thought. I looked at him and started laughing and asked what he was doing. He said, "OH, I thought you were praying." I looked at him and laughed and said: "Nah, I'm just chilling." He looked behind me probably thinking there was a chair right here. Before he got up, he said *"AMEN."* Every time after that when he comes into my room, he would ask if I was praying.

One day, I was off, and I found myself in a place when I needed direction and guidance. It was right before I moved into my own apartment. Everything was happening so fast, and I was unsure if this was meant to be because I wanted it to or if it was truly God. I found myself walking into my room and kneeling down at my bed to pray. Once I got comfortable, I opened my mouth and said, *"sigh…Dear God…"* I couldn't even finish when I heard the Lord clearly say to me; *"SEE, I was just training you to kneel, that way, when it's time to pray bowing before me will be easy, it would become so natural for you."* Y'all that revelation hit me so hard my face hit the bed and uncontrollable tears started to flow; and a song by Fred Hammond came to me *'Show Me Your Face'*. To this day I kneel, to just chill but most importantly – TO PRAY!

The only way you can ***Get the HELL Out*** of your life and situation is by prayer. THIS KIND can only get out by prayer. Prayer can fix it!! I'm a BELIEVER, SURVIOR and a WITNESS!

If my story leads you to think that you or someone you know maybe in an abusive/compromising relationship.

If you need to talk it over, feel free to reach out to

The Hotline 24/7/365 by phone at 1-800-799-SAFE (7233) or by online chat at www.thehotline.org

Acknowledgments

FIRST! Jesus, GOD. Daddy! I LOVE YOU! Thank you Lord for your love and protection and faithfulness. God, thank you for allowing me to go through this storm, so I may be able to tell the world that trails may come, life will definitely happen BUT there is nothing too hard for YOU! It was nothing but your GRACE and MERCY that brought me over and carried me though. Thank you for never leaving my side even when I strayed away, doubted, didn't trust and even questioned you. Lord you are SO AMAZING! I just thank you for my LIFE and for keeping me.

To my parents, Billy and Tonja Gabriel! I love ya'll man! THANK YOU, THANK YOU, THANK YOU! For those many and extra prayers while all of this was going on. Even though you all wanted to beat me upside the head at times – well most of time; but you remembered how pretty my face was and let me slide. hahaha. No for real, that was God's GRACE and MERCY!

Fawbio! Thank you for being my ultimate protector and always having my back and being ready to go to war at any time. For teaching me how to put furniture together, check the oil in my car, WASH MY CAR and be independent without being dependent on a man. Thank you for showing me how I NEED to be treated! Even though in this case I let my guard down and forgot my VALUES and WORTH. I got it NOW! Thank you for always being there for Mom, BJ and myself, especially when things got rough. I can honestly say that we never saw the struggle or lack. You are simply an amazing husband, father and provider! I pray that my son(s) will have the same heart, drive, passion and smarts like you. Well I don't know about the heart; because it's so big and I would hurt someone taking advantage of my babies. Lol I'd go straight "La Qunita" on em. But seriously, Fawbio, thank you for loving me and instilling those life lessons. I will never forget it, even though you let me fall of the bike! -Sweets

Mommy! GIIIIIRRRL! Your prayers, your prayers, YOUR PRAYERS! Thank you for always having that door open to freely come and talk to you, even when I don't use it like I should because I think I'mma "G" and "hard" and don't need any help; you never closed the door on me. (Thugs need love too! Lol ok seriously!) I'm going to do better, I promise oh, and did I mention YOUR PRAYERS!?? You have loved me unconditionally; I am so happy you are MY MOMMY! Thank you for teaching me the importance of following God and keeping his Word in my heart and the POWER OF PRAYER! You are such a jewel; I can only pray that when my time comes to become a mommy, I am half the Mother, Woman of God that you are! Thank you for your unconditional love and covering! –Sweetie

B! Little Crit Crit! My Baby, My Twin! HI! Thank you for always being my biggest supporter always pushing me to be GREAT and of course having my back. Growing up was a little rough, you were SOOO ANNOYING! Lol. Never in a million years did I think we'd have a bond this close and tight! I thank God for our "Twin-Vibes" and our love for each other. I remember when I was moving to Dallas, Mom told me with tears in her eyes *"Don't forget your brother! Don't for-get your* (her blow she does when she's about to cry) *brother."* and to this day I hear her voice. I will NEVER, NEVER EVER forget you B, no matter where life takes us (why am I about to cry...UGH!) job wise, family wise, I won't forget you! I don't think you know how much you mean to me! So future girlfriend, sister-n-law, you better come CORRECT! Even though I pray it's J.G.; but only God knows, eh? Keep striving and making Mutttheer, Pawwps and me proud. I appreciate you staying on my ASSprin about getting this book out and done. Especially the chapter I needed to add; thanks for all the sleepovers and Chris Brown concerts— real life and the ones at my house we had to do in order to get me to finish this book! I love you!

MAZE!!! You are the real definition of a BIG BROTHER; you wear that title well. Yeah, I'm the spoiled little sister but you will check me QUICK and give it to me 100! Although we didn't have much communication during THIS relationship, you came in at the RIGHT TIME! I honestly believe God moved you overseas for this time, because if you were in the states it would have been all bad. Marcus, my birthday twin, my brother! I love you so much! You and BJ are my heartbeats, and ya'll love me in spite of my mess and don't judge me, and there to wipe the tears, hug me when I'm sad, and are ready to fight when I get hurt! Maze thanks for never leaving my side bruh, real talk! FAMILY FIRST AND ALWAYS! #100

Auntie London, First I want to say SORRY! Sorry, that you had to see and live this BS with your niece. Never was this my intention to drag you in to this mess! You are more than an Auntie, you're like my sister/ best friend! You literally lived this book with me! It's crazy! I thank God for the bond we have. I'm sorry for putting you through all of this crazy stuff you did so much for me. Thank you for going behind my back at times and letting my Mom know that I was okay. (UGH, the tears!) Thank you for never judging me while I was going through, when you really could have, and turned your back on me and left me out in the cold, when I was screaming and crying for help! I pray that God starts your healing processes for things you've gone through and put on the back burner, just to make sure I was okay and making it! You are precious, I am so grateful to call you my "Auntie London."

Erika, Girl! You already know how I feel about you! THANK YOU FOR COMING WHEN YOU DID! SERIOUSLY! That was nobody BUT GOD! NOBODY! I love you more than pineapple sandwiches. You've never left myside no matter how far away we were; you have ALWAYS been there for me and I love you for that. If I keep going this would turn into another book, but you are my ride or die and my ace boon coon. I love you babe!

My Bestie Boo Bianca, MERRY CHRISTMAS! You are my backbone, we don't see each other; nor talk every day, but when I needed/need you, you have always been there! I thank GOD that H-E-B brought us together. I am so grateful for you, walking me through that whole court process and some of the legal system with this nut and for being there for me after I lost Harper! I know Harper and Paisley are in heaven having their play dates together. I love you so much bwwwest freeeeewwwwn

TRE'!!! Hey! You are a GOD SENT! You are like my godfather, spiritual father, mentor, uncle, big brother, cousin, best friend all in one! You played a BIG and CRUCIAL role in my life in that season; weather you know it or not! Thank you for seeing and pulling out the best in me spiritually, mentally, and emotionally that overflowed into my work life. I know I was a piece of work (and still am) I'm glad you didn't throw me in the "field" the many times I walked in looking crazy! Thank you for telling me like it is and judging me not once. Okay maybe once, lol. BUT you helped me bring it all back together with a palm to my forehead at times. That conviction is something else I tell ya. Also thank you for helping me decided on my logo and the book cover. My consistent prayer for you and your family is that, God continues to pour into you all double for all that you all pour out to me and others. You definitely have a servant's heart; and I am so blessed that I can call and lean on you when I need and to vent. You've changed my life. REAL TALK! Thank you for being obedient to your assignment (s)! Love you! #itsbeenreal

Pastor Jonathan D. Ellis, You have taught of the many lessons and given me so much wisdom down through the years. Having my back and loving me unconditionally. I am so happy you we're able to write the foreword to my book. THANK YOU THANK YOU THANK YOU!! Love, d'Mônjé.

To my lovely SistHER's ya'll are absolutely AH-MAZING! I love each and every one of you! The prayers, support, transparency and vulnerability and the bond that we have is UNBREAKABLE! You all are amazing. Special shout out to my *"Gang Gang SistHER's"* Krissy, Lisa and Court-Court! I LOVE YA'LL MAN! The prayers ya'll send up for your little and big sis, gets me going and gets me through; OK-KUURT! **Lisa,** thank you for fussing at me to get this book done, and having that CRAZY and I mean CRAZY faith to SPEAK those things that are NOT as though they WERE! (I'mma have a jet too!) **Krissy,** you are my motivator and inspiration to reach high and never give up on my goals and no matter what circumstance may rise I can achieve it because of who I am in the Kingdom. Lastly you taught me "DONT QUIT; FINISH STRONG!" **Court Court** my quite little firecracker, thank you for telling me like it is! Correcting me when I'm wrong and hyping me when I'm right! You are literally like the little sister I never had. I love ya'll to pieces man for real!

Kierra Sheard *"Found Me A Real Friend!"* Where do I start? Your ministry from the beginning has truly, truly blessed my whole entire existence. I remember growing up saying I want to be like Kierra Sheard! I wanted to be a Gospel singer and EVERYTHING! I have looked up you to you since day one. You embody grace! You love the Lord so hard! Thank you for creating SistHER! This program came at the RIGHT time. Thank you for creating a place for young women to express their love for God, feel safe and be vulnerable. You never judge us, your always transparent and valuable with us. You are truly the big sister any girl wants and needs to have and I'm so happy to call you MY SISTHER! I love you!!!

Sonora THANK YOU your writing an amazing synopsis to my cover and for being consistent in our friendship! LOVE YOU!

Nicole Ussery GIRL! You are one dope artist! Thank you, thank you, THANK YOU! For being a lifesaver! My logo, merch, graphics and promotional stuff! You are the bomb and are so gifted. GREAT things are in store for you.

Jakarie Ross Thank you for designing my book cover.

My A. Flake, Thank you for being THAT friend. Staying on me, telling me the truth, agreeing and disagreeing with me. Hyping me up, calming me down and most of all being that balance I need. Thank you for encouraging me to finish the book and not give up and throw in the towel especially during this editing process. I wouldn't trade you for the world. Well…JK.

Melinda Watts and M Creative SIS! You are absolutely amazing! Thank you for seeing and hearing my story and being so gentle and delicate with it. Although others wanted to change the tone and sound of *MY STORY!* You reassured me that I didn't have to. Thank you for being patient with me through the editing process. LIFE DEFINATLY HAPPENED for the BOTH OF US! The editing was harder than I thought! BUT I DID IT! Thank you for always, always, always having my back and encouraging me to *"SHINE BABY!"* I am so grateful for you. I AM A PUBLISHED AUTHOUR BECAUSE OF YOU! LOVE YOU SISSY!

Family, Friends and Supporters!! THANK YOU, THANK YOU, THANK YOU! Whether you brought a book, prayed, gave advice or was just there for me. I appreciate you! I pray that my story blessed you and you have a great outlook on how you should be treated and how to

Made in the USA
Monee, IL
21 July 2020